D0146646

SAMUEL JOHNSON
AND THE TRAGIC SENSE

They say miracles are past; and we have our philosophical persons to make modern and familiar, things supernatural and causeless. Hence it is that we make trifles of terrors, ensconcing ourselves into seeming knowledge when we should submit ourselves to an unknown fear.

ALL'S WELL THAT ENDS WELL, II.iii

SAMUEL JOHNSON AND THE TRAGIC SENSE

Leopold Damrosch, Jr.

Princeton University Press
Princeton, New Jersey
1972

Publication of this book has been aided by
the Committee on Small Research Grants
of the University of Virginia
and the Whitney Darrow Publication Reserve Fund
of Princeton University Press

A brief excerpt from Richmond Lattimore's translation
of Aeschylus' *Agamemnon* is reprinted by permission
of the University of Chicago Press

This book has been composed in Linotype Baskerville
Printed in the United States of America
by Princeton University Press

TO THEODORE REDPATH

Contents

Acknowledgments

MY DEBTS of gratitude begin with Theodore
Redpath, to whom this book is very properly
dedicated; it had its origin in an essay written
under his direction, and without his wide-
ranging knowledge and wisdom—to say nothing of his kindness—it would never have been
conceived or carried out. Lawrence Lipking,
who directed the dissertation out of which the
book has grown, set a standard of intellectual
inquiry which is easier to admire than to emulate, and helped me to understand the ways
in which the work could be developed and
improved. A long and unwieldy version received close critical readings from Ralph
Cohen, Irvin Ehrenpreis, and Francis R.
Hart; Stephen Greenblatt read a more finished version and helped me to eliminate still
more of the spurious transitions and self-con-
tradictions which a writer is all but incapable
of detecting for himself. In addition Edward
Berry, Kurt Olsson, Bruce Stovel, and Richard
Waswo were kind enough to read various
chapters and to offer valuable suggestions.
Whatever the present shortcomings of the
book, they would be far greater if it had
lacked the generous attention of such exemplary readers. I also want to thank Michael
Giles and Samuel Mounger for helping with
some of the more tedious details of preparing
a manuscript for publication.

Two summer research grants from the University of Virginia made possible the comple-
tion of the manuscript.

Finally, like other authors, I owe the greatest
debt of all to my wife, both for encouragement and forbearance.

ABBREVIATIONS

Dictionary	Samuel Johnson, *A Dictionary of the English Language*, 2 vols. (London, 1755)
Hawkins	Sir John Hawkins, *The Life of Samuel Johnson, LL.D.*, ed. and abr. Bertram H. Davis (New York, 1961)
Hazen	*Samuel Johnson's Prefaces and Dedications*, ed. Allen T. Hazen (New Haven, 1937)
Hooker	*The Critical Works of John Dennis*, ed. Edward N. Hooker, 2 vols. (Baltimore, 1939-43)
Letters	*The Letters of Samuel Johnson*, ed. R. W. Chapman, 3 vols. (Oxford, 1952)
Life	James Boswell, *The Life of Samuel Johnson, LL.D.*, ed. G. B. Hill, rev. L. F. Powell, 6 vols. (Oxford, 1934, 1950). [Vol. v of this edition is Boswell's *Journal of a Tour to the Hebrides*.]
Lives	*The Lives of the Poets*, ed. G. Birkbeck Hill, 3 vols. (Oxford, 1905). [In the interest of specifying references, these are cited as *Life of Cowley*, etc., except when the specific *Life* is already evident from the context.]
London Journal	James Boswell, *London Journal*, ed. Frederick A. Pottle (New York, 1950)
Miscellanies	*Johnsonian Miscellanies*, ed. G. Birkbeck Hill, 2 vols. (Oxford, 1897)
Nichol Smith	*Eighteenth Century Essays on Shakespeare*, ed. D. Nichol Smith, 2nd ed. (Oxford, 1963)
Oxford Poems	*The Poems of Samuel Johnson*, ed. D. Nichol Smith and E. L. McAdam (Oxford, 1941)
Preface	*Preface to Shakespeare*, in Yale *Works*, vol. vii
Rasselas	Samuel Johnson, *The History of Rasselas, Prince of Abissinia*, ed. R. W. Chapman (Oxford, 1927). [I have however altered Chapman's chapter numbers to accord with the customary ones; he follows the second edition so scrupulously as to retain the mistake by which two chapters were numbered 28, making the total 48 instead of 49.]
Thraliana	*Thraliana, The Diary of Mrs. Hester Lynch Thrale*, ed. Katharine C. Balderston, 2 vols. (Oxford, 1951)
Watson	John Dryden, *Of Dramatic Poesy and Other Critical Essays*, ed. George Watson, Everyman's Library, 2 vols. (London, 1962)

ABBREVIATIONS

1825 *Works*   *The Works of Samuel Johnson, LL.D.*, 9 vols. (Oxford, 1825)

Yale *Works*   *The Yale Edition of the Works of Samuel Johnson* (New Haven, 1958–). [Johnson's poems, diaries, periodical essays, and Shakespeare criticism are all quoted from this edition.]

Zimansky   Thomas Rymer, *Critical Works*, ed. Curt A. Zimansky (New Haven, 1956)

I. THE PROBLEM OF TRAGEDY
IN THE EIGHTEENTH CENTURY

CHAPTER 1

Introduction

AMONG the older literary historians it was a common-place that the eighteenth century exhibits what Oliver Elton called "the sterility of the tragic sense." This circumstance, if true, accounts so neatly for the undoubted decline of dramatic tragedy during the period that it is hard to say which idea comes first: the death of the tragic sense proving the impossibility of tragedy, or the failure of tragedy proving the absence of a tragic sense. Whichever way one comes at the assumption, its implications are far from flattering to the age. In F. R. Leavis's view, for example, "It is significant that that century, which went in so much for formal tragedy, should have shown itself so utterly incapable of attaining the tragic."[1] The issue is not simply that a particular art form had ceased to produce masterpieces (just as *Paradise Lost* was the last great epic), but rather that an essential element of human experience was forgotten or denied. What is implied is a profound failure of imagination.

More recent scholars have tended to lose interest in castigating *Jane Shore* or *Cato* for being less tragic than *King Lear*, and have invited us to see the tragic sense as displaced into other literary forms; it is detected in the *Dunciad*, in *Gulliver's Travels*, in *The Vanity of Human Wishes*, and even in *The Decline and Fall of the Roman Empire*. The value of this tendency is obvious, both in revealing a greater range of implication in these works than scholars used to perceive, and in resisting the notion that "the eighteenth century" could

---

[1] Elton, *A Survey of English Literature, 1730-1780* (London, 1928), I, 311. Leavis, *The Common Pursuit* (Penguin Books, 1962), p. 130.

3

ever be reduced to a single view of life. Its defect, on the other hand, lies in a possible overemphasis of modern notions of the tragic at the expense both of eighteenth-century ideas on the subject and of untragic but important elements in the works themselves.

The present study aims to do two things: first, to argue that although the tragedies of the period were indeed bad, intelligent people were still capable of a genuine appreciation of earlier tragedies; and second, to explore the nature and limitations of the tragic sense as it appears in a specific writer, Samuel Johnson. In his own century Johnson could be called "the Coryphaeus of Literature"[2]—its leader or chief—but I do not insist that he was central to the age as a whole, or even to a more limited Age of Johnson. Although he was an important figure, he was a highly individual and in some ways eccentric one. Nonetheless, he offers exceptional advantages for an investigation of this kind. Over and over again we are told, and rightly so, that he had a tragic sense of life. The only tragedy he wrote, however, is a feeble one, and his best creative work has as many affinities with satire as with tragedy. And there is the further problem of his literary criticism, which often seems obtuse about the fundamental nature of tragic drama. Can the criticism be reconciled with the "tragic sense," or are the two contradictory in some important way?

For reasons to be explained shortly, no elaborate definition of terms will be undertaken at this point; but something must be said about the crucial distinction between tragedy as genre and the tragic sense. No such

[2] A reviewer of *Dr. Johnson's Table-talk* called him "the Coryphaeus of Literature" in the *Gentleman's Magazine*, 68 (1798), 326. The phrase was perhaps borrowed from Burney's statement that "the publications respecting this literary Coryphaeus have been very numerous," in a review of Mrs. Piozzi's *Anecdotes* in the *Monthly Review*, 74 (1786), 374.

distinction was understood in the eighteenth century, which followed Aristotle in conceiving tragedy as imitating certain kinds of actions, and as arousing or otherwise influencing certain emotions in the spectator or reader. Aristotle himself was willing to call any play a tragedy which fitted his formal definitions, even a play like the *Iphigenia in Tauris* which we would probably consider wholly untragic.

In the nineteenth century a new line of thinking developed which may be summed up by Unamuno's famous phrase, "the tragic sense of life," a subject about which Aristotle has nothing to say. Unamuno denounces philosophical detachment as a denial of "the man of flesh and bone"; he is concerned with man's place in an inimical universe, in the tradition of Pascal. Such an attitude certainly has affinities with those very tragedies to which Aristotle devoted his Linnaean classification, and indeed may be said to have pervaded Greek thought. Unamuno quotes the story of the pedant who reproached Solon when he wept for the death of his son, asking "Why do you weep thus, if weeping avails nothing?" Solon replied, "Precisely for that reason—because it does not avail." In Unamuno's view, we inhabit a hostile universe, and no philosophical consolation is of any use to us; "It is as if one should say to a man whose leg has had to be amputated that it does not help him at all to think about it." This tragic sense may be found in literature of many kinds; Unamuno calls Spinoza's *Ethics* "a despairing elegiac poem."[3]

Between Aristotle's and Unamuno's positions an enormous range of theories has evolved, emphasizing either the generic form or the metaphysical view according to the predisposition of the theorist, but generally assuming some degree of connection between the two, and warning against using the term "tragic" too

[3] Miguel de Unamuno, *The Tragic Sense of Life*, trans. J. Crawford Flitch (New York, 1954), pp. 17, 31.

5

loosely. A useful example is Stephen Dedalus' famous definition: "Pity is the feeling which arrests the mind in the presence of whatsoever is grave and constant in human sufferings and unites it with the human sufferer. Terror is the feeling which arrests the mind in the presence of whatsoever is grave and constant in human sufferings and unites it with the secret cause." Here Aristotle's classic terms are developed in an eloquent statement which manages to suggest, in the haunting phrase "the secret cause," the cruel but perhaps not wholly arbitrary mystery at the heart of tragic experience. Stephen continues his exposition with a negative illustration:

> A girl got into a hansom a few days ago, he went on, in London. She was on her way to meet her mother whom she had not seen for many years. At the corner of a street the shaft of a lorry shivered the window of the hansom in the shape of a star. A long fine needle of the shivered glass pierced her heart. She died on the instant. The reporter called it a tragic death. It is not. It is remote from terror and pity according to the terms of my definitions.[4]

One sees very well what is meant, and yet the story may contain more of the tragic than Stephen is prepared to concede. When one of Hakluyt's seafarers writes "Our voyage ended tragically," he is responding to something that everyone feels. Bradley put it well when he suggested that "this central feeling is the impression of waste."[5] While the anecdote of the girl in the hansom is far less tragic than *Antigone* or *Othello*, it does not follow that it is not tragic at all. It involves death, and also the sense (minimal, since Stephen has

[4] James Joyce, *A Portrait of the Artist as a Young Man* (New York, 1964), ch. 5, pp. 204, 205.

[5] Hakluyt, *Voyages*, cited in the *OED*; A. C. Bradley, *Shakespearean Tragedy* (London, 1905), ch. 1, p. 23.

6

only sketched the story) of what Bradley calls "waste."
In addition I should like to argue that every experience
which we call tragic is made so by the imaginative
grasp with which it is apprehended. Joyce's example is
not imaginatively neutral, just because of the way he
has chosen to tell it. Its organization, its rhythms, and
even its imagery ("shivered the window of the hansom
in the shape of a star") conspire to present a story
which, although brief, has a form and a resonance
which it would not have received in an ordinary news-
paper account. In miniature it is the imitation of an
action.

In such an example as Joyce's, the term "tragic" is understood to be inappropriate because the action is not
represented at any length, because the girl is unimpor-
tant until we know more about her, and because the
occasion of her death is a fortuitous accident rather
than an intelligible event. One may perhaps disagree
with such a position, but there is no question of refuting
it, for this is not a subject where right and wrong have
absolute meaning. I have touched upon it simply as a
means of indicating my own working assumption, that
tragedy as a literary form is something quite different
from a tragic sense, and that the latter is capable of
much wider (and no doubt vaguer) application than the
former. At its furthest remove from generic tragedy it
dwells upon the simple fact of human suffering, expressly distinguishing it as a *condition* from the kinds
of *actions* that find embodiment in art. In Wordsworth's
language,

> Action is transitory—a step, a blow, . . .
> Suffering is permanent, obscure and dark,
> And shares the nature of infinity.[6]

[6] *The Borderers*, III.v. Coleridge quotes these lines in "The
Character of Hamlet," in *Shakespearean Criticism*, ed. T. M.
Raysor (London, 1960), I, 34.

Something like this is implied in Joyce's "secret cause," and in the Shakespearean "unknown fear" which appears in my epigraph. As applied to Johnson and his contemporaries, both phrases suggest a mystery which at once intensifies dread and limits analysis. Lacking terms to elucidate an unknown fear, the moralist or critic may only imperfectly understand his own insights, or may choose to redefine them in less unsettling ways.

But granting that this tragic sense has a real existence, it can go only a little way toward explaining the peculiar power of the great tragic masterpieces. My principal reason for avoiding any formal theory of tragedy here is not to deny its value, but rather to resist prejudgment. Men in the eighteenth century approached the whole subject so differently from ourselves that, as I shall try to show, they could scarcely have understood it as we do. If therefore they were to be measured against any modern theory—and my own would carry no particular authority—they would be found hopelessly lacking before the investigation was well under way. My intention therefore is to examine their ideas in something like their own terms, and to criticize their inadequacies in specific contexts. The problem of the definition of tragedy will receive fuller treatment in the concluding chapter.

Finally, it is well to recall Huxley's observation that tragedy is not the whole truth.[7] A dispassionate view might suppose that life has in it both happy and unhappy elements from which the artist selects, and that he may sometimes create tragedy out of the latter. But if we aspire to rescue the eighteenth century from the stigma (assuming that it is a stigma) of the Peace of the Augustans, we may be inclined to dwell upon some ele-

[7] Aldous Huxley, "Tragedy and the Whole Truth," in *Collected Essays* (New York, 1959), pp. 96-103.

ments of its art at the expense of others. Thus the spacious comedy of *Tom Jones*, where no Blifil can triumph forever, and where Sophia is forever beautiful and young, is described as a consciously imaginary alternative to the depressing reality of life as it is actually lived. Sterne's wit is interpreted as the desperate heroism of a dying man: Yorick the death's head as well as jester. The satiric glee of Pope and Swift is seen as the product of their deeper gloom. And Johnson becomes a tragic hero. All of these interpretations carry a measure of truth, but none perhaps the whole truth. Johnson's tragic sense certainly exists, but it is not necessarily the same as ours, it does not inform all of his works equally, and he himself might have been quite indignant at our desire to identify it in him.

CHAPTER 2

Tragic Theory and Its Limitations

1. The Definition of Tragedy

CRITICS before the nineteenth century only touch occasionally and obliquely on the metaphysical aspect of tragedy. Now and then an extraordinary passage will stand out from the page, as when Sidney remarks that tragedy "openeth the greatest woundes, and sheweth forth the *Ulcers* that are covered with Tissue." Racine has a profound phrase which John Dennis thought good enough to copy, "cette tristesse majestueuse qui fait tout le plaisir de la tragédie." The infrequency of such passages forbids us to make too much of them; and yet what do we learn if we concentrate on the preferred topics of the neoclassical critics?[1]

The critic, to be sure, does not necessarily speak for all of his contemporaries, and in an important sense he does not even speak for himself. He reduces his relatively intuitive and unreflecting literary response to a conventional form of discourse in which he is obliged to use a set of inherited terms, many of which he takes so much for granted that he never thinks of examining them. Pope, pondering one of the self-perpetuating staples of neoclassical criticism, pointed out that it owed more to polemical opportunism than to reality.

> It is ever the nature of Parties to be in extremes; and nothing is so probable, as that because *Ben Johnson* had much the most learning, it was said on the one hand that *Shakespear* had none at all;

[1] Sidney, *Defence of Poesie*, in *Prose Works*, ed. Albert Feuillerat (Cambridge, 1962), III, 23. Racine, preface to *Bérénice*; Dennis borrows the phrase in the preface to his *Iphigenia* (1700): "that majestick Sadness which makes the pleasure of Tragedy" (Hooker, II, 390).

and because *Shakespear* had much the most wit
and fancy, it was retorted on the other, that *Johnson* wanted both. . . . Nay the spirit of opposition
ran so high, that whatever those of the one side ob-
jected to the other, was taken at the rebound, and
turned into Praises; as injudiciously as their antag-
onists before had made them Objections.

(*Preface to Shakespeare*, Nichol Smith, p. 50)

The repetitive quality of much of the dramatic criticism should warn us against regarding all of it with
equal respectfulness. An original mind like Dryden or
Dennis amply repays study, while a Gildon or a
Welsted may occasionally swell the chorus on some dis-
puted point, but seldom with much originality or
interest.

Furthermore, the elaborate "rules" of the more strictly neoclassical critics, which used to excite the solemn
outrage of literary scholars, were in general the obses-
sion of bookish theorists rather than of playwrights or
audiences.[2] Warburton rightly observed that most
of the champions of these rules hardly deserve
consideration:

Tho' it be very true, as Mr. *Pope* hath observed,
that *Shakespear is the fairest and fullest subject for*

[2] The last book to undertake in detail the subject of my intro-
ductory essay is Clarence C. Green's *The Neo-Classical Theory
of Tragedy in England During the Eighteenth Century* (Cambridge, Mass., 1934). This work, which still invariably appears in
bibliographies, is organized on the assumption that "the rules"
were first promulgated and then attacked. There is virtually no
reference to actual plays, and no attempt to ask why a particular
critic would make a particular statement or to distinguish intelligent writers from parrots.

I should mention that I attach no specific set of limiting
definitions to the term "neoclassicism," but use it loosely to refer
to the prevailing tendencies of critical discourse in the late seventeenth and early eighteenth centuries in England and France.

11

criticism, yet it is not such a sort of criticism as
may be raised mechanically on the Rules which
Dacier, Rapin and *Bossu* have collected from Antiquity; and of which, such kind of Writers as
Rymer, Gildon, Dennis and *Oldmixon,* have only
gathered and chewed the Husks. . . . The kind of
criticism here required is such as judgeth our Author by those only Laws and Principles on which
he wrote, NATURE, and COMMON-SENSE.[3]

To be sure, Dryden began his career under the spell of
French aesthetics, and declared in an early prologue,

He who writ this, not without pains and thought,
From French and English theatres has brought
Th' exactest rules by which a play is wrought.
(Secret Love, Watson, I, 107)

But if one examines Dryden's dramatic works (apart
from *All for Love*), it is hard to feel that a faithful ob-
servance of the rules is their leading characteristic.
"Many a fair precept in poetry," he wrote when his
career as a playwright was almost over, "is like a seeming demonstration in the mathematics: very specious in
the diagram, but failing in the mechanic operation"
(Preface to *Sylvae,* Watson, II, 19).

Let us suppose that the technical complications of
neoclassical theory are swept aside. What idea of tragedy remains? In the popular imagination, it has always
been defined by its subject matter, rather than by Aristotelian considerations of structure or effect. To borrow
Martin Opitz's comprehensive statement of 1624, it is
concerned with "royal decisions, manslaughter, despair,
infanticides and patricides, conflagrations, incest, wars
and rebellions, lamenting, screaming, sighing and the

[3] Preface to *The Works of Shakespeare* (1747), Nichol Smith,
p. 97.

like.["4] In Johnson's *Dictionary*, on the other hand, the definition of *tragedy* is much more limited: "1. A dramatick representation of a serious action. 2. Any mournful or dreadful event." The second illustration for the latter is, "I look upon this now done in England as another act of the same *tragedy* which was lately begun in Scotland. K[ing] Ch[arles]." On the analogy of tragedy on the stage, the mournful or dreadful events of life can be seen as tragic. But when he is actually defining literary tragedy, Johnson simply speaks of "a serious action." There is nothing here about metaphysical terror, nothing about fate, nothing even about lamenting, screaming, sighing and the like.

In Dryden's case, we have no definition of tragedy, and there are serious inadequacies in his famous definition of a play. "Lisideius, after some modest denials, at last confessed he had a rude notion of it; . . . he conceived a play ought to be *A just and lively image of human nature, representing its passions and humours, and the changes of fortune to which it is subject, for the delight and instruction of mankind*" (*Essay of Dramatic Poesy*, Watson, I, 25). Crites quite sensibly objects that this is a definition *a genere et fine*, but nobody seems to mind very much, and by the end of the colloquy we find Dryden/Neander accepting it as his own (p. 122). That is to say, here is a definition of a play which in no way restricts it to the drama, even though for most of the *Essay* Dryden is concerned with specifically dramatic problems: the value of the unities, the suitability of rhyme. For Aristotle tragedy was first and foremost

[4] *Buch von der deutschen Poeterey*, as quoted by Karl S. Guthke in *Modern Tragicomedy* (New York, 1966), p. 7. Opitz goes on to say that comedies are about "weddings, festivities, gambling, the cheating and roguishness of servants, vainglorious mercenaries, love affairs, the wantonness of youth, the avarice of old age, pandering and such things as happen daily among common people."

the imitation of an action; for Dryden it is an image of human nature. He even betrays a remarkable kind of antitheatrical prejudice, as if the only true literature existed on the printed page: "In a playhouse, everything contributes to impose upon the judgment: the lights, the scenes, the habits, and, above all, the grace of action, which is commonly the best where there is the most need of it, surprise the audience, and cast a mist upon their understandings" (Preface to *The Spanish Friar*, Watson, I, 275).

When he undertook to distinguish between tragedy and comedy, the best Dryden could manage was the idea that tragedy is elevated and impressive. "Were there neither judge, taste, nor opinion in the world, yet they would differ in their natures; for the action, character, and language of tragedy would still be great and high; that of comedy lower and more familiar; admiration would be the delight of one, and satire of the other" (*Defence of An Essay . . .* , Watson, I, 119). This description of tragedy, like Lisideius' definition of a play, would apply with equal justice to epic, and in fact Dryden saw tragedy and epic as much the same thing. Neander notices no great difference between them except that tragedy has actors who speak dialogue (*Dramatic Poesy*, Watson, I, 87-88), and late in life—with some support from Aristotle—Dryden saw the distinction as chiefly one of scale: "Tragedy is the miniature of human life; an epic poem is the draught at length" (Preface to the *Aeneis*, Watson, II, 226). There is nothing unusual in this identification, which is found in Hobbes in 1650, Kames in 1762, and Cumberland in 1807. Even Aristotle's venerable pair of tragic emotions could be applied to epic, as in Gibbon's account of his youthful reaction to Pope's Homer: "In the death of Hector, and the shipwreck of Ulysses, I tasted the new emotions of terror and pity."[5]

[5] Hobbes, in his *Answer to D'Avenant's Preface to Gondibert*:

14

This attempt to assimilate tragedy to epic recurred because epic was officially the most admired of all literary forms, and because for many readers it apparently did afford the fullest satisfaction of their literary tastes. The heroic plays which for a time embodied their ideal have an extravagant vitality and charm, and the cleverness of Buckingham's *Rehearsal* should not be allowed to obscure the pleasure they can give. But as Pope's Homer was a pretty thing but not Homer, so many of these tragedies are not really tragedies. This is no grounds for reprobation; it is only evidence that Dryden, for example, however much he may have talked about tragedy, did not mean what we do by the term. More generally, there are two notions here which ought not to be confused: (1) that people at that time had an inadequate idea of what tragedy is (which is quite possibly true); (2) that if we could only take them aside and explain it to them, they would be grateful, and would stop wanting to see plays that resemble epics.

To complicate matters further, the critical language of the Restoration lived on to haunt the eighteenth century long after the death of the heroic drama to which it had been related, even while Dryden's ideal of "admiration" gave way to a consistent emphasis on pity as

---

"For the Heroique Poem narrative, such as is yours, is called an Epique Poem. The Heroique Poem Dramatique is Tragedy"; Kames, in *Elements of Criticism*, ch. 22; Cumberland in his *Memoirs* (London, 1807, II, 260): "The tragic drama may be not improperly described as *an epic poem of compressed action.*" Gibbon is quoted from the *Memoirs*, ed. Georges A. Bonnard (New York, 1969), p. 37. As Robert D. Hume observes, Dryden was interested all his life in the heroic, and when he came to see that the drama should be more naturalistic than he had once maintained—thus accepting, for example, Sir Robert Howard's attack on rhyming plays—he transferred this abiding interest to the epic, where in a way it had always belonged (*Dryden's Criticism* [Ithaca, 1970], ch. 6).

the central emotion of tragedy. Addison declared that tragedies "cherish and cultivate that Humanity which is the Ornament of our Nature. They soften Insolence, sooth Affliction, and subdue the Mind to the Dispensations of Providence" (*Spectator* 39). Together with emotionalism, a didactic function is assumed (to which we shall return in a moment). As for the emphasis on pity, which could certainly be exploited by a shallow sentimentalism, it need not always be seen as contemptible. Part of our difficulty lies in the hyperbole into which criticism, or rather appreciation, was drawn. A writer in 1763 says that *Arden of Feversham* shows "a great deal of that nature and simplicity which characterized the works of Lillo." This is sensible enough; but he continues, "No man knew better how to seize the heart; to wring it with contending passions; to melt it into pity; to rouse it to horror; and to torture it with remorse."[6]

Yet we may reflect that Lillo, for all his melodramatic excesses and bathetic sinkings, does exhibit a real sense of the tragedy of fate. And I believe that this reviewer is trying to tell us so, although his assumptions and his vocabulary impel him to concentrate on the wringing, melting, and torturing of the heart. When Addison objects to the mingling of tragedy and comedy, he does so not on arbitrary formal grounds, but for fear that "the tide of sorrow" will be broken (*Spectator* 40). This does not sound like ignorance of what matters in tragedy. Even lesser writers may deserve the benefit of the doubt, as when Thomas Davies discusses the plays of John Home: "It has been questioned, by the critics, whether his genius is warm enough to correspond with the true ends of tragedy; whether he is capable of great energy of sentiment, and of exciting those feelings that never fail to accompany representations of distress, and

[6] Review of *Arden of Feversham* in the *Critical Review*, 15 (1763), p. 134.

16

which melt an audience into tears."[7] Here is a whole catalogue of conventional terms: *warm, energy of sentiment, distress, melt into tears.* Yet Davies knows what he is talking about; he has genuinely felt the untragic limitations of Home's plays, even though he describes his doubts in the language of emotionalism.

2. *Didacticism: Poetic Justice*

While eighteenth-century discussions of the moral function of tragedy took many forms, a brief investigation may profitably center on that notorious subject, the idea of poetic justice. One suspects that at times it was an embarrassment to playwrights, as Charmion's speech near the end of *All for Love* suggests:

> Be juster, Heav'n: such virtue punish'd thus,
> Will make us think that Chance rules all above,
> And shuffles with a random hand, the Lots
> Which Man is forc'd to draw. (v.i.1-4)

To some extent Dryden is being ironic—Cleopatra is rightly punished by poetic justice—but to some extent he is not, since his defense of "the excellency of the moral" in his play seems a little disingenuous: "The chief persons represented were famous patterns of unlawful love; and their end accordingly was unfortunate" (Watson, I, 222). As Dennis pointed out, the play ends with the lines, "And Fame to late Posterity shall tell, / No Lovers liv'd so great, or dy'd so well" (letter to Steele, Hooker, II, 163).

However inconvenient poetic justice may sometimes have been for playwrights, its foundations in critical theory were secure.[8] Rymer, who invented the term

[7] *Memoirs of the Life of David Garrick* (1780), I, 214.
[8] Two valuable discussions are: Richard H. Tyre, "Versions of Poetic Justice in the Early Eighteenth Century," *Studies in Philology*, 54 (1957), 29-44; and Aubrey Williams, "Poetical Jus-

(Zimansky, p. 27), tells us that his real objection to *Othello* is a religious one.

> We may ask here what unnatural crime *Desde-mona*, or her Parents had committed, to bring this Judgment down upon her; to Wed a Black-amoor, and innocent to be thus cruelly murder'd by him. What instruction can we make out of this Catas-trophe? Or whither must our reflection lead us? Is not this to envenome and sour our spirits, to make us repine and grumble at Providence; and the gov-ernment of the World? If this be our end, what boots it to be Vertuous?
>
> (*Short View of Tragedy*, Zimansky, p. 161)

One notices that Rymer takes the Brabantio view of the affair: "to Wed a Black-amoor" is in itself a hideous misfortune, the penalty no doubt for some unnatural crime. And clearly enough this is the tragedy of Desde-mona, not of Othello. Having behaved monstrously, Othello dies, which presumably satisfies Rymer; but Desdemona ought to have lived happily on, as Cordelia does in Tate's *Lear*. Tragedy, Rymer said in the earlier essay, should exhibit "that constant order, that harmony and beauty of Providence" by which virtue and vice are ultimately rewarded and punished (*Tragedies of the Last Age*, Zimansky, p. 75).

This religious emphasis dominates most serious dis-cussions of poetic justice throughout the century. It is not just that we like to see the "good" characters come out all right, but that the poet is expected to act almost as the agent of the Almighty. The central idea is stated by Dennis, its most eloquent proponent, in a single sen-

---

tice, the Contrivances of Providence, and the Works of William Congreve," *English Literary History*, 35 (1968), 540-65. Williams shows that a number of divines described the unseen operation of Providence in real life in exactly the way that it appears in the drama.

tence: "The great Design of Arts is to restore the Decays that happen'd to human Nature by the Fall, by restoring Order" (*The Grounds of Criticism in Poetry*, Hooker, I, 336). In its conception, this is anything but shallow. Dennis is aware that "order" is a fundamental preoccupation of his age, and in his admiration for Longinus and "passion" he epitomizes the desire to have (in Martin Price's terms) energy without sacrificing order.[9] More than this, he perceives that art characteristically creates order, that the great tragedies give shape to the terrible elements of life. Plays that present a wholly irrational and cruel universe—Euripides' *Orestes*, many Jacobean tragedies, many of the modern French variations on Greek themes—may have great interest and force, but seem to lie somewhere on the fringe of tragedy. But noble as Dennis's ideal may be at its best, it gravely misconceives the nature of tragedy. The genres best suited to restoring the decays of fallen man are pastoral and, to some degree, comedy. Tragedy, if it permits a religious context at all, is almost by definition about fallen man.

And here is the central issue: that although theories of this kind do recognize the importance of the problem of justice in tragedy, they are unwilling to leave it unresolved. In effect, art is being asked to illustrate dogma —almost, indeed, to become theodicy. One might divide theorists of poetic justice into two groups. Either they accept the view of Eliphaz the Temanite, "Remember, I pray thee, who ever perished, being innocent? or where were the righteous cut off?" (Job 4 : 7), or else they echo Job's charge against God, "Is it good unto thee that thou shouldest oppress, that thou shouldest despise the work of thine hands, and shine upon the counsel of the wicked?" (10 : 3); and they seek to re-

[9] *To the Palace of Wisdom: Studies in Order and Energy from Dryden to Blake* (New York, 1964).

19

dress the balance in art. One can argue a significance for tragedy in eighteenth-century trivializations of the Book of Job. "I went to Mayfair Chapel," Boswell records, "and heard prayers and an excellent sermon from the Book of Job on the comforts of piety" (*London Journal*, p. 45). Cotton Mather shamelessly recommends the text of Bildad the Shuhite, "Though thy beginning was small, yet thy latter end should greatly increase" (Job 8 : 7), and even Johnson was capable of selective quotation from Job.[10]

Not surprisingly, writers who in theory opposed the requirements of poetic justice were generally unwilling to confront a universe in which innocence is allowed to suffer; they might show that it does not suffer in vain, or they might redefine and restrict the nature and scope of the suffering itself. Thus Addison, whose attack on poetic justice is well known, did little in his *Cato* to suggest the possible dimensions of tragic experience. He had argued against Dennis that "Good and Evil happen alike to all Men on this Side the Grave" (*Spectator* 40), and had made the sensible observation that if an audience knew the hero would end happily, they would not be sufficiently moved by the injustice of his suffering. Like Dennis he was concerned with ultimate justice, but he did not believe that the drama should furnish a literal copy of it. The application of these ideas in his play, however, is most disappointing. There is no question in *Cato* of an inscrutable fate, let alone a cruel one; the problem of evil does not arise. "These are not ills," Cato explains to Juba, "else would they never fall / On

[10] Mather, "Opportunities to Do Good," in *Bonifacius: Essays to Do Good* (1710). Johnson writes in *Rambler* 32, "A settled conviction of the tendency of every thing to our good, and of the possibility of turning miseries into happiness, by receiving them rightly, will incline us to 'bless the name of the Lord, whether he gives or takes away.'" He is alluding to Job 1 : 21, at the very beginning of the book, and of course he does not mention Job's heroic resistance later on.

20

heav'n's first fav'rites, and the best of men" (ii.iv.52-53). Altogether the effect is much less tragic than the one Pope seems to imply (alluding to Addison's Senecan epigraph) in his prologue to the play, "A brave man struggling in the storms of fate, / And greatly falling with a falling state."

The most untragic aspect of neoclassical theory is not so much that virtue is rewarded, as that evil—monstrous, unmitigated evil—is not permitted to exist. By a kind of economy of energy, a villain should be no more wicked than is strictly necessary to keep the plot in motion. From this follows Rymer's irritation with the needlessly unlimited cruelty of "Jago" in *Othello*, and on this point Dryden and Dennis agreed.[11]

But moving away from theory, it may be that readers and critics, however prescriptively they wished that playwrights would observe poetic justice, were by their very sensitivity to the issue able to feel imaginatively the injustice in existing tragedies. One need not accept Lord Kames' premises to recognize the perceptiveness of his conclusion:

> Where a person of integrity is represented as suffering to the end under misfortunes purely accidental, we depart discontented, and with some obscure sense of injustice: for seldom is man so submissive to Providence, as not to revolt against the tyranny and vexations of blind chance; he will be tempted to say, This ought not to be. Chance, giving an impression of anarchy and misrule, pro-

---

[11] For Rymer, see Zimansky, pp. 135-36 and 163; for Dennis, Hooker, ii, 53 (arguing a similar point with reference to Syphax and Sempronius in *Cato*). In *The Grounds of Criticism in Tragedy* Dryden says, "To produce a villain, without other reason than a natural inclination to villainy is, in poetry, to produce an effect without a cause; and to make him more a villain than he has just reason to be, is to make an effect which is stronger than the cause" (Watson, i, 248).

duces always a damp upon the mind. I give for an example the *Romeo and Juliet* of Shakespeare, where the fatal catastrophe is occasioned by Friar Laurence's coming to the monument a minute too late: we are vexed at the unlucky chance, and go away dissatisfied.[12]

Desdemona might not have dropped the handkerchief; help might have reached Cordelia a moment sooner. But these apparent accidents are terrible just because we cannot feel them as truly accidental: they reveal the working out of a pattern, though a far from comforting one. What Kames describes as a damp upon his mind is, for us, an insight into the nature of tragic experience.

3. Catharsis

Ever since Renaissance commentators began trying to understand what Aristotle could have meant by his maddeningly elliptical reference to catharsis, theorists of tragedy have felt it necessary to say something about the subject. In the seventeenth and eighteenth centuries a series of writers attacked the paradox of "the pleasures of tragedy," as E. R. Wasserman calls it in his definitive survey of the topic.[13] Why do we enjoy in the theater what would be painful in real life? Johnson, though he understood the subject, was almost completely uninterested in it, and it seems to have influenced the ordinary intelligent reader only in the vaguest and most general way. Hume's impressive essay was received by the *Critical Review* in this manner:

The title of Mr. *Hume's* third dissertation, *of Tragedy,* flatter'd us with the hopes of much pleasure and instruction, and when we had, as it were,

---

[12] *Elements of Criticism* (1762), ch. 22. I quote from the 9th ed. (Edinburgh, 1817), II, 338.

[13] "The Pleasures of Tragedy," *English Literary History,* 14 (1947), 283-307.

prepared our appetites for one dish, we were a little disappointed at being obliged to sit down to another. Instead of an essay on the construction of several parts of the drama which we expected, we meet only with a cold philosophical enquiry into the cause of that "unaccountable pleasure which the spectators of a well wrote tragedy receive from sorrow, terror, anxiety, and other passions which are in themselves disagreeable and uneasy."[14]

Quite possibly the bankruptcy of analysis of "the construction of several parts of the drama" had helped to impel the Scottish aestheticians toward their new kind of study; instead of endlessly defining the parts of a literary form, they wanted to know how it operated on its audience.

I do not say that the new theories were without effect, but that they were typically received in a diluted and muddled fashion. Indeed there is something a bit quixotic in the search for "the" tragic pleasure, as if there were any reason why people should not react in different and even contradictory ways. On the other hand, this quest for a single truth usually characterizes the best thinkers, and while they should perhaps have remembered Imlac's aphorism, "Inconsistencies cannot both be right, but, imputed to man, they may both be true" (*Rasselas*, ch. 8), it was no solution to cram as many theories as possible into a single paragraph. Such is the method, if it deserves that name, of the critic whom Walpole called "insipid Bishop Hurd":

Not only our attention is rouzed, but our moral instincts are gratified; we reflect with joy that they are so, and we reflect too that the sorrows which call them forth, and give this exercise to our humanity, are but fictitious. We are occupied, in a

14 *Critical Review*, 3 (1757), 212.

word, by a *great* event; we are melted into tears by a *distressful* one; the heart is relieved by this burst of sorrow; is cheared and animated by the finest moral feelings; exults in the consciousness of its own sensibility; and finds, in conclusion, that the whole is but an illusion.[15]

The reason for all this confusion is that most people were not really concerned with explaining why we enjoy plays about lamentable events; they were looking for reasons to support what they hoped was true, that going to plays makes us better men. "The peculiar province of *Tragedy*," Theobald wrote in 1715, "is to refine our Souls, to purge us of those Passions that hurry us into Misfortunes, and correct those Vices that make us incur the Wrath of Heaven, and Condemnation of our Fellow-Creatures."[16] Insofar as catharsis could support a didactic view, there was no objection to adding it to the list of tragedy's virtues. Conversely, it might well seem an unwieldy and dubious ally which didacticism did not really need.

On this subject Dryden is especially interesting. Publicly he saw fit to show great respect to Rymer, and to follow him in saying that "the end or scope of tragedy" is "to rectify or purge our passions, fear and pity" (*Grounds of Criticism in Tragedy*, Watson, I, 245). But in his unpublished notes for an answer to Rymer he suggested that the catharsis of pity and fear was a needlessly limiting doctrine.

To return to the beginning of this enquiry: consider if pity and terror be not enough for tragedy

---

[15] Horace's *Epistolae ad Pisones, et Augustum,* ed. Richard Hurd, 5th ed. (1776), pp. 101-102. I owe the reference to Wasserman, who identifies the various sources of Hurd's farrago (p. 296). Walpole is quoted from a letter to William Mason, 9 June 1783.

[16] *The Censor,* no. 7 (25 April 1715).

to move; and I believe, upon a true definition of tragedy, it will be found that its work extends farther, and that it is to reform manners by delightful representation of human life in great persons, by way of dialogue. If this be true, then not only pity and terror are to be moved as the only means to bring us to virtue, but generally love to virtue and hatred to vice; by shewing the rewards of one, and punishments of the other; at least by rendering virtue always amiable, though it be shown unfortunate; and vice detestable, tho' it be shown triumphant. (Watson, I, 212-13)

If this is not exactly poetic justice, it certainly resembles it, and clearly lays stress on tragedy as a moral lesson rather than a health-giving experience. But, as always, what Dryden is really interested in can be done better by epic than by tragedy, and late in life he was willing to state as much.[17]

Among ordinary people the idea of catharsis filtered down simply as one more proof that drama is moral, and as a useful corroboration for the idea of sentimental sympathy. "Pity" usually receives most of the stress in the Aristotelian formula of pity-and-fear, which appears over and over again as an unexamined catch phrase. In Arthur Murphy's *Life of Garrick*, for instance, it serves as a convenient substitute for analysis. We are told that both Garrick and Mrs. Pritchard "made the spectators pant with terror and pity." When

---

[17] "What virtue is there in a tragedy which is not contained in an epic poem, where pride is humbled, virtue rewarded, and vice punished; and those more amply treated than the narrowness of the drama can admit? . . . Ill habits of the mind are like chronical diseases, to be corrected by degrees and cured by alternatives; wherein, though purges are sometimes necessary, yet diet, good air, and moderate exercise have the greatest part" (Preface to the *Aeneis*, Watson, II, 227-29). Clearly Dryden doubts the value of violent emotional excitement.

Barry competed with Garrick in playing Romeo, Barry excelled in some respects, but Garrick "raised such terror and pity in the catastrophe, that the public opinion was much divided." During a visit to Paris Garrick impersonated a bereaved father who had been the model for his interpretation of Lear, and a celebrated French actress "did not hesitate to declare, that with such a performer the English stage must be the spot where terror and pity were the great passions of the drama."[18]

We have already noticed that the objections to poetic justice were arguments from experience: "Life isn't like that." The ultimate government of Providence was never at issue. What finally killed poetic justice, and likewise caused catharsis to be interpreted in drastically new ways, was the appearance in the next century of theories of tragedy which rested on entirely different assumptions about the universe. Hegel and Bradley saw good emerging from waste and defeat, even though good men are destroyed; Schopenhauer made tragedy an adjunct of his philosophical pessimism; Nietzsche located the "pleasures of tragedy" not in social sympathy but in a flood of Dionysiac emotion.

The limitations of tragic theory in the eighteenth century are in part reflected by the very assumption that we feel *pleasure* in tragedy. Obviously some pleasure is involved, but is there really no pain as well? Hume tried to account for both elements,[19] and through this kind of analysis the Scottish school began to open the way to a breakdown of the old assumptions. One of the *Mirror* papers in 1780, discussing the fact that we desire things more intensely in proportion as they are dif-

[18] *The Life of David Garrick* (1801), I, 170, 194-95; II, 17. Murphy quotes Young's statement that terror and pity are "the two pulses of tragedy" (I, 38).

[19] Hume's ideas are expounded by Ralph Cohen in "The Transformation of Passion: A Study of Hume's Theories of Tragedy," *Philological Quarterly*, 41 (1962), 450-64.

ficult to obtain, suggests that this may tell us something about a psychological need that poetic justice *not* be satisfied. We admire and feel for a virtuous character all the more strongly if he meets with "undeserved calamities," and conversely, "with regard to the vicious, nothing excites so strongly our indignation against vice, or our desire that it should be punished, as our beholding the vicious successful, and, in the midst of his crimes, enjoying prosperity."[20]

This writer fully accepts the view that we should admire the virtuous and abhor the wicked, but he hasn't the slightest interest in an emotional acceptance of the outcome in calm of mind, all passion spent. Far from it; he is concerned with an exacerbation of our feelings, which will enhance the moral effect of tragedy. There is much to be said for this line of thought. At the end of *Hamlet*, who really feels joy at the healing of Denmark, and the future prospects of Fortinbras the fighter for eggshells? Who does not feel something like outrage at Hamlet's death? I do not suppose that the writer in the *Mirror* had all of this in mind; but his discussion at least suggests a welcome liberation from the shackles of hand-me-down thought.

[20] *Mirror*, no. 77 (1 Feb. 1780).

CHAPTER 3

Tragedy Perceived: Other Evidence

1. *The Greeks*

THREE great bodies of tragic drama were available to the eighteenth century: the Greek (with Seneca thrown in), the Elizabethan, and the French. The latter two were less than a century old, but the ancients occupied a position of venerable remoteness, and received their share of routine praise from writers who thought it necessary to admire them. At the same time playwrights frequently saw fit to alter them, by implication for the better. A good deal can be learned about conceptions of tragedy in the eighteenth century if we give some attention to discussions of the Greeks, and then to two representative alterations.

While one should not exaggerate the ignorance of Greek literature among literate men, there are grounds for wondering just how extensively the plays were known. Parson Adams called Sophocles "the greatest genius who ever wrote tragedy," but then *Cato* was the only English tragedy he had ever read, and Homer is the poet he chooses to expound upon. Joseph Warton commented on the absence of the tragedians from the six great authors in Pope's *Temple of Fame*, and explained, "The truth is, it was not fashionable in POPE's time, nor among his acquaintance, attentively to study these poets." Yet Warton himself elsewhere illustrates the claim that the basic literary themes are invariable with this example: "A Jew will nearly resemble a Grecian, when placed almost in the same situation; that is, the Ioas of Racine in his incomparable Athalia, will be very like the Ion of Euripides."[1] Such a remark suggests

[1] Fielding, *Joseph Andrews*, III.ii and v. Warton, *An Essay on the Genius and Writings of Pope*, 4th edn. (1782), I, 379; cf. Geof-

a very imperfect knowledge of at least one of these plays; he doubtless knew the general plot of the *Ion*, but had given little thought to its ironic and even comic implications. Let us begin with Rymer's discussion in *The Tragedies of the Last Age Consider'd and Examin'd by the Practice of the Ancients, and by the Common Sense of All Ages*, which Dryden in his private notes called "the best account I have ever seen of the Ancients" (Watson, I, 218). As the title suggests, Rymer is determined to admire Greek tragedy in order to use it as a stick with which to beat the Elizabethans. He offers first a garbled account of the *Phoenissiae* of Euripides, and next a hasty plot-summary of Sophocles' *Antigone* which is notable for the vagueness of its conclusion: "In this we have every thing *just*, every thing *surprizing*, every thing *passionate* to extremity" (Zimansky, p. 34). He says nothing whatever about Antigone's spiritual heroism, except to mention that "the piety of *Antigone* could not digest so hard a Law" (p. 33). We are told that Creon punishes her, but not that Creon in his own way—as Hegel was to emphasize—argues that he is upholding what the gods desire. What Rymer does dwell upon is the successive suicides of Creon's son and wife—the most visible aspect of the plot, and the most sensational.

Rymer on the *Hippolytus* of Euripides is more penetrating, but again finally disappointing. His long analysis includes extended translations of speeches, and he makes much of the psychological naturalness of Phaedra's behavior and the subtlety with which her guilty secret is extracted by the amoral Nurse. He quite properly remarks on the comparative crudity of Seneca's version, and suggests—with some exaggeration—what

---

frey Tillotson's extended quotation and comment in vol. II of the Twickenham edition of Pope's *Poems* (London, 1940), p. 230. The final quotation from Warton is from *Adventurer*, no. 63 (12 June 1753).

the Jacobeans might have done with it: "Had some Author of the last age given us the character of *Phedra*,
they (to thicken the *Plot*) would have brought her in
burning of Churches, poisoning her Parents, prostitut-
ing her self to the Grooms, solliciting her Son face to
face, with all the importunity and impudence they
could imagin" (p. 55). But a few pages later, during his
discussion of *The Maid's Tragedy*, he pauses to make
the extraordinary observation,

> The *Phedra* in *Euripides* told us truly that it is *not
> Natural to do evil when we know good*. Therefore
> vice can never please unless it be painted and
> dress'd up in the colours and disguise of vertue,
> and should any man knowingly and with open eyes
> prefer what is evil, he must be reckon'd the great-
> est of Monsters, and in no wise be lookt on as any
> image of what is Natural, or what is suitable with
> humane kind. (P. 62.)

In spite of having himself translated Phaedra's speech,
which clearly states that men cannot help doing wrong
even when they know it to be wrong, Rymer thus takes
the Socratic line with which Euripides was no doubt
disillusioned: that we have only to know the good in
order to do it. In spite of his recognition of some important effects in the play, his moralism has imposed a
conception of ideal tragedy which causes him to distort
the meaning of the very passage he has just translated.

Finally, Rymer takes up Aeschylus' *Persae*, that rare
and wonderful feat of sympathy with a vanquished
enemy, and sees it as nothing more than an occasion for
Greek self-congratulation. His sketch for an English
play along the same lines, to be called *The Invincible
Armado* (p. 91), illustrates at once his superficial interest in the simplicity of Greek drama and his total un-
awareness of its tragic implications. Indeed it is far less
tragic than the projected play of Scaliger from which,

30

as his editor tells us, he borrowed the idea (p. 239). If this is the champion of Greek tragedy, one can understand Dryden's statement in 1693 (when hostility to Rymer had stung him to frankness) that "the Greek writers only gave us the rudiments of a stage which they never finished; that many of the tragedies in the former age amongst us were without comparison beyond those of Sophocles and Euripides" (Preface to *Examen Poeticum*, Watson, II, 160).

One comes to see that try as they might, critics had too rudimentary an historical sense to achieve an imaginative reconstruction of a drama and world view so different from their own. Consider Dennis's treatment of the *Antigone* in his youthful *Impartial Critick*:

> When she was condemn'd to the severest Punishment, which was to be buried alive, the thing that lay most heavy upon her Heart was, that she was to go to Hell with her Maiden-head. I think, *Sir*, I need not take pains to demonstrate, that this passage would have been laugh'd at with us. Now what reason can be given, why that should appear so contemptible to us, which mov'd the *Athenians* so much? The only Reason that can be assign'd, is the difference of Climate and Customs. The *Athenians* by using their Women, as the Modern *Italians* do theirs, plainly declared their Opinion of them; which was, that Passion was predominant over Reason in them; and that they were perpetually thinking, how they might make some Improvement of the Talent which NATURE had given their Sex. (Hooker, I, 12)

Though he attempts to illustrate the idea that ancient and modern drama differ, Dennis offers a facile and unimaginative explanation which is scarcely redeemed by the attempt at jolly raillery.

One more example may be mentioned. Rowe in his

31

preface to Shakespeare noticed long before Gilbert Murray that "*Hamlet* is founded on much the same Tale with the *Electra* of *Sophocles.*" Against the ghost's warning, "Nor let thy soul contrive / Against thy mother aught," Rowe contrasts the horrible behavior of both Orestes and his sister: Electra hears her dying mother's cries for mercy, and yet "encourages her Brother in the Parricide" (Nichol Smith, p. 18). Now, the spectacle of Electra urging her brother on is indeed shocking, and Rowe has perceived a real crux in the interpretation of the play. But he has no notion of trying to explain it, as the modern critic has trained himself to do. Today we ask *why* this shocking incident should occur, and try to see whether anything in the structure of the play or the assumptions of Sophocles' time can be found to justify it. (Such a procedure will probably lead us to conclude that Electra is affirming her solidarity with Orestes in the fated retribution.) In addition, we recognize that Sophocles' conception of the legend is involved; he is not just retelling a story, but using the story to say something about the nature of justice and guilt.

I would not pursue this question if it were impossible for a reader of Rowe's time to understand it. My point is that all readers were not alike, and that a sufficiently reflective one could well have perceived something of what the modern scholar finds in the *Electra*. Rowe simply concludes that Sophocles has made a mistake in introducing horror, while Shakespeare wisely confines himself to terror (p. 19). In other words, he perceives the true nature of the Sophoclean scene, but sees no reason why it should be defended. A reviewer of a translation of Sophocles in 1759, however, while granting that "What Electra utters on this occasion is truly horrible," understands that this is essential to the poet's treatment of the legend.

Surely, nothing was ever so calculated to excite horror, as the catastrophe of this tragedy, which is, in all respects, tremendously sublime. Every body knows that Orestes, at the instigation of Electra, sacrifices his own mother Clytemnestra to the manes of his father Agamemnon. Sacrifices her on the very spot where his father fell. There is something dreadful in the circumstance of a son's imbruing his hands in the blood of his parent; but this emotion rises to all the solemnity of horror, when we consider him as executing the vengeance of the gods, by the express command of the oracle.[2]

This writer, who seems to echo Rowe's statement that "*Orestes* embrues his Hands in the Blood of his own Mother" (Nichol Smith, p. 18), accepts the term "horror" without accepting the view that horror is necessarily bad. An appeal to the sublime helps him to argue a quite original case.

Whoever this writer was, his open-minded perceptiveness places him in a small minority. Thomas Franklyn, the translator whom he was reviewing, published in the next year a rigorously standard account of Greek tragedy under more or less Aristotelian categories, with not the slightest awareness of tragic feeling. In the concluding chapter Franklyn makes the remarkable claim that "too strict an attention to the unities hath fettered and confined it," which suggests that he could only see Greek drama through the eyes of neoclassical commentators, though he repudiates their admiration for the unities which it was supposed to obey. He goes on to object that "the same story, the same characters and sentiments, even the same expressions too often occur in different tragedies," thus revealing that he has no

---

[2] Review of Thomas Francklin's translation of *The Tragedies of Sophocles* in the *Critical Review*, 7 (1759), pp. 515-16.

idea of different interpretations of a legend—a story is a story, regardless of treatment. And there is no hint of a mythic world; the plays give us "a most exact and faithful picture of the manners of Greece," including "it's religious and civil policy."[3]

Considering the vagueness and prejudice which many writers showed toward Greek tragedy, it is not surprising that as time went on voices were openly raised against it. Owen Ruffhead, reviewing Franklyn's book, expressed his doubt "whether their pieces, founded mostly on fabulous absurdities, are, at this time, proper entertainments for rational and enlightened minds."[4] And more specific objections began to be based not on neoclassical abstractions but on common sense. The chorus, for instance, had often been criticized on the grounds of probability—why would so large a group of people be present at private discussions?—but Richard Cumberland in the 1780's goes beyond this to attack the earnest fatuousness which the chorus sometimes betrays. While it does not occur to him that this may at times be intended by the poet, he is at least reflecting on how the chorus speaks, not simply on the fact that it exists. When Cassandra bursts into her great prophetic rhapsody in the *Agamemnon*,

The chorus I confess stand the shock with wonderful presence of mind, but the phlegm and apathy of a Greek chorus is proof against every thing. . . . I take the character of a true Greek chorus to be such, that if Apollo himself had come in person to tell them, that the earth would open and swallow them up, if they did not instantly remove from the spot on which they stood, they would have stopped

[3] Thomas Franklyn [or Francklin], *A Dissertation on Ancient Tragedy* (1768 ed.), pp. 79, 81. The title page identifies the author as "Late Greek Professor in the University of Cambridge."
[4] *Monthly Review*, 23 (1760), p. 7.

to moralize, or hymn an ode, in strophe and antistrophe, to Jupiter or Venus, or the gods below to whom they were descending, though the ground was cleaving under their feet.

(The Observer, no. 134)

Years later, writing in his *Memoirs*, Cumberland takes it for granted that the Greeks were strict adherents of the neoclassical rules, and expresses shame for his boyish admiration: "I well remember, when I was newly come to college, with what avidity I read the Greek tragedians, and with what reverence I swallowed the absurdities of their chorus, and was bigoted to their cold character and rigid unities."[5]

Much can be learned as well from the attempts of playwrights to transform what even scholars could hardly understand into the terms of contemporary drama. Consider, for example, the *Oedipus* of Dryden and Lee (1678 or 1679). This is a frenetic and overwritten play, with plunges into bathos (especially in the parts written by Lee) which it would be a waste of time to examine here. There are also exaggerated specimens of Restoration horror, and the play ends with a grotesque medley of murders and suicides. But as it was performed almost every year from 1700 to 1730, and often thereafter, it cannot very well be dismissed as a transitory phenomenon. Viewed as a version of Sophocles, it is a travesty; taken in itself, it is a lively attempt to make a modern drama out of one of the most haunting and baffling of all legends.

Addison quoted a crucial passage in *Spectator* 40 as being "very natural, and apt to move compassion" in contrast to some of the rant:

[5] *Memoirs* (1807), I, 116. Cumberland mentions that in writing the *Observer* papers on Greek literature he had the use of notes inherited from his grandfather, the great Richard Bentley (I, 94-95).

To you, good Gods, I make my last appeal;
Or clear my Vertues or my Crime reveal:
If wandring in the maze of Fate I run,
And backward trod the paths I sought to shun,
Impute my Errours to your own Decree;
My hands are guilty, but my heart is free.[6]

Here certainly is the central paradox of the Oedipus story: why is a man punished for what he never knew he was doing, and indeed seems to have been pre-destined to do? Corneille confessed himself thoroughly puzzled in his discussion of Aristotle's principle that the hero should fall through his own fault.[7] Further discussions—including Johnson's, which we shall look at later —all turn upon this point. In order to make Oedipus more reprehensible, Corneille made him, in Dryden's words, "suspicious, designing, more anxious of keeping the Theban crown than solicitous for the safety of his people" (Preface to *Oedipus*, Watson, I, 233). Dryden in turn tried to restore Oedipus to his original virtue, and to de-emphasize the obligatory subplot. "Making Oedipus the best and bravest person, and even Jocasta but an underpart to him, his virtues and the punishment of his fatal crime drew both the pity and the terror to himself" (*Grounds of Criticism in Tragedy*, Watson, I, 250). But either extreme has its drawbacks,

[6] Act III, in *Dryden: The Dramatic Works*, ed. Montague Summers (London, 1932), IV, 397-98.

[7] "[Oedipus] seems to me to commit no fault at all, even though he kills his father, since he didn't know him, and since he does nothing more than dispute the road, like a man of courage [*homme de coeur*], against the attack of a stranger who has the advantage on his side. Nonetheless, as the Greek word *hamártema* may extend to a simple failure of recognition such as his was, let us admit it with this philosopher, even though I am unable to see of what passion we are to be purged, or how we can correct ourselves by his example" (*Discours II: De la tragédie* [1660], para. 6).

and Dennis presently argued that Dryden's Oedipus is too perfect and excites horror rather than terror, while the Sophoclean hero was justly if enormously punished for his curiosity, pride, and violent temper (*The Impartial Critick*, Hooker, I, 19-22).

These difficulties do not arise from simple misreading of the Greek original, but rather from a philosophical chasm between Sophocles and postclassical times. It is possible to say that Oedipus is *de facto* guilty of incest and patricide even though in our sense his conscience is clean, and this may be the assumption of the play; in the later *Oedipus at Colonus*, however, Sophocles makes his hero insist on his innocence in terms reasonably congruous with our own. Evidently he has no intention of furnishing easy answers to an intolerable dilemma; but be that as it may, his lack of emphasis on psychological analysis (such as Euripides might have employed) allows him to limit the issue of willed and unwilled crime. In this connection Theobald's discussion of the play is highly relevant. Like everyone else he struggles with the problem of how Oedipus can deserve his punishment, and like Dennis he settles on "Pride, Anger, Violence, Temerity, and Imprudence," making the preposterous suggestion that Oedipus might have lived happily ever after with Jocasta if only he had not asked unnecessary questions. But then, surprisingly, he launches into a much more persuasive point about *Othello*: "The Crimes and Misfortunes of the *Moor* are owing to an impetuous Desire of having his Doubts clear'd, and a Jealousie and Rage, native to him, which he cannot controul, and which push him on to Revenge."[8]

In other words, all of these critics are at a loss when they try to interpret a play that lacks naturalistic psy-

[8] *The Censor*, no. 36 (12 Jan. 1717).

chology, and only by the introduction of such psychology—an almost impossible feat—can the Oedipus story be made intelligible. While Dryden and Lee load their play with every device they can think of to add variety and interest, the incest theme is the dominant one, and is explored with such fascination as to enhance our admiration for Sophocles' restrained treatment of it.[9] And if fate is still unjust—Oedipus and Jocasta have not consciously willed their sin—this psychological kind of determinism is more palatable than the kind which would seem to accuse Heaven of injustice.

A brief glance at Thomson's *Agamemnon* (1738) will demonstrate that this solution is not confined to the hectic drama of the Restoration. Aeschylus' play, one of the richest and most extraordinary of all tragedies, involves its characters in a hopelessly tangled web of fate, and gives little evidence that their crimes, monstrous and punishable as they are, could possibly have been averted by their own volition. Seneca's chief contribution was to intensify the physical horror of the murder, in which Thomson is not tempted to follow him, but he also has a scene in which a temporarily re-

[9] Two instances will suffice: the labored irony of

OEDIPUS.   No pious Son 'ere lov'd his Mother more
Than I my dear *Jocasta*.
JOCASTA.   I love you too
The self same way. . . .
And when I have you in my arms, methinks
I lull my child asleep. (Act I, p. 369)

and the clinical account of the inhibitions experienced by a man who has married his mother:

Nay, she is beauteous too; yet, mighty Love!
I never offer'd to obey thy Laws,
But an unusual chillness came upon me;
An unknown hand still check'd my forward joy,
Dash'd me with blushes, tho' no light was near:
That ev'n the Act became a violation. (Act II, p. 377)

38

pentant Clytemnestra tries to dissuade Aegisthus from
their evil designs. From this circumstance Thomson
probably seized the idea of his play, in which Clytemnestra's psychological struggle receives the main focus.
In addition an intrigue is devised to contribute suspense, and the agency of fate is exonerated from blame
for the destruction of the innocent. All moral ambi-
guities are swept away. The death of Iphigenia at Aulis,
which is a complicating factor in the versions of all
three Greek tragedians, is explained by Thomson's
Agamemnon with the claim that Clytemnestra herself
would have despised any evasion of "The mingled
voice / Of honour, duty, glory, public good, / Of the
commanding gods" (II.ii, pp. 134-35).[10] There is no hint
that the gods may sometimes command what is wrong;
in the next scene Electra sees her sister's death as an
enviable martyrdom: "Who would not die to gain immortal fame, / Deliver *Greece,* and crown a father's
glory?" (II.iii, p. 139).

The emphasis of the play is upon Clytemnestra's
struggle. In her anguish before the murder she becomes
Hamlet:

My sole remaining hope
Is death, kind death, that amiable sleep,
Which wakes no more,—at least to mortal care—
But then the dark Hereafter that may come.—
There is no anchor that against this storm,
This mighty sea of doubts and fears, can hold.

(IV.iv, p. 177)

Once the deed is done she raves deliriously, denounces
Aegisthus, and faints upon seeing a vision of her husband. "Ah! What avails it where the guilty fly, / Since
from themselves they cannot!" (v.viii, p. 202). One may

[10] I quote from the text in Thomson's *Works* (1750), vol. III.

39

compare her calm statement in Aeschylus, "There will be no tears in this house for him."[11]

Bad as Thomson's play is, its intention at least suggests tragic possibilities. Since the admirable Agamemnon has died, and since the eventual triumph of Orestes is only distantly sketched, poetic justice is not fully satisfied even though Clytemnestra is clearly guilty. This Thomson defends in conventional terms, by an appeal to sensibility.

> Sweet source of every virtue,
> O sacred sorrow! He who knows not thee,
> Knows not the best emotions of the heart,
> Those tender tears that humanize the soul,
> The sigh that charms, the pang that gives delight.
>
> (v.iii, p. 194)

That Thomson's play has at least a potentiality for tragic feeling is illuminated by the obtuseness of Aaron Hill, who wrote to Pope, "*Agamemnon*, who gives *moral* and *name* to the Play, ought to have animated, and stood obvious in every part of it. All the evil he *suffers*, should be an effect of some act which he *does*."[12] In addition to adding various sorts of "business," Hill would support his emphasis on Agamemnon by making Clytemnestra entirely innocent of the plot against him. This version would have been a strenuously active play, but Thomson's, though it is anything but Greek, has the rudiments of genuine tragedy. And like the Dryden-Lee *Oedipus* it depends for its effect on translating ancient myth into naturalistic psychology. That such a translation seemed desirable or necessary suggests how much that is central to classical trag-

[11] Line 1554 of the translation by Richmond Lattimore, in the Chicago edition of the Greek tragedies.
[12] Letter of 8 Nov. 1738, in Hill's *Works*, 2nd ed. (1754), II, 42ff.

edy was simply unavailable to readers in the eighteenth
century.

2. Shakespeare

While in a sense "Shakespeare idolatry" swelled like
a flood during the eighteenth century, in another sense,
as is well known, he had always been admired, and it
was really the terms of admiration that changed. In fact
the best known attacks on Shakespeare, from Rymer on
down, are essentially the polemical gestures of conservative intellectuals who do not even pretend to
speak for the majority. If one looks for them, such pro-
nunciamentos are by no means confined to the earlier
part of the century. Walpole in 1775 explicitly used the
inspired-idiot metaphor: "He seems to recall the
Mahometan idea of lunatics, who are sometimes inspired, oftener changelings." Gibbon in his *Autobiog-
raphy* ambiguously mentions "the Gigantic Genius of
Shakespeare," an idolatry of which "is inculcated from
our infancy as the first duty of an Englishman." Arthur
Murphy in 1801 still saw Shakespeare as lacking regularity, and approved a version of *The Winter's Tale* in
which Garrick "with great judgement, extracted from
the chaos before him a clear and regular fable." And an
interesting testimony to the ideal of uniformity of taste
is furnished by the pompous Cumberland, who recalls
that in his boyhood in the 1740's his mother (a daughter
of Richard Bentley) had taken pains to form his appreciation of Shakespeare:

> I well remember the care she took to mark out for
> my observation the peculiar excellence of that un-
> rivalled poet in the consistency and preservation
> of his characters, and wherever instances occurred
> amongst the starts and sallies of his unfettered
> fancy of the extravagant and false sublime, her dis-

41

cernment oftentimes prevented me from being so dazzled by the glitter of the period as to misapply my admiration, and betray my want of taste.[13]

Further discussion of this conservative tradition may be delayed until we take up Johnson's criticism of Shakespeare. It cannot be dismissed as negligible, for men like Walpole, Gibbon, and Johnson are certainly not negligible, but neither can it be said to reflect the mainstream view of Shakespeare in the eighteenth century. The much-maligned adaptations, for example, while they did make various concessions to "regularity," were chiefly intended to bring forward the effect of pathos.[14] That this was unfortunate may be admitted, and yet it does not prove that Shakespeare was made wholly untragic, as perhaps he would have been if he had been compelled to march rigidly within the rules.

Those critics who believed in rules had a good deal of difficulty in adjusting their systems to accommodate Shakespeare. The interesting thing is not the simple absurdity of implying that he wrote without knowing what he was doing, but the sense one gets that they felt it to be absurd without quite seeing what to do about it. Dennis in an *Essay on the Genius and Writings of Shakespeare* treats the obligatory theme of Nature as follows: "He had so fine a Talent for touching the Pas-

[13] Walpole, letter to Robert Jephson, Feb. 1775. Gibbon, *Memoirs*, ed. Georges A. Bonnard (New York, 1969), p. 84. Murphy, *The Life of David Garrick* (1801), I, 285. Cumberland, *Memoirs* (1807), I, 55.
[14] Eric Rothstein observes that the Restoration adapters made Shakespeare into a kind of Fletcher: *Restoration Tragedy* (Madison, 1967), p. 55. Accounts of Garrick's emphasis on love and pathos will be found in a series of articles by George W. Stone, Jr., notably "Garrick's Presentation of *Antony and Cleopatra*," *Review of English Studies*, 13 (1937), 20-38, and "Garrick's Production of *King Lear*," *Studies in Philology*, 45 (1948), 89-103.

sions, and they are so lively in him, and so truly in Nature, that they often touch us more without their due
Preparations, than those of other Tragick Poets, who
have all the Beauty of Design and all the Advantage of
Incidents" (Hooker, II, 4). How essential can those "due
Preparations" be when we can be greatly moved without them? How can Shakespeare be assumed to lack all
notion of design? How can "incidents" be so narrowly
defined as not to apply to his plays?

Exactly the same contradictions run through Pope's
Preface:

> The *Power* over our *Passions* was never possess'd
> in a more eminent degree, or display'd in so differ-
> ent instances. Yet all along, there is seen no labour,
> no pains to raise them; no preparation to guide our
> guess to the effect, or be perceiv'd to lead toward
> it: But the heart swells, and the tears burst out, just
> at the proper places: We are surpriz'd, the moment
> we weep; and yet upon reflection find the passion
> so just, that we shou'd be surpriz'd if we had not
> wept, and wept at that very moment.
>
> (Nichol Smith, p. 45)

Pope is awkward here because his critical vocabulary
does not really permit him to say what he wants to say;
fifty years later Maurice Morgann, in his famous essay
on Falstaff, could ironically expose the inconsistency of
"those who firmly believe that this wild, this unculti-
vated Barbarian [Shakespeare] has not yet obtained
one half of his fame," and could repeat the substance
of Pope's argument while drawing exactly the opposite
conclusion from it.

> He scatters the seeds of things, the principles of
> character and action, with so cunning a hand, yet
> with so careless an air, and, master of our feelings,

43

submits himself so little to our judgment, that every thing seems superior. We discern not his course, we see no connection of cause and effect, we are rapt in ignorant admiration, and claim no kindred with his abilities. All the incidents, all the parts, look like chance, whilst we feel and are sensible that the whole is design.

(Nichol Smith, pp. 232, 233)

It is as simple as that: writers like Dennis and Pope have accepted a needlessly limited notion of "design."

However mistakenly they apply this notion, these writers are evidently aware of a fundamental difference between Shakespeare and the dramatists of their own time, who did think it necessary to prepare every effect by careful degrees. "We are surpriz'd, the moment we weep," Pope says; in the drama of his own time we foresee, like the White Queen in *Alice*, that the moment is about to arrive when we shall be weeping. Rymer tells us that the same "springs" move the passions in London that used to move them in Athens, and Warburton makes the mechanical metaphor explicit—one might have thought of watery "springs"—when he praises the "amazing sagacity" with which Shakespeare "investigates every hidden spring and wheel of human Action." In numerous places Dryden shows that this conventional image was supposed to reflect the art of the playwright. Having studied the passions in "natural philosophy, ethics, and history," he can turn this technical knowledge to account, without which indeed his genius would be useless.

A poet may be born with this quality; yet, unless he help himself by an acquired knowledge of the passions, what they are in their own nature, and by what springs they are to be moved, he will be subject either to raise them where they ought not

44

to be raised, or not to raise them by the just degrees of nature, or to amplify them beyond the natural bounds, or not to observe the crisis and turns of them, in their cooling and decay: all which errors proceed from want of judgment in the poet, and from being unskilled in the principles of moral philosophy.

The egregious Aaron Hill brings out the degree to which this seemed to provide a foolproof science of playwriting. "The *Passions* are, (in a Tragedy where well *mark'd*, and *express'd*) what the *Keys* are, in a *Harpsichord.* —If they are aptly and skilfully *touch'd*, they will *vibrate* their different *Notes*, to the Heart, and awaken in it the *Musick* of *Humanity*."[15]

In these discussions of the mastery of the passions, what is implied is not so much a psychological analysis of the characters as the rhetorical power to move the more generalized emotions of an audience. And even though critics like Dennis and Pope believed Shakespeare to be ignorant of this technical skill, one perceives that they really didn't mind very much. If he moved them by surprise, they cannot help but imply, he is imparting pleasure as great or greater than that of the more methodically studied tragedies. In this lay the point of the endless equations of Shakespeare with

[15] Rymer, *Tragedies of the Last Age* (Zimansky, p. 19). Warburton, Preface to *The Works of Shakespeare* (Nichol Smith, p. 100). Dryden, *Grounds of Criticism in Tragedy* (Watson, I, 248 and 254). Hill, *The Prompter*, no. 64 (20 June 1735).
Two further examples of mechanical "springs" may be given: in the early "To my Honored Friend, Sir Robert Howard, On his Excellent Poems" (1660), Dryden says that dull readers of Howard's poetry are unable to see "what hidden springs within the Engine be" (line 22); in his indecent explanation of Henri IV's militarism Swift asks, "What secret wheel, what hidden spring could put into motion so wonderful an engine?" (*A Tale of a Tub*, sec. ix).

Nature and Jonson with Art: that the kind of art Shakespeare lacked is not of a crucially important kind.[16]

The great defect of the exaltation of "nature" was that it emphasized certain aspects of Shakespeare while obscuring others. With exceptional inappropriateness Dennis quoted Milton's lines, "So Shakespeare, Fancy's sweetest child, / Warbles his native wood notes wild," in the prologue to his adaptation of *Coriolanus* (Hooker, II, 407); and Joseph Warton in the *Enthusiast* demands, "What are the lays of Artful Addison, / Coldly correct, to Shakespeare's warblings wild?" The wild woodnote warbler does not at once suggest *Othello* or *King Lear*. Pathos and romance gain prominence as Shakespeare's leading characteristics; a reviewer in 1767 says that the only English poets worthy to be compared with him are Milton, Otway, and Spenser.[17]

But vocal as the admirers of the "romantic" were, critics like Johnson continued to mean human nature when they spoke of Shakespeare's "nature." In Dryden's noble encomium, "Shakespeare had an universal mind, which comprehended all characters and passions" (*Grounds of Criticism*, Watson, I, 260). And most important, the dismissal of his "art," however patronizing and contradictory it now seems, allowed critics to ignore the kind of technical skills that their contemporaries boasted of—not just the "rules," but the labored management of "springs of passion"—in order to relocate the discussion in the feelings which the plays arouse.

I should like to conclude this part of my discussion

[16] Thus Johnson in the *Drury Lane Prologue*:

Then JOHNSON [i.e. Jonson] came, instructed from the school,
To please in method, and invent by rule;
His studious patience, and laborious art,
By regular approach essay'd the heart.

[17] Review of a translation of Metastasio—who is likewise compared with Shakespeare—in the *Critical Review*, 24 (1767), 52.

by quoting at length from an essay of John Hughes in 1713, a sensitive account of a great play which makes nonsense of the idea that no one could understand the meaning of Shakespearean tragedy. And this long, connected passage will illustrate the point that brief critical dicta—Shakespeare the barbarian, Shakespeare the warbler—do not always give us a full idea of what intelligent men thought and felt.

Hughes' thesis is that Othello's love "is tempestuous, and mingled with a wildness peculiar to his character, which seems very artfully to prepare for the change which is to follow."

> How savage, yet how ardent, is that expression of the raptures of his heart, when, looking after Desdemona as she withdraws, he breaks out,

> > Excellent wench! [*sic*] perdition catch my soul,
> > But I do love thee; and when I love thee not,
> > Chaos is come again.

> The deep and subtle villany of Iago, in working this change from love to jealousy, in so tumultuous a mind as that of Othello, prepossessed with a confidence in the disinterested affection of the man who is leading him on insensibly to his ruin, is likewise drawn with a masterly hand. Iago's broken hints, questions, and seeming care to hide the reason of them; his obscure suggestions to raise the curiosity of the Moor; his personated confusion, and refusing to explain himself, while Othello is drawn on, and held in suspense till he grows impatient and angry; then his throwing in the poison, and naming to him, in a caution, the passion he would raise,

> > —O beware of jealousy!

> are inimitable strokes of art, in that scene which has always been justly esteemed one of the best

47

which was ever represented on the theatre.

To return to the character of Othello. His strife of passions, his starts, his returns of love, and threatenings to Iago, who puts his mind on the rack, his relapses afterwards to jealousy, his rage against his wife, and his asking pardon of Iago, whom he thinks he had abused for his fidelity to him, are touches which no one can overlook that has the sentiments of human nature, or has considered the heart of man in its frailties, its penances, and all the variety of its agitations. The torments which the Moor suffers are so exquisitely drawn, as to render him as much an object of compassion, even in the barbarous action of murdering Desdemona, as the innocent person herself who falls under his hand.

But there is nothing in which the poet has more shown his judgment in this play, than in the circumstance of the handkerchief, which is employed as a confirmation to the jealousy of Othello already raised. What I would here observe is, that the very slightness of this circumstance is the beauty of it. How finely has Shakespeare expressed the nature of jealousy in those lines, which, on this occasion, he puts into the mouth of Iago,

> Trifles light as air
> Are to the jealous confirmations strong
> As proofs of Holy Writ.

It would be easy for a tasteless critic to turn any of the beauties I have here mentioned into ridicule; but such an one would only betray a mechanical judgment, formed out of borrowed rules and common-place reading, and not arising from any true discernment in human nature, and its passions.

(*Guardian* 37, 23 April 1713)

This essay raises so many valuable points in the light of our earlier discussion that it may be useful to list some of them, in approximately the order in which they occur.

1. Hughes admires "the subtle villany of Iago." Not just Rymer but Dryden and Dennis as well had argued on dogmatic grounds that a tragedy cannot countenance so monstrous a villain. Hughes is more interested in why the play is so good than in whether it obeys arbitrary laws, and consequently he does not reject the villainy which in fact reflects the problem of evil, a problem which so many critics were not willing to see tragedy explore.

2. To understand the play as a psychological combat between Iago and Othello is an enormous advance from hunting out inconsistencies in the plot, or deducing a moral lesson which it is supposed to convey. Again, it directs our attention to what happens in the play, not to what doesn't. And the relations between Iago and Othello are quite subtly described. Hughes perceives that Iago is really playing on Othello's inherent weakness, his potentiality to *be* jealous.

3. All of this is described as "strokes of *art*," not as unaccountable assaults on our emotions; and this art is understood to be wholly compatible with Shakespeare's mastery of "nature," which is also praised.

4. Furthermore, "nature" mainly refers to the psychological depths of characterization—the wildness *"peculiar"* to Othello's character, not the broad, vague feelings of an audience. One need not deny that plays do work rhetorically on audiences to see that this is much more interesting and valuable than the mechanical idea of the playwright and his harpsichord of the passions.

5. Othello is just as much an "object of compassion" as Desdemona is. This is a notable step forward from criticism conditioned by the notion of poetic justice, ac-

cording to which Othello deserves to die and Desdemona does not. In a deeper sense neither deserves to die, and, what is at least as important, this is the tragedy of Othello. Desdemona, like Ophelia, is so moving because her case is clear and simple, and finally limited; it is best suited to the pathos admired by eighteenth-century audiences, as exemplified by the "she-tragedies" of Rowe. But Hughes has a real sense of what a tragic hero can be.

6. The handkerchief, much derided by Rymer, is not an inept device at all, but dramatically successful by "the very slightness of this circumstance," which could not achieve its effect if Iago had not carefully poisoned the mind of Othello.

7. Hughes quotes some lines on "the nature of jealousy," but whereas many writers were fond of lifting bits of poetry out of context (and still are: "To thine own self be true"), he recognizes that they are spoken by Iago "on this occasion." They may have universal application, but they are not abstracted as a self-contained *sententia*, Shakespeare on Jealousy.

8. Finally, Hughes uses the conventional term "beauties" to describe what he has been analyzing; but clearly he does not mean fragmentary anthology-pieces by the term, as many writers did. He is talking about the effect that *Othello* really has on us, in explicit contrast to a mechanical and derivative criticism that is divorced from living aesthetic experience.

The last thing I would claim is that Hughes' essay is representative. The heart of my argument is that it is not, but that the foolishness of minor writers and the misguidedness of major ones should not tempt us to pronounce that an entire century had forgotten what tragedy is all about. At the time of Rowe and Hughes it seems incontrovertible that some people did understand it, even if their critical language was not very well suited to expressing it. At the end of the century, developing the emphasis on character rather than plot, a school of psychological criticism extended and deepened these insights.[18]

Finally, we should remember that a large canon of tragedy was seen on the stage, and that a series of celebrated actors, however artificial their style might seem to us today, must have helped to give it life for the ordinary spectator. Garrick's Lear, for example, was one of the most famous of all roles, and some of the accounts of it give a sense of impressive strength and feeling. Joseph Warton's essays on the play include a warm tribute to Garrick (*Adventurer* 113), which suggests that the actor's interpretation had contributed to Warton's. And Thomas Wilkes's tribute rises to the level of an imaginative recreation:

> I never see him coming down from one corner of the stage, with his old grey hair standing, as it were, erect on his head, his face filled with horror and attention, his hands expanded, and his whole frame actuated by a dreadful solemnity, but I am astounded, and share in all his distresses. . . . Methinks I share in his calamities, I feel the dark drifting rain, and the sharp tempest.[19]

Who will presume to say that, Tate's version notwithstanding, this was not a tragic *King Lear*?

3. General Observations

The evidence presented in this chapter has shown, I hope, that even if new tragedies of considerable stature were no longer being written, the ability to understand tragedy was not extinct. But something ought to be said about the larger indictment that is implied when people say that the eighteenth century had lost the tragic sense of life, or that it evaded the problem of

[18] This subject will receive further discussion in Chapter 8.
[19] *A General View of the Stage* (1759), p. 234.

evil. On the material and social level, there were great hopes for the progress of mankind (especially in France); on the metaphysical level, the universe was conceived of as making sense, as a system in which evil had a strictly limited and necessary place, like toilets.

So huge an indictment can scarcely receive an answer here, especially since it contains so many elements of truth. In the next chapter some of its implications will be examined in detail as they relate to Johnson. What can be said at present is that all men were not alike, and that deeply reflective if not tragic notes occur in many of the best thinkers. D'Alembert, the great *Encyclopédiste*, wrote in a somber moment to a king:

> When, weary of labor or company, which often happens, I find myself alone, and isolated as I am in this best of possible worlds, my solitude frightens and chills me, and I am like a man who sees before him a great desert to be crossed, and the abyss of destruction at the end of that desert, with no hope of finding there a single being who will be sorry to see him fall into that abyss, and who will remember him after he has fallen.[20]

In England various manifestations reflect a similar view, though when they are taken in general rather than in individuals their depth and interest suffers. The vogue of so-called graveyard poetry, for example, is highly miscellaneous and varied, but it surely reflects a need to engage the fact of mortality. That it is sometimes macabre and usually sentimental does not mean that the need was not genuine. An eighteenth-century reader of *The Grave* may have enjoyed a *frisson* for which we feel little enthusiasm, but that does not prove it to have been a factitious *frisson*.

[20] Letter to Frederick the Great, 27 Feb. 1777, in *Œuvres* (1805), XVIII, 102-103.

Or again, it is interesting that many people found the traditional metaphor of life as a tragedy to be vital and significant. The Civil War especially attracted it, as in Marvell's lines in the *Horatian Ode*:

> That hence the *Royal Actor* borne
> The *tragic scaffold* might adorn,

or in Hume's reference to "the tragic death of Charles."[21] Boswell calls the martyrdom of Charles I "this tragical event" (*London Journal*, p. 173).

At the very end of the century this metaphor achieves classic statement in Burke's *Reflections on the Revolution in France*. Paul Fussell has discussed the way in which *King Lear* haunted Burke, and in the *Reflections* there is a direct allusion to the play: "The wardrobe of a moral imagination, which the heart owns and the understanding ratifies as necessary to cover the defects of our naked, shivering nature. . . ." (Perhaps a similar allusion is intended in Johnson's *Rambler* 129: "Reflections that may drive away despair, cannot be wanting to him who considers how much life is now advanced beyond the state of naked, undisciplined, uninstructed nature.") For Burke the Revolution was a disastrous event that would reduce all men to forked animals again. A few pages after this passage he rises to a brilliant evocation of life as tragic drama:

> We are so made as to be affected at such spectacles with melancholy sentiments upon the unstable condition of mortal prosperity and the tremendous uncertainty of human greatness. . . . When kings are hurled from their thrones by the Supreme Director of this great drama and become the objects of insult to the base and of pity to the good, we behold such disasters in the moral as we should behold a miracle in the physical order of things.

[21] *History of England* (Edinburgh, 1792), VII, 148.

53

> We are alarmed into reflection; our minds (as it has
> long since been observed) are purified by terror
> and pity, our weak, unthinking pride is humbled
> under the dispensations of a mysterious wisdom.[22]

This majestic vision, like the often strident *Reflections*
as a whole, is a kind of valediction to a dying way of
looking at life.

Finally, to hazard a large generalization, it is no accident that the eighteenth century was a golden age of
comedy and satire. My argument has been intended to
show that a genuine tragic sense could exist, and in
some writers could even find expression in literary criticism. But in an age whose prevailing urge was to establish harmony and order, it is not surprising that
tragedy, with its tendency to undermine norms and
confront the unknown, should have been forced into a
particularly rigid and conventionalized form. Comic
and satiric literature, which assume the validity of
norms and the possibility of resolution, luxuriated
meanwhile in an imaginative freedom from form; it was
in tragedy that disruptive elements had to be carefully
controlled.

In consequence the sense of the tragic tended to be
displaced into genres where it need not be the sole or
dominant theme—one thinks of much Augustan satire
—or to find expression in unliterary or subliterary
modes. Johnson's *Irene* is his least tragic piece of writing, less tragic even than the final paragraph of the
Preface to the *Dictionary*. *The Vanity of Human
Wishes*, ostensibly a satire imitating a satire, is deeply
colored by tragic feeling; Johnson's private prayers and

[22] *Reflections on the Revolution in France* (1790), ed. Thomas
Mahoney (New York, 1955), pp. 87, 91. See Paul Fussell, *The
Rhetorical World of Augustan Humanism* (Oxford, 1965), pp.
15, 39-42, and 228-29.

meditations are the most tragic of all. His deficiencies as a critic of dramatic tragedy, moreover, are due not so much to his aesthetic assumptions as to the view of life which they reflect; profoundly conscious as he was of the existence of the tragic, he did not like to see it openly explored in art.

II. THE TRAGIC
IN JOHNSON'S LIFE AND WORKS

CHAPTER 4

Johnson's Tragic Sense of Life

1. Johnson as Tragic Hero

DESCRIBING Johnson's character as a writer, Robert Alves wrote in 1794,

> A certain sublimity, as well as melancholy of imagination, marks even his earliest productions. He was more struck with the terrible and tragic than the beautiful or gay. In nature he always described the most awful or solemn scenes; and in the moral world he took most delight in the recital of human misery, the fall of greatness, the disappointments of ambition, or misfortunes from levity or extravagance in the lower spheres of life.[1]

Here, stated only a decade after his death, is a theme which runs through many modern studies of Johnson: he was acutely conscious of human misery; this consciousness is in some way "tragic"; and it is discernible in both his works and his life.

Recent scholarship emphasizing this theme may be said to have begun with W.B.C. Watkins' *Perilous Balance: The Tragic Genius of Swift, Johnson and Sterne*, which first laid emphasis on the darker side of Johnson, and represented as tragic a life spent in heroic struggle against the threat of insanity. A few quotations will illustrate the general recognition of the tragic dimension in later works on Johnson's moral thought: Walter Jackson Bate speaks of Johnson's "tragic exploration of man's destiny"; Robert Voitle identifies "an awareness of the tragedy of human existence and of the more comprehensive evil surrounding man, which cannot be suc-

---

[1] *Sketches of a History of Literature* (Edinburgh, 1794), pp. 287-88. Alves' account of Johnson is highly derogatory.

cessfully faced alone"; and Arieh Sachs sees *hope* and *fear*, two central terms in Johnson's writing, as summing up "the tragic restlessness inherent in man's temporal being, his mind's constant over-reaching of his body."[2]

As these writers use the term, it is certainly appropriate to Johnson. We all understand the sense in which a powerful mind, oppressed by emotional disability, is said to be tragic; or the sense in which the inevitable limitation of human happiness, and the certainty that all life must end in death, are said to be tragic. But as soon as one pursues the question further, important complications and qualifications appear. Above all we should not forget that however deeply he may have suffered, Johnson always strove in his role as moralist to conquer tragedy, or at least to go beyond it. In Bate's terms, his "achievement" is the transmutation of personal anguish into stability, order, control. In this chapter I shall try to examine what we mean when we talk of Johnson's tragic sense, considering first his life, then his religious and philosophical views, and finally the antitragic elements of his moral writing.

Knowing very well that "Nothing . . . is more common than to call our own condition, the condition of life" (*Rasselas*, ch. 45), Johnson nonetheless believed that his moral writing possessed general validity, and that what he called "the general sense or experience of

---

[2] Bate, *The Achievement of Samuel Johnson* (New York, 1961), p. 136; Voitle, *Samuel Johnson the Moralist* (Cambridge, Mass., 1961), p. 108; Sachs, *Passionate Intelligence: Imagination and Reason in the Work of Samuel Johnson* (Baltimore, 1967), p. 45. Watkins' book was published at Princeton in 1939. In addition to the published works cited in this chapter, I want to record that Rodman D. Rhodes, "Samuel Johnson and the Problem of Evil" (Harvard diss., 1963) was of particular value to me when I was setting out on my investigation, helping me to define my approach and suggesting many passages for discussion.

mankind" (*Life of Dyer*, III, 345) was everywhere the same. As he wrote in an essay on the uses of biography,

> There is such an uniformity in the state of man, considered apart from adventitious and separable decorations and disguises, that there is scarce any possibility of good or ill, but is common to human kind. . . . We are all prompted by the same motives, all deceived by the same fallacies, all animated by hope, obstructed by danger, entangled by desire, and seduced by pleasure. (*Rambler* 60)

The multifarious events of ordinary life are characteristically abstracted here into a few great recurring principles: hope, danger, desire, pleasure. Viewed in this light, what is true for Samuel Johnson, or more accurately for Johnson as he appears as the Rambler, will be equally true for all men.

But the world has never been willing to take Johnson's works apart from their writer, nor is it likely that it could. Carlyle long ago presented him as a moral hero: "Nature, in return for his nobleness, had said to him, Live in an element of diseased sorrow." Even in his lifetime he seems to have been admired in this way: in the words of a minor poet in 1766,

> . . . Envy owns thro' ev'ry arduous stage,
> His life, a brighter lesson than his page.[3]

More recently, this picture has been elaborated and darkened to produce a tragic Johnson. In *Perilous Balance* Watkins emphasizes Johnson's awareness of evil, his horror of death, and his unending struggle to hold

[3] Thomas Carlyle, *On Heroes and Hero-Worship*, ch. 5, "The Hero as Man of Letters." "The Authors," a poem by D. Hayes, Esq., was discovered by D. J. Greene, who describes it in "No Warbler He—A Contemporary Tribute to Johnson," *Notes and Queries*, 198 (1953), 243-44.

madness at bay. Such an interpretation, like any other, requires the selective use of quotation from the vast body of Johnsonian material, but it manifestly deals with matters central to Johnson's personality, and is sometimes able to explain episodes which were obscure even to Boswell. Thus Watkins quotes the extraordinary scene of Johnson's gigantic mirth at the thought of Langton making his will: "He then burst into such a fit of laughter, that he appeared to be almost in a convulsion; and, in order to support himself, laid hold of one of the posts at the side of the foot pavement, and sent forth peals so loud, that in the silence of the night his voice seemed to resound from Temple-bar to Fleet-ditch" (*Life*, II, 262). Watkins very appropriately cites Lear's speech, "Hysterica passio! down, thou climbing sorrow! / Thy element's below."[4]

Once our imaginations have been awakened to this aspect of Johnson, it is impossible, even if it were desirable, to banish it from our minds when we read his works. And indeed parallels between his moral reflections and his own experience are everywhere to be found. His fear of madness and his technical knowledge of it are most fully displayed in the account of the astronomer in *Rasselas*, and appear over and over in less extended form.[5] Johnson's term for his condition was

[4] *Perilous Balance*, p. 70.
[5] E.g., in *Rambler* 5: "It may be laid down as a position which will seldom deceive, that when a man cannot bear his own company there is something wrong." Sir Joshua Reynolds wrote that "solitude to him was horror; nor would he ever trust himself alone unemployed in writing or reading. He has often begged me to accompany him home with him to prevent his being alone in the coach" (*Portraits by Sir Joshua Reynolds*, ed. F. W. Hilles [New York, 1952], pp. 76-77). Johnson told Mrs. Thrale, "The solitary Mortal, is certainly luxurious, probably superstitious, and possibly mad: the mind stagnates for want of Employment; grows morbid, & is extinguished like a Candle in foul Air" (*Thraliana*, I, 180).

"melancholy," which meant essentially a state of mental anguish accompanied by paralysis of the will, in which imaginary pleasures are preferred to "the bitterness of truth" (*Rasselas*, ch. 44). His endless resolutions to rise early in the morning are not mere scruples against wasting time, but an effort to overcome the constitutional indolence which he feared as the first step toward insanity and despair.

The ending of *The Vision of Theodore, the Hermit of Teneriffe*, which to modern taste is a rather labored effort at allegory but which Johnson considered "the best thing he ever wrote" (*Life*, I, 192), is an eloquent evocation of his own condition:

> They wandered on from one double of the labyrinth to another with the chains of Habit hanging secretly upon them, till, as they advanced, the flowers grew paler, and the scents fainter; they proceeded in their dreary march without pleasure in their progress, yet without power to return; and had this aggravation above all others, that they were criminal but not delighted. . . . They crawled on reluctant and gloomy, till they arrived at the depth of the recess, varied only with poppies and nightshade, where the dominion of Indolence terminates, and the hopeless wanderer is delivered up to Melancholy; the chains of Habit are rivetted for ever; and Melancholy, having tortured her prisoner for a time, consigns him at last to the cruelty of Despair. (1825 *Works*, IX, 174-75)

Johnson's diaries and personal poems are full of references to this terrible state, of which he grimly wrote, "This is not the life to which Heaven is promised" (*Diaries*, Yale *Works*, I, 78).

Whether or not this is tragic depends on how loosely one wishes to use the word. If suffering in itself is not tragic, then Johnson's melancholy in itself is not. But it is easy to carry the analysis further, and to see his battle against it as a genuinely tragic spectacle. Curiously enough William Richardson, one of the pioneers of Shakespearean character-criticism, described Macbeth's ambition in language that seems to be directly taken from *The Vision of Theodore*: "Imaginary representations, more even than real objects, stimulate our desires. . . . Melancholy, brooding over images of misery and disappointment, is tortured with anguish, and plunges into despair."[6] Can Johnson be seen not simply as tragic sufferer but as tragic hero?

Johnson Agonistes (as Bertrand Bronson has called him) lived his life as a contest against hostile forces in himself and in the world around him. According to one of Boswell's most impressive characterizations,

> His mind resembled the vast amphitheatre, the Colisaeum at Rome. In the centre stood his judgement, which, like a mighty gladiator, combated those apprehensions that, like the wild beasts of the *Arena*, were all around in cells, ready to be let out upon him. After a conflict, he drove them back into their dens; but not killing them, they were still assailing him.   (*Life*, II, 106)

His unpredictable outbursts of rudeness and abuse were, as Boswell observed to Reynolds, symptoms of this internal warfare, which he likened to a mutiny on shipboard: "I said, 'Dr. Johnson's harsh attacks on his freinds arrise from uneasiness within. There is an insurrection aboard. His loud explosions are guns of distress.' " Against this rebellion Johnson strove to enforce order by whatever means he could command, notably by redirecting his energies outward instead of try-

[6] "On the Character of Macbeth," in *Essays on Some of Shakespeare's Dramatic Characters* (1774; 5th ed., 1798), p. 42.

ing to "think down" thoughts which could not be suppressed.[7]

For this notion of life as warfare there is ample evidence in Johnson's writings, in the spirit of his deathbed vow, "I will be conquered; I will not capitulate" (*Life*, IV, 374). Underlying this is doubtless the idea of fighting the good fight, but with the premise that, try as one may, victory is by no means inevitable.

> To strive with difficulties, and to conquer them, is the highest human felicity; the next, is to strive, and deserve to conquer: but he whose life has passed without a contest, and who can boast neither success nor merit, can survey himself only as a useless filler of existence; and if he is content with his own character, must owe his satisfaction to insensibility. (*Adventurer* 111)

That this language is not confined simply to mental fight, to the soul's struggle to make itself acceptable to God, is shown by Johnson's suspicion of monasticism as a pusillanimous escape. Since he cannot very well counsel a man to be destroyed by what he might have avoided, he makes Imlac say, "Perhaps, every one is not able to stem the temptations of publick life; and, if he cannot conquer, he may properly retreat" (*Rasselas*, ch. 47). But as a rule he takes the opposite position.

---

[7] The analogy of the mutiny is quoted from an isolated note for 5 June 1784, reprinted in Geoffrey Scott's *The Making of the Life of Johnson*, vol. VI of *Private Papers of James Boswell* (New York, 1936), p. 62. It follows immediately upon the story of Langton as Johnson's "confessor" which appears in the *Life*, IV, 280-81. The second reference is to a conversation in which Boswell suggested trying to "think down" distressing thoughts: "No, Sir," Johnson replied, "To attempt to *think them down* is madness. . . . To have the management of the mind is a great art, and it may be attained in a considerable degree by experience and habitual exercise" (*Life*, II, 440).

Discussing monks in one of his sermons, he declares, "Surely it cannot be said that they have reached the perfection of a religious life; it cannot be allowed, that flight is victory; or that he fills his place in the creation laudably, who does no ill, *only* because he does *nothing*" (Sermon 3, 1825 *Works*, IX, 313).

Johnson's emphasis on activity and achievement in the face of despair has a truly tragic quality. It is not *mere* suffering, but something closer to what William Arrowsmith has called "the dignity of significant suffering which gives man the crucial victory over his own fate."[8] In religious terms, we find here a vision like that of Pascal, whom Johnson much admired: the struggle of the indomitable human will against a hostile universe, in the hope of eventual salvation. In secular terms, we may think of Johnson's contempt for Gray, which derives in part from his attitude toward Gray's quasi-monastic retirement at Cambridge, and which may be taken as indirect self-condemnation, for similarities to Johnson himself are apparent:

> BOSWELL. "But, Sir, why don't you give us something in some other way?" GOLDSMITH. "Ay, Sir, we have a claim upon you." JOHNSON. "No, Sir, I am not obliged to do any more. No man is obliged to do as much as he can do." . . . BOSWELL. "But I wonder, Sir, you have not more pleasure in writing than in not writing." JOHNSON. "Sir, you *may* wonder."
> (*Life*, II, 15)

His embarrassment is evident as he defiantly takes a position opposite to his usual one. And in his usual posture of aggressive combat it is easy to see a kind of tragic hero, just as monastic or Cantabrigian retirement

---

[8] "The Criticism of Greek Tragedy," *Tulane Drama Review*, 3 (March 1959), 57.

can represent a failure of engagement without which tragedy is not possible.

2. The Religious Question

I have tried to present a fair review of some well-known facts about Johnson's life, and to suggest ways in which it is quite right to describe that life as tragic. One need not, however, imply that it was unremittingly and devastatingly tragic, and in fact it is worth asking whether such a description would have made sense to Johnson. If he were to accept our account of his mental and emotional history, would he also accept the interpretation we have been placing upon it?

The most obvious problem is the depth and centrality of Johnson's religious faith, and his almost homiletic conception of his role as a writer, which he saw as that of a moralist in the classic Christian tradition. I do not pretend to supply a definitive answer to the vexed question of whether tragedy is compatible with Christianity, but clearly it needs to be examined with some care. At first sight, and not only at first sight, it may appear that Johnson's view of the human condition *would be* tragic except for the final victory of salvation and life everlasting.

> Piety is the only proper and adequate relief of decaying man. He that grows old without religious hopes, as he declines into imbecillity, and feels pains and sorrows incessantly crowding upon him, falls into a gulph of bottomless misery, in which every reflexion must plunge him deeper, and where he finds only new gradations of anguish, and precipices of horrour. (*Rambler* 69)

This passage is full of the imagery of Johnson's poems: one writer has noticed the use of "crowd" in *The Vanity of Human Wishes*, and another the frequency with

67

which Johnson associates "gulphs" with damnation.[9] He presents, then, a powerfully imaginative picture of man's tragic fat?, but of a fate that need not prevail. Piety is a "proper and adequate relief"; through piety the gulphs and the precipices may be escaped. Is this not the avoidance of tragedy?

So far as doctrine goes, the Christian believes that any miseries to be endured in the present life are only temporary, and that because of Christ's sacrifice the Fall of Man was paradoxically fortunate and human life a *commedia* instead of a tragedy. "O death, where is thy sting?" Suffering may be taken as a necessary discipline or even as an authentication of grace, and death is the entrance to a happier state. A writer who means to inculcate pious lessons may therefore, like Samuel Richardson, devote many pages to proving that the world is not good enough for a virtuous soul. As Richardson wrote to one of the female admirers of *Clarissa*, "But why . . . is Death painted in such shocking Lights, when it is the common Lot? If it is become so terrible to human Nature, it is Time to familiarize it to us— Hence another of my great Ends, as I have hinted."[10]

In a time of personal grief, Johnson expressed this orthodox argument in the sermon intended to be preached at his wife's funeral. "To Christians the celebration of a funeral is by no means a solemnity of barren and unavailing sorrow," because "religion will inform us, that sorrow and complaint are not only vain, but unreasonable and erroneous" (Sermon 25, 1825

[9] For "crowd," see Bate, *The Achievement of Samuel Johnson*, p. 19; for "gulphs," see Voitle, *Samuel Johnson the Moralist*, pp. 42-43. Voitle observes that in his poems and even in the choice of examples for the *Dictionary* Johnson seems to associate "gulphs" with damnation.

[10] Letter to Lady Bradshaigh, 26 Oct. 1748, in *Selected Letters*, ed. John Carroll (Oxford, 1964), p. 95.

Works, IX, 521-22). It is as if he were playing on the idiom in which a religious ceremony is "celebrated." And two years earlier he had written, "The frequent contemplation of death, as it shows the vanity of all human good, discovers likewise the lightness of all terrestrial evil. . . . The soul cannot long be held in prison, but will fly away, and leave a lifeless body to human malice" (*Rambler* 17). The world may indeed be a terrible place, the home of malice which is indignant when death robs it of its prey, but the soul has only to spread its wings and "fly away."

So Johnson sometimes writes; but this is by no means his invariable emphasis when he confronts the idea of death, either in conversation or in print. He argued heatedly with the Rector of St. Andrews that sorrow is not "murmuring against the dispensations of Providence," but that on the contrary it is "inherent in humanity" (*Life*, V, 64). In one of the *Rambler*s he expresses the same sentiment as Solon's when he wept for the death of his son: "Heaven seems to indicate the duty even of barren compassion, by inclining us to weep for evils which we cannot remedy" (*Rambler* 59). Whatever he may have tried to make himself feel in a sermon at the time of his wife's death, Johnson generally gives full weight to the burden of irrevocable loss.

> For sorrow there is no remedy provided by nature; it is often occasioned by accidents irreparable, and dwells upon objects that have lost or changed their existence; it requires what it cannot hope, that the laws of the universe should be repealed; that the dead should return, or the past should be recalled.
>
> (*Rambler* 47)

The relation of man to God is of central importance. The logical difficulties involved in the idea of a deity who created man "Sufficient to have stood, though free to fall" (*Paradise Lost* III.99) have always proved baffling if not insoluble, and it may possibly be granted that Christianity, in the imagination if not in the intellect, has frequently had some taint of Manichaeism. The world has often been regarded as a sort of occupied territory where mankind, though affirming allegiance to God, is at the immediate mercy of implacable enemies. This is indeed a universe where innocence can suffer, and all that religion can offer is the belief that it will not suffer forever.

The bitter reality of this suffering is, in Johnson's view, itself an argument for the existence of that happy future state.

> It is scarcely to be imagined, that Infinite Benevolence would create a being capable of enjoying so much more than is here to be enjoyed, and qualified by nature to prolong pain by remembrance and anticipate it by terror, if he was not designed for something nobler and better than a state, in which many of his faculties can serve only for his torment, in which he is to be importuned by desires that never can be satisfied, to feel many evils which he had no power to avoid, and to fear many which he shall never feel: there will surely come a time, when every capacity of happiness shall be filled, and none shall be wretched but by his own fault. (*Adventurer* 120)

The point about Christ's sufferings, despite the fact that he was God, is that he did indeed suffer. "All the distresses of persecution," as Johnson goes on to say in the same essay, "have been suffered by those, 'of whom the world was not worthy' [Hebrews 11 : 38]; and the Redeemer of mankind himself was 'a man of sorrows and acquainted with grief' [Isaiah 53 : 3]."

To the extent that Christianity postulates ultimate happiness, it doubtless negates the force of tragedy, but

70

I am suggesting that this need not be the case when the imagination is fixed on the present world, where we are everywhere confronted with the waste of individual lives, often as the direct result of "the tragical or fatal effects . . . of private malignity" (*Rambler* 11). All the same, when we have recognized the irrevocable nature of suffering, is it not all the more obvious that the Christian must welcome the death that releases him from it? Probably so, for a saint like Richardson's Clarissa, but not for Johnson; and not, in Johnson's view, for mankind in general. "The fear of death has always been considered as the great enemy of human quiet, the polluter of the feast of happiness, and embitterer of the cup of joy": so he introduces the sermon which is intended to counsel against the fear of death (Sermon 25, 1825 *Works*, IX, 518). His own horror of death is well known. "The whole of life," he told Boswell, "is but keeping away the thoughts of it" (*Life*, II, 93), and late in life he said that "he never had a moment in which death was not terrible to him" (*Life*, III, 153). One of his sternest rebukes to Boswell was called forth by persistent badgering on this subject; he became very agitated, said "Give us no more of this," and forbade his admirer to visit the next day (*Life*, II, 107).

Clearly Johnson's fear of death was an intensely personal experience, and quite probably he felt it with greater agony than most men. To this extent he was wrong, no doubt, in projecting his feelings upon mankind in general. In any case, there is nothing surprising in finding such fears entertained by a religious man, and they are certainly not evidence of a basic intellectual skepticism. John Wesley wrote to his brother in a remarkable letter, "If I have any fear, it is not of falling into hell, but of falling into nothing."[11]

[11] Letter to Charles Wesley, 27 June 1766, in *John Wesley*, ed. Albert C. Outler (New York, 1964), p. 82.

Whether or not Johnson sometimes feared falling into nothing, he violently feared falling into hell. A number of excellent studies have demonstrated how deeply his religion was permeated by disquietude, fear, and even despair.[12] The reason for his fear of death is eloquently expressed in *Rambler* 110:

> If he who considers himself as suspended over the abyss of eternal perdition only by the thread of life, which must soon part by its own weakness, and which the wing of every minute may divide, can cast his eyes round him without shuddering with horror, or panting for security; what can he judge of himself but that he is not yet awaked to sufficient conviction, since every loss is more lamented than the loss of the divine favour, and every danger more dreaded than the danger of final condemnation?

In the last year of Johnson's life his friend Dr. Adams, master of Pembroke College, objected to this kind of fear, on the grounds that God is infinitely good. Johnson retorted that a good God must nevertheless punish wicked individuals:

> "As I cannot be *sure* that I have fulfilled the conditions on which salvation is granted, I am afraid I may be one of those who shall be damned." (looking dismally.) DR. ADAMS. "What do you mean by damned?" JOHNSON. (passionately and loudly) "Sent to Hell, Sir, and punished everlastingly."
>
> (*Life*, IV, 299)

Even if the Christian were certain to be rewarded with eternal felicity, his sufferings on this earth might

[12] See esp. J. H. Hagstrum, "On Dr. Johnson's Fear of Death," *English Literary History*, 14 (1947), 308-19, and Arieh Sachs, "Reason and Unreason in Johnson's Religion," *Modern Language Review*, 59 (1964), 519-26.

still seem tragic; but in Johnson's case we can add that the specter of everlasting punishment is almost unarguably so. It would be a curious doctrine that denied the name of tragedy to *Doctor Faustus*, and perhaps there is an even more tragic spectacle in the good man who is persuaded that God has rejected him. One thinks of the terrible knowledge of eternal reprobation that lies behind Cowper's gentle suburban concerns,

> But I beneath a rougher sea,
> And whelm'd in deeper gulphs than he.

When Johnson writes in a sermon, "It is always to be remembered, that nothing but wickedness makes death an evil" (Sermon 5, 1825 *Works*, IX, 335), he has hardly said that death is therefore never an evil. For his own part, he brooded constantly upon the implications of the parable of the talents.

> The solemn text, "of him to whom much is given, much will be required" [Luke 12 : 48], seems to have been ever present to his mind, in a rigorous sense, and to have made him dissatisfied with his labours and acts of goodness, however comparatively great; so that the unavoidable consciousness of his superiority was, in that respect, a cause of disquiet. He suffered so much from this, and from the gloom which perpetually haunted him, and made solitude frightful, that it may be said of him, "If in this life only he had hope, he was of all men most miserable" [I Corinthians 15 : 19].
>
> (*Life*, IV, 427)

Sometimes Johnson alludes directly to this theme,[13] and often it is present by implication. Much of the pathos

[13] E.g., "He that neglects the culture of ground, naturally fertile, is more shamefully culpable than he whose field would scarcely recompence his husbandry" (*Rambler* 154).

in the noble elegy for his obscure friend Levet derives from the implied contrast with Johnson himself:

> His virtues walk'd their narrow round,
> Nor made a pause, nor left a void;
> And sure th' Eternal Master found
> The single talent well employ'd.
>
> *(Poems, p. 315)*

No Biblical text appears oftener in Johnson's works than the one which he had engraved in Greek on the dial-plate of his watch: "The night cometh, when no man can work."[14]

Even more poignant than these fairly obvious cases of self-reproach are those in which Johnson warmly praises men who achieved what he could not. Among other instances, the *Life of Boerhaave* is Johnson's tribute to a moral hero, with whom he probably noticed even a physical resemblance,[15] whose application to his studies was as intense as Johnson's was not, and who consequently achieved wonders in two professions.

It is, I believe, a very just observation, that men's ambition is, generally, proportioned to their capac-

[14] *Life*, II, 57. The text is John 9 : 4. Johnson also quotes it in *Adventurer* 120, in his fourth and twenty-fifth sermons (1825 *Works*, IX, 330 and 525), and in a prayer "Imploring Diligence" (Yale *Works*, I, 118).

[15] "Thus died Boerhaave, a man formed by nature for great designs, and guided by religion in the exertion of his abilities. He was of a robust and athletick constitution of body, so hardened by early severities, and wholesome fatigue, that he was insensible of any sharpness of air, or inclemency of weather [just as Johnson would deride Boswell for this kind of sensibility]. He was tall, and remarkable for extraordinary strength. There was, in his air and motion, something rough and artless, but so majestick and great, at the same time, that no man ever looked upon him without veneration, and a kind of tacit submission to the superiority of his genius" (1825 *Works*, VI, 288).

Paul Fussell discusses the parable of the talents and the auto-

ity. Providence seldom sends any into the world with an inclination to attempt great things, who have not abilities, likewise, to perform them. To have formed the design of gaining a complete knowledge of medicine, by way of digression from theological studies, would have been little less than madness in most men, and would have only exposed them to ridicule and contempt. But Boerhaave was one of those mighty geniuses, to whom scarce any thing appears impossible, and who think nothing worthy of their efforts, but what appears insurmountable to common understandings.

(1825 *Works*, VI, 275)

This encomium was written in 1739, when Johnson was just setting out on his London career; but he had already been obliged to leave Oxford without the degree that would have made a profession accessible, had failed in an attempt to establish a little school, and was struggling to make a living at miscellaneous journalism of which the *Life of Boerhaave* was an instance. "Mighty genius" is strong language—at the end of his life Johnson applied the phrase to Shakespeare (*Life of Gray*, III, 437)—and it must have been painful to reflect that, like Boerhaave, he had both the inclination and the ability to perform great things, but seemed unlikely to achieve as much as he might have done.

But when we pursue considerations like these, are we doing what Johnson could have approved? When we ransack his private diaries and the records of his private conversation or read autobiographical feeling into the life of a Dutch physician, we may indeed be describing a tragic Johnson, but not Johnson as he presented himself to the world. While I should like to postpone

biographical aspect of the *Life of Boerhaave* in *Samuel Johnson and the Life of Writing* (New York, 1971), pp. 95-108.

a full discussion of the antitragic aspect of Johnson as moralist, the fundamental paradox of his specifically religious thought should be noticed: that he attempts to transform a personal religion of torment and even despair into an eminently *rational* model of belief. As scholars have lately begun to point out, he is at great pains to represent the fear of death as rational: the more that worldly enjoyments can be shown to be inadequate, the more certain it is that man was meant for a different fate. The fear of death demonstrates an active concern with the most important of all things, one's eternal destiny, as opposed to a beast-like indifference to it.[16] In the language of *Rasselas*, the hunger of imagination can be appeased by no human enjoyments, and must be redirected to the choice of eternity.

In this sense, Johnson's awareness of the misery in life is the very opposite of a confrontation with the irrational, such as we find in much tragedy. There is no question of existential despair according to this interpretation, and Johnson Agonistes, whatever the nature of his *agon*, is not the hero who imposes his will upon the *néant*. He is simply Christian, who fights the good fight and looks forward to obtaining his crown of glory at the end of the journey. Each setback, each sorrow that he encounters is only so much evidence that God

---

[16] See Sachs' *Passionate Intelligence* and Chester F. Chapin's *The Religious Thought of Samuel Johnson* (Ann Arbor, 1968), particularly the final chapter of each work. Chapin cites *Rambler* 41: "We have no reason to believe that other creatures have higher faculties, or more extensive capacities, than the preservation of themselves, or their species, requires; they seem always to be fully employed, or to be completely at ease without employment, to feel few intellectual miseries or pleasures, and to have no exuberance of understanding to lay out upon curiosity or caprice, but to have their minds exactly adapted to their bodies, with few other ideas than such as corporal pain or pleasure impress upon them.

has prepared something infinitely better for those he loves.

But it is not necessary to reiterate Johnson's grave doubts that he was one of those, doubts which cause an element of paradox in all his treatments of religion. The fear of death, for example, is perfectly rational according to his intellectual system, but at the same time it is obsessive and debilitating in his emotional life. One notices how conventional his descriptions of eternal bliss are in comparison with those of damnation. It is not that he is of the devil's party without knowing it, but rather that his imagination does not often dwell in the realms of light. Consider these questions from a sermon on the subject of God's tender mercy:

> Were there not mercy with him, were he not to be reconciled after the commission of a crime, what must be the state of those, who are conscious of having once offended him? A state of gloomy melancholy, or outrageous desperation; a dismal weariness of life, and inexpressible agonies at the thought of death; for what affright or affliction could equal the horrours of that mind, which expected every moment to fall into the hands of implacable Omnipotence? (Sermon 2, 1825 *Works*, IX, 302)

What must be the state of those? The description that follows sounds very much like Johnson himself; he is offering consolation for others even while he cannot feel it for himself. To Boswell he questioned whether even an apostle could be certain of salvation: "St. Paul, though he expresses strong hope, also expresses fear, lest having preached to others, he himself should be a cast-away" (*Life*, IV, 123). And in a solemn discussion with Hawkins in the last days of his life, "he uttered this passionate exclamation,—'Shall I, who have been a teacher of others, myself be a castaway?'" (Hawkins, p. 257).

3. The Problem of Evil

From the subject of Johnson's religion as it relates to the question of salvation, we may proceed to an aspect of it which lies near the heart of an investigation of tragedy. His discussions of the problem of evil are remarkable in that they seek neither to explain nor to explain away. He cannot claim an emotional satisfaction with the universe as it is, but he categorically refuses to invent philosophical justifications for what can never be known, much less intelligibly justified. One may even doubt whether he thought it worth while to conceive of evil as a metaphysical entity—as a force, that is, independent of the particular acts in which it is embodied. In the *Dictionary* he gives the following definitions:

1. Wickedness; a crime.
2. Injury; mischief.
3. Malignity; corruption.
4. Misfortune; calamity.
5. Malady; disease: as, the *king's evil* [with which Johnson himself was afflicted].

Of these, the third definition is the closest to a general one, and is illustrated with a verse from Ecclesiastes, "The heart of the sons of men is full of *evil*" [9 : 3]. Elsewhere Johnson seems almost to insist on the nature of evil as particular. "There is no evil but must inhere in a conscious being, or be referred to it; that is, evil must be felt, before it is evil."[17]

---

[17] Review of Jenyns, 1825 *Works*, VI, 50. Very likely Johnson has in mind the traditional ontological definition of evil as nothingness, hence perceivable only in specific acts which *result from* the condition of privation (which is very different from thinking of privation as simply the lack of something we wish we had: we wish we were richer, that man had angelic powers, etc.). As the preacher John Preston illustrates the point in 1632: "Though all sinne bee a meere privation, yet it is in an operative subject,

In *Idler* 89 Johnson observes,

> How evil came into the world; for what reason it is that life is overspread with such boundless varieties of misery; why the only thinking being of this globe is doomed to think merely to be wretched, and to pass his time from youth to age in fearing or in suffering calamities, is a question which philosophers have long asked, and which philosophy could never answer.

He goes on to offer the orthodox answer: "Religion informs us that misery and sin were produced together." As he told Boswell in Scotland, "Moral evil is occasioned by free will, which implies choice between good and evil" (*Life*, v, 117). Or again, in a sermon:

> It will appear upon examination, that though the world be full of misery and disorder, yet God is not to be charged with disregard to his creation; that if we suffer, we suffer by our own fault, and that "he has done right, but we have done wickedly" [Nehemiah 9 : 33].
>
> (Sermon 5, 1825 *Works*, IX, 332)

Perhaps more often than not, when a man asserts that frail reason must not question the unsearchable mysteries of Providence, his attitude will be remote from any conceivable sense of tragedy. Besides, this world is a temporary station on the journey to a state which

---

and thence it comes to passe that sinne is fruitfull in evill workes: as for example: take an horse and put out his eyes, as long as hee stands still there is no error: but if he begins to runne once, he runnes amisse, and the longer hee runnes, the further he is out of the way wherein he should doe, and all this because hee wants his eyes, which should direct him: So it is with sinne, though it in its selfe bee but a meere privation, yet it is seated in the soule, which is alwaies active" (*An Elegant and Lively Description of Spirituall Life and Death*, p. 5). I owe the point and the illustration to my colleague Richard Waswo.

will amply make up for whatever was suffered here. But Johnson, for whom the comforts of such a faith were agonizingly difficult of attainment, always showed a profound sympathy for the sufferings of the present life. In consequence he was not simply indignant at theories that pretended to explain the problem of evil, but expressed his indignation in such a way as to reveal a horror at the malignity of evil that bears close affinity to the great tradition of literary tragedy.

Everyone knows that Johnson attacked a minor moralist named Soame Jenyns for an essay on the origin of evil, and some passages of brilliant invective from his attack are a staple of anthologies. I should now like to present an investigation not of the metaphysical but of the imaginative aspect of that review. On the face of it Johnson is simply mocking a preposterous theory that postulates needless cruelty to explain the evil whose existence is apparent enough without it. But more than that, the review has, to a remarkable degree, resonances throughout his other writings. It is as though it lay at the center of a cluster of associations which reflect Johnson's deepest instinctive response to the fact of evil in human life, a fact which, though it could not be explained, was not at all to be palliated.

Since Jenyns' argument depends in part on the idea of the Great Chain of Being, and since literary scholarship has taught us to admire the use of this idea by the poets, something should be said about Johnson's undisguised hostility to it. He was not, as might be supposed, unaware of its poetic value; in a rather extraneous apostrophe in *Irene*, he refers to the British Constitution as being "Unbroken as the sacred chain of Nature, / That links the jarring elements in peace" (i.ii.63-64). (One remembers that the "jarring atoms" reduced to order had been a favorite image of Dryden's.) What Johnson disliked was the *literal* application of this imaginative conception, taking it not as a metaphor for cosmic harmony, but as a metaphysical explanation of why the universe has to be as it is. He had in fact serious reservations about metaphysics in general, as an observation six years before the Jenyns review attests: "The philosopher has the works of omniscience to examine; and is therefore engaged in disquisitions, to which finite intellects are utterly unequal" (*Rambler* 122).

Jenyns' *Free Enquiry into the Nature and Origin of Evil* attracted enough attention to arrive at four editions within a year, and Johnson's review in turn "was read with such eagerness, when published in the Literary Magazine [in 1757], that the author was induced to reprint it in a small volume by itself" (1825 *Works*, VI, 47). An expert judge, A. O. Lovejoy, calls Johnson's criticism of the Chain of Being concept "profound and dialectical"; but with this aspect of the review we are not here concerned.[18] What matters most at present is the vehemence with which Johnson asserts the reality of grief and suffering.

> Life must be seen, before it can be known. This author and Pope, perhaps, never saw the miseries which they imagine thus easy to be borne. The poor, indeed, are insensible of many little vexations, which sometimes imbitter the possessions, and pollute the enjoyments, of the rich. They are not pained by casual incivility, or mortified by the mutilation of a compliment; but this happiness is like that of a malefactor, who ceases to feel the cords that bind him, when the pincers are tearing his flesh. (1825 *Works*, VI, 54-55)

[18] Lovejoy says that Johnson's attack is "more profound and more dialectical" than Voltaire's, and adds that it "reached very nearly to the root of the matter" by exposing the logical contradictions within the theory itself (*The Great Chain of Being* [New York, 1960], ch. 9, pp. 253-54).

The best-known passage in Johnson's review is the one in which, with brilliant satire, he elaborates on Jenyns' unlucky suggestion that our sufferings may be of some use to a superior race of beings.

> He might have shown, that these "hunters, whose game is man," have many sports analogous to our own. As we drown whelps and kittens, they amuse themselves, now and then, with sinking a ship, and stand round the fields of Blenheim, or the walls of Prague, as we encircle a cockpit. As we shoot a bird flying, they take a man in the midst of his business or pleasure, and knock him down with an apoplexy. . . . Many a merry bout have these frolick beings at the vicissitudes of an ague, and good sport it is to see a man tumble with an epilepsy, and revive and tumble again, and all this he knows not why. (64-65)

The offensiveness of this idea of Jenyns' was noticed by the *Critical Review*, but the solemn calmness of its refutation helps us to appreciate the intensity of Johnson's response: "Our author seems to have forgot that these beings, whatever they are, if superior to us, must be rational, and that in a much higher degree than ourselves, and consequently incapable of feeling such necessities, or enjoying such pleasures, as he has assigned them."[19] This is no more than to play Jenyns' own game.

[19] *Critical Review*, 3 (1757), 443. The sentence which I have quoted is immediately preceded by the observation that Jenyns' superior beings "may feed upon us, as we do on sheep, oxen, &c. hunt us as we do hares, set us a fighting as we do game-cocks, or torture us as we do worms on a fish-hook, for their diversion." Clearly either this writer or Johnson saw the other's review before writing his own. One is tempted to suppose that Johnson's came first, since the notice in the *Critical Review* is so much weaker and more perfunctory; but it hardly matters which. William Rose in the *Monthly Review*, 16 (1757), summarizes Jenyns' argument and concludes that even if God "could not

If we are to take turns at assigning qualities to these nonexistent beings, who is to say which account is right? Johnson quite rightly places his emphasis not on argument but on satire. He asks, in effect: What kind of beings would these be, if they were exactly as Jenyns imagines them? and perhaps even: What sort of man would wish to imagine such beings as these?

Many readers have perhaps supposed that Johnson was taking rhetorical liberties in seizing upon this point, and that he made ridiculous what in Jenyns had been clothed in the dispassionate language of reason, even if not very well thought out. Anyone who looks at Jenyns' work, however, will discover that Johnson is simply asking us to reflect on the implications of what the author very frankly declares: that these superior beings "deceive, torment, or destroy us, for the ends only of their own pleasure or utility."[20] They not only use our suffering, but they enjoy it! Jenyns conceives of this race of torturers by analogy with the conduct of mankind, and this is what most fully arouses Johnson's wrath. In effect Jenyns has chosen to bring forward the very aspects of man that prove him most vicious and evil, and has projected them gratuitously upon an order of "intermediate beings" who exist only so that evil may be more prevalent.

Here is Jenyns' account:

> Man is one link of that vast chain. . . . If we look downwards, we see innumerable species of inferior Beings, whose happiness and lives are dependent on his will; we see him cloathed by their spoils, and fed by their miseries and destruction, inslav-

---

absolutely exclude evil from the best possible system of things, yet it is impossible for us to prove this, our faculties being evidently inadequate to such researches" (p. 316).

[20] *A Free Inquiry* . . . , Letter iii, "On Natural Evils," in *Miscellaneous Pieces* (1761), ii, 96.

ing some, tormenting others, and murdering millions for his luxury or diversion; is it not therefore
analogous and highly probable, that the happiness
and life of Man should be equally dependent on
the wills of his superiors?[21]

To be sure, Jenyns is not talking about what men do to
each other, but rather about what men do to animals.
But this is enough to enrage Johnson, not because of
sentimentality about animals, but because of what it reveals in human nature. A year after the Jenyns review
he wrote,

Among the inferiour professors of medical knowledge, is a race of wretches, whose lives are only
varied by varieties of cruelty; whose favourite
amusement is to nail dogs to tables and open them
alive; to try how long life may be continued in various degrees of mutilation, or with the excision or
laceration of the vital parts; to examine whether
burning irons are felt more acutely by the bone or
tendon; and whether the more lasting agonies are
produced by poison forced into the mouth or in-
jected into the veins.   (*Idler* 17)

One begins to suspect that Johnson's description of
Jenyns' "frolic beings" is more than an imaginary *re-
ductio ad absurdum* of his argument; they represent
the unlimited evil of which man is capable, not in order
to satisfy any particular need, but simply to gratify his
enjoyment of cruelty.

[21] *Ibid.*, pp. 94-95. In his preface Jenyns unrepentantly dis-
misses the opposition to his work as "the united force of ignorance, and malevolence, of faction, bigotry, and enthusiasm" (p.
xxx). He maintains that doubts about the existence of his "superior beings" are "like the incredulity of the ignorant peasant,
who can scarce be perswaded to believe that there is any thing
in the world, some specimen of which he has not beheld within
the narrow limits of his own parish" (p. ix).

And so, after a brief satiric attack on Jenyns himself, Johnson returns to his theme in a passage closely parallel to the description of the vivisectionists in the *Idler*. We are in effect being told, he says,

> That a set of beings, unseen and unheard, are hovering about us, trying experiments upon our sensibility, putting us in agonies, to see our limbs quiver; torturing us to madness, that they may laugh at our vagaries; sometimes obstructing the bile, that they may see how a man looks, when he is yellow; sometimes breaking a traveller's bones, to try how he will get home; sometimes wasting a man to a skeleton, and sometimes killing him fat, for the greater elegance of his hide.
>
> (1825 *Works*, VI, 66)

Any being that could inflict madness or disease must, in view of Johnson's feelings about these afflictions, be hideously depraved. Leaving aside madness—the condition he feared most of all—the voluntary imposition of disease is sufficiently reprehensible. In a moving passage in the *Life of Boerhaave* we are told, "He related, with great concern, that once his patience so far gave way to extremity of pain, that, after having lain fifteen hours in exquisite tortures, he prayed to God that he might be set free by death" (1825 *Works*, VI, 287). We can guess at the depth of Johnson's anger when he asks us to imagine such exquisite tortures inflicted for sport.

By now he is certainly going beyond the theory as Jenyns develops it, but he is not going beyond that region of human nature from which Jenyns has drawn his material. He is talking about the problem of evil not just as a vague entity that plays some obscure part in the Great Chain of Being, but as a monstrous deformation of man as he everywhere surrounds us. What I have called the imaginative cluster of the Jenyns review reappears with surprising frequency in Johnson's writing during the next couple of years, always in illustration of man's inhumanity to man. Thus two years later he has an Indian chief describe the European conquest of his country: "Those invaders ranged over the continent, slaughtering in their rage those that resisted, and those that submitted, in their mirth" (*Idler* 81). In the same year a much fuller expansion of the theme occurs unexpectedly in the midst of a generally factual introduction which Johnson contributed to a collection of voyages—apparently intended for the edification of children[22]—called *The World Displayed*:

> On what occasion, or for what purpose cannons and muskets were discharged among a people harmless and secure, by strangers who without any right visited their coast; it is not thought necessary to inform us. The *Portuguese* could fear nothing from them, and had therefore no adequate provocation; nor is there any reason to believe but that they murdered the negroes in wanton merriment, perhaps only to try how many a volley would destroy, or what would be the consternation of those that should escape. (Hazen, p. 227)

Again and again during this period Johnson seems to have reflected on the malice and cruelty which are so rooted in man that there is no hope of eradicating them. All that he could do was to appeal to the conscience of those not wholly inured not merely to human suffering

---

[22] Hazen does not suggest that *The World Displayed* was particularly aimed at the young, and this notion may well be wrong. The *Critical Review*, however, in noticing the work, speaks as follows of the publisher Newbery: "Numberless are the compendious little volumes he has published to facilitate science, by adapting it to the capacities of young people. . . . He here publishes the first volume of a work perfectly suited to the purpose intended; that of engaging the attention and opening the understanding of children" (*Critical Review*, 8 [1759], 486).

in general but to the suffering which they themselves had caused.

> Surely, he whose debtor has perished in prison, though he may acquit himself of deliberate murder, must at least have his mind clouded with discontent, when he considers how much another has suffered from him; when he thinks on the wife bewailing her husband, or the children begging the bread which their father would have earned. If there are any made so obdurate by avarice or cruelty, as to revolve these consequences without dread or pity, I must leave them to be awakened by some other power, for I write only to human beings.   (*Idler* 38)

One hears an echo of this in a note to *Cymbeline*—quite possibly written during the same period—where vivisection is again denounced as the work of "a race of men that have practised tortures without pity, and related them without shame, and are yet suffered to erect their heads among human beings."[23]

That man is inclined to evil Johnson thought too obvious to require proof.

> None of the axioms of wisdom which recommend the ancient sages to veneration, seems to have required less extent of knowledge or perspicacity of penetration than the remark of Bias, that . . . "the majority are wicked." The depravity of mankind is so easily discoverable, that nothing but the desert or the cell can exclude it from notice.
>
> (*Rambler* 175)

[23] Note to *Cymbeline*, I.v.23, in Yale *Works*, VIII, 881. Bertrand Bronson in his introduction (vol. VII) gives evidence that the edition was largely completed by the spring of 1758, so that this note could well have been written at much the same time as the

As he pursues the subject in this essay, it becomes clear as usual that he is talking about immediate and concrete acts of evil at the expense of our fellows, like the sailors' wanton murder of the Negroes. When an inexperienced young man or woman enters the world, "Perhaps, among all those who croud about them with professions and flatteries, there is not one who does not hope for some opportunity to devour or betray them, to glut himself by their destruction, or to share their spoils with a stronger savage."

This view of man stood in direct opposition to the powerful tide of self-congratulatory benevolism, and was regarded by many as a grotesque distortion of reality. Shortly after the publication of the *Rambler* Johnson visited Richardson's correspondent Miss Mulso, who wrote to a friend, "I had the assurance to dispute with him on the subject of human malignity, and wondered to hear a man who by his actions shews so much benevolence, maintain that the human heart is naturally malevolent, and that all the benevolence we see in the few who are good, is acquired by reason and religion."[24] Here precisely lay Johnson's opposition to Rousseau, who believed that human nature is fundamentally good but has been perverted by society. According to Johnson, men like Rousseau were totally mistaken about the nature of man. "Pity," he said, "is not natural to man. Children are always cruel. Savages are always cruel. Pity is acquired and improved by the cultivation of reason" (*Life*, I, 437). And civilization it-

---

Jenyns review, the *Idler* papers, and the introduction to *The World Displayed*.

[24] Hester Mulso (later Mrs. Chapone) in a letter to Elizabeth Carter in 1753; reprinted in her *Works* (1807), I, 73. When *Rasselas* came out she wrote, "Alas! poor Mr. Johnson has, I fear, considered the worst side of the character of human nature, and seems to be but little acquainted with the best and happiest of its affections and sensations" (*Ibid.*, p. 111).

self can do little more than regulate the passions it cannot uproot.[25]

Here, then, are some important ways in which Johnson was receptive to a tragic sense of life, while many of his contemporaries were not. He thought that fallen man was inherently wicked, and that it is man's lot to suffer. "He that wanders about the world," as he wrote to Mrs. Thrale, "sees new forms of human misery, and if he chances to meet an old friend, meets a face darkened with troubles" (*Letters*, I, 340). It is absolutely characteristic that after giving an extremely gloomy picture of human life—"a chaos of unhappiness, a confused and tumultuous scene of labour and contest, disappointment and defeat"—he is able to go on to say, "But by him that examines life with a more close attention, the happiness of the world will be found still less than it appears" (*Adventurer* 120). He celebrates sleep because "Life is to most, such as could not be endured without frequent intermissions of existence" (*Adventurer* 39). This conviction prompted his magnificent answer to the querulous Mrs. Williams when she deplored excessive drinking, saying, "I wonder what pleasure men can take in making beasts of themselves!" "I wonder, Madam," Johnson retorted, "that you have

[25] "Men are at first wild and unsocial, living each man to himself, taking from the weak, and losing to the strong. In their first coalitions of society, much of this original savageness is retained. . . . The ferocity of our ancestors, as of all other nations, produced not fraud, but rapine. They had not yet learned to cheat, and attempted only to rob. As manners grow more polished, with the knowledge of good, men attain likewise dexterity in evil. Open rapine becomes less frequent, and violence gives way to cunning. Those who before invaded pastures and stormed houses, now begin to enrich themselves by unequal contracts and fraudulent intromissions" (*Life*, II, 198-99). So Johnson wrote in a legal argument prepared for Boswell's use. If this position is very much like that of Hobbes, it is because Johnson, like Hobbes, had a low view of man's inherent capacity for goodness.

not penetration enough to see the strong inducement to this excess; for he who makes a *beast* of himself gets rid of the pain of being a man" (*Miscellanies*, II, 333). When he was asked if a man is not sometimes happy in the present moment, he replied, "Never, but when he is drunk" (*Life*, II, 351).

Very well; it is amply evident that Johnson believed in the wickedness of man (though not in total depravity in the Calvinist sense).[26] His view of life is pessimistic in the extreme. But is it tragic? The answer will largely depend on how one chooses to define "tragic." The more generalized the definition, the more obviously it applies to Johnson. The more strictly the definition is confined to the characteristics of literary tragedy—to great actions, let us say, performed by men above the common stature, and endowed with unity and coherence by the artistic imagination—the less it will be appropriate to Johnson's Christian pessimism. Of the tragedy of great heroes, especially, he has little to say. But insofar as these ideas can be transferred to the humbler sufferings of ordinary lives, he can truly be said to possess a tragic vision.

4. Domestic Tragedy

Johnson's imagination was filled with a literary tradition through which everyday events, however insignificant in themselves, could be apprehended with larger meaning. Again and again he uses literary allusion to emphasize the pathos of man's mortality, for example in his complex deathbed reference to Ovid and Tibullus, in the story of Xerxes weeping which he ap-

[26] Johnson's opposition to the doctrine of total depravity is one of the points of contention in his very interesting correspondence with Miss Hill Boothby, a highly pious Evangelical lady whom at one time he seems to have hoped to marry. For a full discussion see Chapin's *The Religious Thought of Samuel Johnson*, ch. 4.

plied to the thoughtless pleasure-seekers at Ranelagh,[27] or again in the letter to a young girl which reports the death of a cat: "Miss Porter has buried her fine black cat. So things come and go. Generations, as Homer says, are but like leaves; and you now see the faded leaves falling about you" (*Letters*, I, 287). The line from Homer is used as motto for *Rambler* 161, and is perhaps alluded to in *The Vanity of Human Wishes*.[28]

That man must die was for Johnson a tragic fact. His statement that "the passions rise higher at domestick than at imperial tragedies" is often quoted, but the context is not; it occurs in a letter to Mrs. Thrale in which he is discussing not eighteenth-century drama but the sentiments aroused by a visit to his native town.

Many families that paid the parish rates are now extinct, like the race of Hercules. Pulvis et umbra

[27] To Bennet Langton "he tenderly said, *Te teneam moriens deficiente manu*" [When dying may I hold you with my failing hand"; Tibullus I.i.60] (*Life*, IV, 406). Thirty years before, in *Adventurer* 58, Johnson pointed out that Ovid had quoted the line, which Tibullus addressed to his mistress, in his own elegy on the death of Tibullus.

When Boswell was speaking of *The Vanity of Human Wishes*, Johnson remarked, "When I first entered Ranelagh, it gave an expansion and gay sensation to my mind, such as I never experienced any where else. But, as Xerxes wept when he viewed his immense army, and considered that not one of that great multitude would be alive a hundred years afterwards, so it went to my heart to consider that there was not one in all that brilliant circle, that was not afraid to go home and think; but that the thoughts of each individual there, would be distressing when alone" (*Life*, III, 199). The anecdote about Xerxes is also mentioned in Sermon 14 (1825 *Works*, IX, 418).

[28] In *The Vanity of Human Wishes*: "Year chases year, decay pursues decay / Still drops some joy from with'ring life away" (305-306). The similarity is noted by Susie I. Tucker and Henry Gifford, "Johnson's Poetic Imagination," *Review of English Studies*, n.s. 8 (1957), 242-43. The immediate source, however, is Pope's version of Horace's Epistle II.ii.72-73.

sumus. What is nearest us, touches us most. The passions rise higher at domestick than at imperial tragedies. I am not wholly unaffected by the revolutions of Sadler street, nor can forbear to mourn a little when old names vanish away, and new come into their place. (*Letters*, i, 240)

Pulvis et umbra sumus: the phrase comes from an ode of Horace which Johnson translated, with brilliant conciseness, in the last month of his life.

> Her losses soon the moon supplies,
> But wretched man, when once he lies
> Where Priam and his sons are laid,
> Is naught but ashes and a shade.
>
> (Yale *Poems*, p. 343)

The ode is a classic expression of the contrast between the eternal youth of nature and the inevitable death of individual man. At the time of his translation Johnson was solemnly preparing himself for a death of Christian tranquility, but at the same time he strove to go on living—he protested to his doctors, "I want length of life, and you fear giving me pain" (Hawkins, p. 273)—and was evidently willing to ponder a pagan poem which regards death as utterly final.

On many occasions Johnson speaks of domestic tragedy in the sense of his letter to Mrs. Thrale, referring to the suffering and death of ordinary people. This is the burden of a passage in which he actually uses the phrase "the tragedy of life."

> The most indifferent or negligent spectator can indeed scarcely retire, without heaviness of heart, from a view of the last scenes of the tragedy of life, in which he finds those who in the former parts of the drama were distinguished by opposition of conduct, contrariety of designs, and dissimilitude of personal qualities, all involved in one common

distress, and all struggling with affliction which they cannot hope to overcome.   (*Rambler* 69)

There is even a hint of the formal construction of literary tragedy. Instead of a continuing static condition ("one common distress"), there is from another point of view a drama composed of a series of "scenes" in which people of all kinds are conducted toward an inescapable fate.

In some such way as this, Johnson seems to have been accustomed to brood upon the succession of little unregarded tragedies that constantly occur in ordinary life. Here is a fine example, from a letter to Mrs. Thrale in which he describes the death of one of his amanuenses, a "humble assistant" who only barely disturbed the periphery of Boswell's consciousness.[29]

Poor Peyton expired this morning. He probably during many years for which he sat starving by the bed of a Wife not only useless, but almost motionless, condemned by poverty to personal attendance, and by the necessity of such attendance chained down to poverty, he probably thought often how lightly he should tread the path of life without his burthen. Of this thought the admission was unavoidable, and the indulgence might be forgiven to frailty and distress. His Wife died at last, and before she was buried he was seized by a fever, and is now going to the grave.

Such miscarriages when they happen to those on whom many eyes are fixed, fill histories and trag-

[29] "The sixth of these humble assistants was Mr. Peyton, who, I believe, taught French, and published some elementary tracts" (*Life*, I, 187); Boswell was once "entertained by observing how [Johnson] contrived to send Mr. Peyton on an errand, without seeming to degrade him" (*Life*, II, 155). He also prints a short letter to Langton in which Johnson asks assistance for "an old amanuensis in great distress," quite likely Peyton (*Life*, II, 379).

edies and tears have been shed for the sufferings,
and wonder excited by the fortitude of those who
neither did nor suffered more than Peyton.

(*Letters*, ii, 120)

Unlike the earlier Augustans, who reproached themselves for not being heroes, Johnson constantly reminds
us that heroes are only men. By "domestic tragedy" he
does not mean simply the tragedy of insignificant people; as we shall see when we examine his Shakespeare
criticism, he is interested in the "domestic" aspect of
Hamlet and *King Lear*. Human nature, whatever its
superficial differences in individual men, is in its fundamental passions everywhere the same.

He that is most elevated above the croud by the
importance of his employments or the reputation
of his genius, feels himself affected by fame or
business but as they influence his domestick life.
The high and low, as they have the same faculties
and the same senses, have no less similitude in
their pains and pleasures. The sensations are the
same in all, tho' produced by very different occasions. The prince feels the same pain when an in-
vader seizes a province, as the farmer when a thief
drives away his cow. (*Idler* 84)

Johnson has deliberately chosen an ignoble example—
he could have said that the farmer and the prince
equally mourn when a loved one dies—so that there
will be no doubt that he means what he says.

To appreciate what Johnson is doing here, it is instructive to compare the superficially similar use of the
same analogy in a more aristocratic tradition. Webster's
Bosola cynically observes, "Some would think the souls
of princes were brought forth by some more weighty
cause than those of meaner persons: they are deceived,
there's the same hand to them; the like passions sway

them; the same reason that makes a vicar to go to law
for a tithe-pig and undo his neighbours, makes them
spoil a whole province, and batter down goodly cities
with the cannon" (*Duchess of Malfi*, II.i.115ff.). Or again
Swift, more briefly: "The very same principle that influences a bully to break the windows of a whore who
has jilted him, naturally stirs up a great prince to raise
mighty armies, and dream of nothing but sieges, bat-
tles, and victories" (*Tale of a Tub*, sec. ix). Two distinctions should be noticed: first, that Johnson is interested
in emotion as felt internally, whether by prince or farmer, while these passages are concerned with the aggressive actions (by implication contemptible) that issue
from those emotions; second, that they mean to belittle
"greatness" when they make the comparison, just as
Fielding belittles Walpole as the "great man" Jonathan
Wild. Johnson is really saying that all men, great or
small, feel emotion equally in their "domestic" life, and
if anything he is attempting to raise littleness, not to belittle greatness.

According to an influential view of tragedy, some
degree of heroic elevation is necessary before suffering
can be called tragic. As Bradley explains it, "A tale, for
example, of a man slowly worn to death by disease,
poverty, little cares, sordid vices, petty persecutions,
however piteous or dreadful it might be, would not be
tragic in the Shakespearean sense."[30] This may be true,
and yet the tale might still be tragic in a different
sense. Such a notion, in precisely the way that Johnson
conceives it, has become so familiar in the last two hundred years that statements like Bradley's are really attempts to argue us out of it, or at least to warn us not
to apply it to Sophocles and Shakespeare. This latter
caution might easily be appropriate, without automatically implying that it is a grave mistake to call anyone

[30] *Shakespearean Tragedy* (London, 1905), ch. 1, p. 8.

but heroes tragic. Real difficulties arise only if one asserts that minor figures are *as tragic* as the gigantic Oedipus or Othello. But there is no need to make such a claim, any more than it is necessary to confine the idea of tragedy only to its grandest manifestations. Surely it is an advance of the human spirit to perceive that the profound emotions of the greatest tragedy have their echo in the lives of humble people.

In the classical tradition adopted by the Augustans, the misfortunes of men no better than ourselves, and especially of those to whom we feel superior, are almost by definition comic. When Pope wrote a rather inflated epitaph on a pair of rural lovers who were killed by a thunderbolt, Lady Mary Wortley Montagu responded with derision, and after overseeing the provision of a memorial tablet Pope could not resist composing a further couplet on the event:

> Here lye two poor Lovers, who had the mishap
> Tho' very chaste people, to die of a Clap.[31]

Johnson's attitude is much more like that of George Eliot;[32] he knew well that most of life is not passed in

[31] Lady Mary wrote, "I must applaud your good-nature in supposing that your pastoral lovers (vulgarly called haymakers) would have lived in everlasting joy and harmony if the lightning had not interrupted their scheme of happiness." Her letter is quoted in an interesting discussion by James Sutherland in *A Preface to Eighteenth Century Poetry* (Oxford, 1948), p. 96. For the details of the affair, see vol. vi of the Twickenham edition, Pope's *Minor Poems*, ed. Norman Ault and John Butt (London, 1954), pp. 197-201.

[32] "Some discouragement, some faintness of heart at the new real future which replaces the imaginary, is not unusual, and we do not expect people to be deeply moved by what is not unusual. That element of tragedy which lies in the very fact of frequency, has not yet wrought itself into the coarse emotion of mankind; and perhaps our frames could hardly bear much of it. If we had a keen vision and feeling of all ordinary human life, it would be like hearing the grass grow and the squirrel's heart beat, and

episodes of intense experience but rather in a succession of little incidents, and that we are chiefly affected not by "the more awful virtues" that moralists usually discuss, but by "those petty qualities, which grow important only by their frequency, and which though they produce no single acts of heroism, nor astonish us by great events, yet are every moment exerting their influence upon us, and make the draught of life sweet or bitter by imperceptible instillations" (*Rambler* 72).

That this is deeply tragic there is no need to declare. Rather it is tragic in the Chekhovian sense, in which sympathy and amusement may be mingled with pity, and in which fear, in the classical sense, is not very immediately present. Every domestic tragedy is chiefly tragic to its participants, without involving the fate of an entire people as in Hamlet's Denmark or Oedipus' Thebes. For those not immediately concerned, life goes on as before, unless it happens that they too are actors in their own small tragic drama.

> Thousands and ten thousands flourish in youth, and wither in age, without the knowledge of any other than domestick evils, and share the same pleasures and vexations whether their kings are mild or cruel, whether the armies of their country persue their enemies, or retreat before them. While courts are disturbed with intestine competitions, and ambassadours are negotiating in foreign countries, the smith still plies his anvil, and the husbandman drives his plow forward; the necessaries of life are required and obtained, and the successive business of the seasons continues to make its wonted revolutions.   (*Rasselas*, ch. 28)

---

we should die of that roar which lies on the other side of silence. As it is, the quickest of us walk about well wadded with stupidity" (*Middlemarch*, ch. 20).

97

Here is a detached perspective like that of Auden's "Musée des Beaux Arts." But of course to the people who happen to be involved in suffering, it is in no way minimized by the fact that the seasons continue to revolve. If the husbandman who drives his plow forward discovers that a thief has driven away his cow, he will feel just as much pain as the prince does at a military defeat; he will feel even more pain when he encounters sickness and death. The converse of the fact that life goes on even during public disaster is that in times of public prosperity, when "all is triumph and exultation, jollity and plenty," it remains true that "the condition of individuals is very little mended by this general calm; pain and malice and discontent still continue their havock, the silent depredation goes incessantly forward, and the grave continues to be filled by the victims of sorrow" (*Adventurer* 120).

From Johnson's sympathy for the quotidian tragedy of such people as "poor Peyton," there are yet further conclusions to be drawn. To say that Peyton is not so tragic as Lear is beside the point, true though it obviously is. A five-act *Tragedy of Peyton* would not be likely to succeed, but that is no reason why a one-paragraph account of Peyton cannot arouse genuinely tragic emotion. Furthermore Johnson is able to express, and perhaps even to understand, the tragedy of Peyton better than Peyton himself could do it. Peyton is the victim of inexplicable suffering, and only a victim; his death so soon after that of his invalid wife is a cruel irony of fate. We have no way of knowing what Peyton made of his circumstances, but we do possess Johnson's moving description which gives those circumstances a kind of artistic shape. Through language he has assimilated them to the tragic view which may be gathered (together with many other things) from *Rasselas* and the *Ramblers*.

There are, then, two points which I wish to empha-

98

size: that Johnson in effect gives us Peyton's tragedy, which in other hands could just as well have been pathetic, or tragicomic, or boring; and that in his large perspective it is part of the unceasing tragedy of everyday lives, less terrible and certainly less intense than the tragedies we know in art. In a way he is anticipating the untheatrical tragic effects of the novel: instead of admiring figures whose humanity is more awesome and wonderful than our own, we learn to perceive the kind of tragic feeling that prevails in life as we actually live it.

It will be apparent that I wish to focus the discussion on Johnson rather than on Peyton, or whatever other humble person he may describe from time to time. The point is not whether the character is objectively "important," as Peyton, for example, was not important to Boswell. What matters is whether he is made to seem important *to us*. And this is accomplished not in the hortatory manner of a sermon, by declaring that all men are valuable in the eyes of God, but by encouraging in us an empathy that feels the man's suffering as real suffering, his tragedy as real tragedy. In the fate of Peyton, of whom we know nothing more than the little Johnson tells us, we receive an intimation of the fate of all men, which of course includes our own.

For the larger purposes of the present book, however, two reservations must be made. The first is that however fully Johnson may have appreciated the tragedies of ordinary men, he is not thereby empowered to criticize those of Shakespeare or the Greeks, and indeed may be handicapped in his criticism. The second is that while the idea of quotidian tragedy is a prominent theme in his writing and conversation, it is only a theme; it coexists with others that may counteract or even contradict it, and to analyze it in detail is to bring forward what for Johnson himself was largely in the background. If we permit him to choose his own emphases, he will choose them differently, and the burden of his moral thought is intended, insofar as it confronts the problem of tragedy, to be virtually antitragic in implication.

5. The Antitragic Moralist

The last words of the *Rambler* are, "I shall never envy the honours which wit and learning obtain in any other cause, if I can be numbered among the writers who have given ardour to virtue, and confidence to truth" (*Rambler* 208). At the beginning of the enterprise, Johnson had written that "men more frequently require to be reminded than informed" (*Rambler* 2), and he always regarded his public role in this light. "He that communicates truth with success, must be numbered among the first benefactors to mankind" (*Adventurer* 95). Several writers have discussed Johnson's work as "wisdom literature," and there is no doubt that in daily life as well as in writing he attempted to act the part of the "wise man."[33] "His discourse," says Hawkins, "through life was of the didactic kind" (Hawkins, p. 71).

The purpose of this wisdom was not to shock men into an awareness of their existential predicament, as tragedy or for that matter Pascal's *Pensées* may be said to do, but to help them live better lives. Johnson was not writing *Pensées* intended to undermine man's faith in himself and his place in any universe except a religious one; on the contrary, he started from the as-

[33] See Ian Watt's "Dr. Johnson and the Literature of Experience," in *Johnsonian Studies*, ed. Magdi Wahba (Cairo, 1962), pp. 15-22; also Matthew Hodgart, *Samuel Johnson and His Times* (London, 1962) esp. pp. 122-24. Mrs. Thrale recalled his influence in these words: "How much cause shall his contemporaries have to rejoice that their living Johnson forced them to feel the reproofs due to vice and folly—while Seneca and Tillotson were no longer able to make impression—except on our shelves" (*Miscellanies*, I, 207).

sumption that man's self-esteem is already undermined, and undertook to provide moral encouragement and consolation. He was attempting to act as an expositor of the wisdom of the race, a wisdom which he did not regard as proceeding merely from personal experience; his experience, rather, served to assure him that the wisdom of the race was genuine.

According to Johnson's more Pascalian passages, man is the despairing prey of an invincible force of habit that betrays him to the merciless tortures of melancholy. According to his more conventionally moralistic passages, the wisdom of the race counsels us to dominate our passions, without, apparently, telling us what we can do if the attempt proves to be impossible. Johnson was perfectly aware of the distinction between his private experience and his public voice. His journals are full of hopeless resolutions to rise early, the failure of which he regarded with evident anguish, but as he told Lady Macleod, "No man practises so well as he writes. I have, all my life long, been lying till noon; yet I tell all young men, and tell them with great sincerity, that nobody who does not rise early will ever do any good" (*Life*, v, 210).

But even in the writings themselves, Johnson does not always speak in the same way. Selective quotation can be used to support widely varying kinds of theories about his moral teaching, not in excerpting dogmatic principles which might contradict each other, for these are not especially prevalent, but in laying emphasis unduly on certain aphoristic phrases at the expense of the context. Everyone has heard, for example, the brief sententious statements that "human life is every where a state in which much is to be endured, and little to be enjoyed" (*Rasselas*, ch. 11), or again, that "misery is the lot of man" (*Rambler* 45 and *Idler* 32). But consider the context of the latter phrase as it appears in *Rambler*

45. A fictitious correspondent is questioning the assertion, made in earlier numbers, that marriage is generally unhappy.

> Every man recounts the inconveniencies of his own station, and thinks those of any other less, because he has not felt them. Thus the married praise the ease and freedom of a single state, and the single fly to marriage from the weariness of solitude. From all our observations we may collect with certainty, that misery is the lot of man, but cannot discover in what particular condition it will find most alleviations; or whether all external appendages are not, as we use them, the causes either of good or ill.

Thus the phrase, in itself so gloomy, is not a bitter cry of despair, but is thrown out as part of a judicious skepticism about human complaining. The point is not that men are unhappy, but that they need not be as unhappy as they think. And so the discussion continues, "It is not likely that the married state is eminently miserable, since we see such numbers, whom the death of their partners has set free from it, entering it again." The real affinity of this passage is not with tragedy, but with Johnson's famous description of a second marriage as "the triumph of hope over experience" (*Life*, II, 128) —a comic or satiric observation.

Insofar as one can generalize about the whole bulk of Johnson's moral writing, its tendency seems to be to dominate or at least to channel the tragic sense of life which appears so vividly in isolated passages. At any rate it is well not to exaggerate the depth of his pessimism. Joseph Wood Krutch has very accurately described him as "a pessimist with an enormous zest for living,"[34] and the sane and healthy strength of his sense

---

[34] *Samuel Johnson* (New York, 1944), p. 1.

of humor is too well known to need discussion here. And of course this, too, is only one aspect of Johnson. That he strove for a detached perspective on himself and his pessimism does not prove that he always achieved it, any more than the amusing quatrain—

> If the man who turneps cries,
> Cry not when his father dies,
> 'Tis a sign that he had rather
> Have a turnep than a father.
>
> (Yale *Poems*, p. 296)

—proves that he was usually frivolous about death. A paradigm of the problems I have been discussing occurs in a speech Johnson made while traveling in the Hebrides, enhanced by an especially felicitous Boswellian description.

"No wise man will be contented to die, if he thinks he is to go into a state of punishment. Nay, no wise man will be contented to die, if he thinks he is to fall into annihilation: for however unhappy any man's existence may be, he yet would rather have it, than not exist at all. No; there is no rational principle by which a man can die contented, but a trust in the mercy of GOD, through the merits of Jesus Christ."—This short sermon, delivered with an earnest tone, in a boat upon the sea, which was perfectly calm, on a day appropriated to religious worship, while every one listened with an air of satisfaction, had a most pleasing effect upon my mind. (*Life*, v, 180)

Johnson intended that it should. If a wise man were to be *contented* to die, Johnson tells where his contentment must be found; but in an indirect sense, as in so many cases, he seems also to be describing himself.

103

What of the man who is not contented, who fears punishment or even annihilation?

One must also recognize that Johnson is simply not consistent throughout a career of nearly five decades, or even, perhaps, at any single moment during that career. By this I do not mean that he was given to logical contradictions, but that his complex view of life is probably not a single "view" at all—the phrase makes one think of the prospect from a single window, always the same—but rather the varied expression of an unusually interesting personality. "Sir, you have not travelled over *my* mind, I promise you," Johnson told Goldsmith (*Life*, IV, 183), and we should not imagine that we have done so either, least of all by abstracting one element from his discourse and declaring it to be the true one. In one of the *Rambler*s, for instance, he takes the line that life may be full of minor vexations but that these need not be dignified with much lamentation. "The main of life is, indeed, composed of small incidents, and petty occurences; of wishes for objects not remote, and grief for disappointments of no fatal consequence; of insect vexations which sting us and fly away, impertinencies which buzz a while about us, and are heard no more" (*Rambler* 68). Yet four months earlier he had written,

> The cure for the greatest part of human miseries is not radical, but palliative. Infelicity is involved in corporeal nature, and interwoven with our being; all attempts therefore to decline it wholly are useless and vain: the armies of pain send their arrows against us on every side, the choice is only between those which are more or less sharp, or tinged with poison of greater or less malignity; and the strongest armour which reason can supply, will only blunt their points, but cannot repel them.
>
> (*Rambler* 32)

6. Conclusion

Among all the qualifications and shifting perspectives, is there any attitude toward tragic experience which Johnson displays more often than others? If I had to express such an attitude in a single sentence, I would define it as a straightforward facing of life. At different times life appears in different lights; the strength and will to face the tragic are not constantly called for. But when they are it must be endured with as much patience and sanity as possible. Indulgence in grief, and above all self-pity, are to be avoided at all costs. "To hear complaints," Nekayah says, "is wearisome alike to the wretched and the happy; for who would cloud by adventitious grief the short gleams of gaiety which life allows us? or who, that is struggling under his own evils, will add to them the miseries of another?" (*Rasselas*, ch. 35). If life is so constituted that it affords no greater happiness than a few "short gleams of gaiety," this is all the more reason not to dwell on its bitterness.

The determination to see life in a true perspective is particularly evident in Johnson's letters of condolence. He was perfectly aware of "the emptiness of rhetorical sound, and the inefficacy of polished periods and studied sentences" (*Rasselas*, ch. 18) as consolations for grief. He knew well that "the state of a mind oppressed with a sudden calamity, is like that of the fabulous inhabitants of the new created earth, who, when the first night came upon them, supposed that day never would return" (*Rasselas*, ch. 35), and that the loss of a loved one "is a state of dreary desolation in which the mind looks abroad impatient of itself, and finds nothing but emptiness and horror" (*Idler* 41). His answer to the fact of grief, as given in *Rambler* 47, is that there is no answer; all one can do is to go on living, so that the sorrow will gradually wear away of itself. "Life is a Tragedy," Swift wrote to a lady who had lost a child, "wherein we sit as Spectators awhile, and then act our own Part in it."[35] We cannot choose not to act.

Johnson's letters of condolence are often deeply moving because they offer no easy consolations, but simply remind the bereaved person that he must continue to live. He wrote to his friend Langton on the death of a relative,

> Let us endeavour to see things as they are, and then enquire whether we ought to complain. Whether to see life as it is will give us much consolation I know not, but the consolation which is drawn from truth, if any there be, is solid and durable, that which may be derived from errour must be like its original fallacious and fugitive.
>
> (*Letters*, I, 111)

And if Johnson consistently recommended an attitude toward life that mitigated, so far as possible, its inevitable sorrows, such an attitude is wholly compatible with a tragic sense that is the more profound for rejecting sentimentality. "All that virtue can afford is quietness of conscience, a steady prospect of a happier state; this may enable us to endure calamity with patience; but remember that patience must suppose pain" (*Rasselas*, ch. 27).

The same sober acceptance lies behind Johnson's religious attitude toward the problem of evil, accepting God's decisions because they must be accepted, not because they are intelligible.

> Implore his aid, in his decisions rest,
> Secure whate'er he gives, he gives the best.
>
> (*Vanity of Human Wishes*, 355-56)

[35] Letter to Mrs. Moore, 7 Dec. 1727, in *Correspondence*, ed. Harold Williams (Oxford, 1963), III, 254.

This position is reached only at the end of a poem which exposes the bitterness of all human ambitions and which presents what is virtually a hypothesis: *if* man is ever to be happy, it cannot be in the present life, and must therefore be in a future one.

Johnson's answer to Pope's famous "Whatever is, is right" is characteristic: "I have heard him strongly maintain," Boswell says, "that 'what is right is so not from any natural fitness, but because God wills it to be right.'" It is interesting to notice the gabble with which Boswell tries to elucidate this remark: "and it is certainly so, because he has predisposed the relations of things so as that which he wills must be right" (*Life*, IV, 31n.). Johnson is not interested in trying to make sense of "the relations of things"; he accepts the belief that God has ordained everything for the best because there is no other way to attain tranquility in a Heraclitean world in which "our minds, like our bodies, are in continual flux" (*Rasselas*, ch. 35).

When Johnson attempts to cope with the tragic condition of man, then, he attains great objectivity and breadth of feeling. Consider for example his *Life of Savage*, which in its way is a true tragedy, but muted by a characteristic blend of compassion and clear-sightedness. It illustrates the effects of the self-delusion that plays so central a role in Johnson's moral thought: "By imputing none of his miseries to himself he continued to act upon the same principles, and to follow the same path; was never made wiser by his sufferings, nor preserved by one misfortune from falling into another" (*Lives*, II, 380). The theme is expressed in many passages where it is hard to say whether the irony or the sympathy is more impressive. Of these the following may stand as an example:

Mr. Savage, however, was satisfied and willing to retire, and was convinced that the allowance, though scanty, would be more than sufficient for him, being now determined to commence a rigid œconomist, and to live according to the exactest rules of frugality; for nothing was in his opinion more contemptible than a man who, when he knew his income, exceeded it; and yet he confessed that instances of such folly were too common, and lamented that some men were not to be trusted with their own money.

Full of these salutary resolutions he left London in July, 1739, having taken leave with great tenderness of his friends, and parted from the author of this narrative with tears in his eyes. (II, 413-14)

The note of compassion deepens as the account proceeds, and it is with true grandeur that Johnson anticipates, at the end, the possible animadversions of the reader. "Those are no proper judges of his conduct who have slumbered away their time on the down of plenty, nor will any wise man presume to say, 'Had I been in Savage's condition, I should have lived or written better than Savage'" (II, 433).

The more one ponders the tragic sense in Johnson, the more one is impressed by largeness and complexity. A mind which continually strives to see life whole is not always amenable to the formulations of a special study; and indeed, as will presently be argued, the very breadth of Johnson's vision is an obstacle to his critical understanding of tragedy in its formal manifestations. But first let us try to come to terms with two of his creative works. Why is *Irene*, his one attempt at writing a tragedy, so lamentably disappointing? And how is it that his imitation of a biting Roman satire strikes many readers as profoundly tragic?

CHAPTER 5

Irene

RECOMMENDING two young Lichfield protégés to a friend in London, Gilbert Walmesley wrote in 1737, "Davy Garrick is to be with you early the next week, and Mr. Johnson to try his fate with a tragedy. . . . Johnson is a very good scholar and poet, and I have great hopes will turn out a fine tragedy-writer" (*Life*, 1, 102). Garrick succeeded in the theater beyond all expectation; Johnson never wrote another play after *Irene*. Yet Walmesley's letter suggests that as a young man he may really have entertained hopes of becoming a "tragedy-writer," which must surely have influenced his later attitude toward tragic drama.

That attitude was in any case powerfully affected by the majestic failure of *Irene*. He had to wait twelve years after coming to London before the play could even be produced. Garrick, who seems to have been personally responsible for keeping it alive for nine performances,[1] was alarmed by its philosophical frigidity, and proposed some enlivening additions which Johnson indignantly rejected. "Sir, (said he) the fellow wants me to make Mahomet run mad, that he may have an opportunity of tossing his hands and kicking his heels" (*Life*, 1, 196). In his Prologue he proudly declares that he "No snares to captivate the judgment spreads; / Nor bribes your eyes to prejudice your heads" (27-28). He may possibly have thought himself vindicated when Garrick insisted on having the heroine strangled onstage with a bowstring, and the offended audience cried out "Murder! Murder!" (*Life*, 1, 197).

This modest success of *Irene* was to be its last. One

[1] Nicoll, in *A History of English Drama, 1700-1750* (Cambridge, 1929), p. 59, gives the play's run as thirteen nights, but he is repeating a mistake of Murphy's; see Boswell's *Life*, 1, 198, n. 1.

of the first reviewers made an effort to censure its departure from historical accuracy on neoclassical grounds,[2] but this was the almost symbolic gesture of a dying critical system. In general *Irene* was dismissed because it was boring, a criticism, as Johnson often observed, against which there is no answer. Boswell recorded in his journal before he had met Johnson, "Dempster, talking of *Irene*, a tragedy written by Mr. Samuel Johnson, said it was as frigid as the regions of Nova Zembla; that now and then you felt a little heat like what is produced by touching ice" (*London Journal*, p. 69). By then, in 1762, Johnson was famous as the poet of *The Vanity of Human Wishes*, the moralist of the *Rambler* and *Rasselas*, and the editor of the *Dictionary*. In the years of Grub Street hackwork, however, we may imagine that he would have written more tragedies if he had seen any prospect of success. Murphy once asked Garrick why he didn't produce another tragedy for Johnson, and Garrick replied—alluding to the *Drury Lane Prologue*—"When Johnson writes *tragedy, declamation roars, and passion sleeps*" (*Miscellanies*, I, 387). This was to be the general verdict of the age, and one which Johnson seems finally to have understood. "At another time, when one was reading his tragedy of 'Irene,' to a company at a house in the country, he left the room; and somebody having asked him the reason of this, he replied, 'Sir, I thought it had been better' " (*Life*, IV, 5).

The plan of my study does not call for a thoroughgoing "reading" of the play, but rather a discussion of it as it bears on Johnson's understanding of tragedy. In simple terms we may conclude that *Irene* is untragic for two principal reasons: first, because it is a kind of set

[2] An anonymous *Essay on Tragedy* (1749) with an "examen" of *Irene* appended. Its argument is summarized by James W. Johnson in *The Formation of English Neo-Classical Thought* (Princeton, 1967), pp. 173-74.

exercise, a bookish and derivative work begun early in the writer's life and tinkered with for years, perhaps never sustaining a serious rethinking of form and theme; secondly, because Johnson did not (for whatever reason) draw upon the deep understanding of the tragic in human life which he was developing during this period and which found moving expression in the *Life of Savage*. It is easy to read a personal repudiation of a restricting idea of drama in a passage written two years before *Irene* finally reached the stage:

> Then crush'd by rules, and weaken'd as refin'd,
> For years the pow'r of tragedy declin'd;
> From bard, to bard, the frigid caution crept,
> Till declamation roar'd, while passion slept.
> *(Drury-Lane Prologue, 29-32)*

To dilate at length on these points would be a negative and finally a circular procedure: *Irene* fails as tragedy because it is untragic. What I propose to do instead is to broaden the investigation, even at the cost of apparent digression from the topic of tragedy, and to ask not simply why *Irene* is a bad tragedy, but why it is a bad play. In attempting to understand why Johnson chose the subject he did and why he handled it in this particular way, we can learn a good deal about his idea of drama; and this will be of value when we come to assess his criticism of tragedies which, unlike *Irene*, are genuinely great.

Whether or not Johnson owed much to earlier plays on the Irene story,[3] his main inspiration was their mutual source, Richard Knolles' *Historie of the Turkes* (1603), an enormous work which qualified its author, in Johnson's opinion, as the best of the admittedly second-rate English historians (*Rambler* 122). In Knolles'

---

[3] See Bertrand Bronson, "Johnson's 'Irene,'" in *Johnson Agonistes and Other Essays* (Berkeley, 1965), pp. 100-18. All subsequent references to Bronson are to this work.

account, the story of Irene is a variation on the Antony and Cleopatra theme—"Mars slept in Venus' lap, and now the soldiers might go play." In order to prove to his restive followers that he was not a slave to passion, the Sultan Mahomet II contrived an instructive spectacle, and "with one of his hands catching the faire Greeke by the haire of the heade, and drawing his falchion with the other, at one blow strucke off her head, to the great terror of them all. And having so done, said unto them: *Now by this judge whether your emperour is able to bridle his affections or not.*"[4] Johnson, on the other hand, presents Mahomet as a civilized and indeed anxiously conscientious monarch who is depressed by the thought that Irene's conversion to his religion is not sincere, and who resolves, upon learning that he has unjustly commanded her death, to "quit the scepter of dominion" forever (v.xii.42ff.).

Why has Johnson made this change? Gibbon, who was inclined to doubt the authenticity of the story of Irene, took it as certain that Mahomet's passions "were at once furious and inexorable; that in the palace, as in the field, a torrent of blood was spilt on the slightest provocation; and that the noblest of the captive youth were often dishonoured by his unnatural lust."[5] And something of this Asiatic monster survives in Johnson's manuscript notes for the play:

Mahomet was learn'd especially in astronomy, could speak Greek Latin Arabick Chaldee and Persian; he loved the arts, and encourag'd a Venetian painter. He was avaritious and irreligious, perfidious, ambitious bloody cruel revengefull crafty and

[4] Quoted in the introduction to *Irene* in the Oxford *Poems*, pp. 233, 234.
[5] *Decline and Fall of the Roman Empire*, ch. 68; in J. B. Bury's ed. (London, 1902), vii, 161. Subsequent references will be given parenthetically in the text.

dissembling. He delighted in reading histories particularly of Alexander and Julius Caesar.

(Yale *Poems*, p. 218)

Here is a highly interesting character: the enlightened monarch whose passions provoke behavior altogether at variance with his cultured sensibility. The example of Nero comes to mind. But Johnson has chosen to eliminate this powerful source of dramatic interest and to internalize a different kind of drama within the minds of the various characters. At the center is Irene, tempted to betray her religion and her friends by the hope of becoming empress; Mahomet is important only as he precipitates this crisis and agonizes over it; Aspasia and Demetrius analyze the morality of using dubious means to attain a desirable end, the liberation of Greece. Before we consider these matters, however, Johnson's choice of subject suggests some general reflections.

The surprising thing in Johnson's encomium of Knolles is that he censures him for precisely this: he might have been truly great if he had written the history of his own nation, instead of employing his genius "upon a foreign and uninteresting subject"; he has "exposed himself to the danger of oblivion, by recounting enterprizes and revolutions, of which none desire to be informed" (*Rambler* 122). One naturally wonders whether Johnson implies some doubt about his own subject in *Irene*. On the whole I think not. Neoclassical tragedy, whether French or English, assumed a certain remoteness in time or space that emphasized the constant truths of human nature. Johnson wrote of Dryden's *Aureng-Zebe*, "His country is at such a distance that the manners might be safely falsified and the incidents feigned; for remoteness of place is remarked by Racine to afford the same conveniencies to a poet as length of time" (*Life of Dryden*, 1, 360). Moreover

113

while comedy could be in prose and could represent vivid English types—writers liked to boast of their country's eccentric "originals"—tragedy had to be heightened into solemn verse and concerned with human types which were not peculiar to a particular time or place. "His [Shakespeare's] story requires Romans or kings, but he thinks only on men" (*Preface*, Yale *Works* VII, 65).

Thus it is not surprising that *Irene* retains almost no traces of the historical detail that Johnson had carefully worked up. The focus is upon certain human beings who are trapped in a situation from which they try to find an honorable means of escape. In consequence Johnson virtually ignores the contrast between two great civilizations, just as Dryden had done when he adapted *Antony and Cleopatra* to the neoclassical form. The religious conflict that remains, crucial as it is, exists only in the minds of the main characters. It is a given element in the dilemma in which Irene finds herself, not a realm of complicated intuitions and responses which we are invited to explore.

In effect Johnson has chosen to write a particular kind of play, one whose official prestige was not matched by popular appreciation. During the half-century at whose end *Irene* made its transitory appearance on the stage, Shakespeare was by far the most popular tragic dramatist, followed by Otway and Rowe, then by the Restoration heroic playwrights, and last of all by the strictly neoclassical ones, whose most famous success was Addison's *Cato*.[6] To the degree that *Cato* furnished Johnson with a model he was laboring under a considerable handicap, but his choice of the neoclassical mode was not automatically an antitheatrical one. The technical disposition of his plot is, if not engrossing, at least not amateurish. Johnson under-

[6] See Nicoll, *History of English Drama*, pp. 59-60.

stands very well the peculiar virtue of the unity-of-time convention, that it can condense the psychological crises of a small group of characters into a single crucial moment in which their essential natures are laid bare.

As for engaging the interest of the audience, there is a reasonable degree of suspense. The plot against Mahomet is discovered, and although he is too distracted by love to smash it at once, the conspirators are running dangerously short of time. Then in successive scenes their own jealousy threatens to upset this unstable state of affairs: first Leontius and Demetrius quarrel over who shall lead the attack, displaying the excess of their patriotic virtue (iv.iii), and next Abdalla's jealousy of Demetrius over the fair Aspasia suggests a similar danger (iv.iv). It is consistent with this kind of plot that there should be little action, only the constant threat of action; Demetrius chafes at necessary delay and the resourceful Cali strives to hold everything together while, as he rather splendidly puts it, "Fate lies crouded in a narrow space" (iii.vi.5). In the end, as in so many French neoclassical plays, the action finally does break like a wave, and proves too powerful for either side to control.

Yet Garrick can be forgiven for wanting an excuse to toss his hands and kick his heels. Despite these theoretical advantages, *Irene* is very boring. Of the various reasons that can be proposed, three seem particularly relevant to our inquiry: first, the characterization is inadequate and wooden; secondly, the language is too generalized and turgid; thirdly, the moral lesson of the play is enforced in a heavy-handed manner, and conceived in a way destructive of tragic feeling.

The question of characterization need not detain us long. Marshall Waingrow has made an admirable effort to discern complexity of motive in Cali and Irene, and has ingeniously found a means of enduring the unfailing perfection of Aspasia.[7] But the main difficulty is that Johnson has chosen to employ an inhuman standard of rigorous virtue. No doubt he had historical support; as Gibbon says, the "noble band of volunteers" that defended Constantinople "was inspired with Roman virtue" (ch. 68, vii, 178). But the artistic liabilities are obvious. In general this kind of character is dramatically interesting only when we are shown its limitations or inner contradictions, as in Shakespeare's Roman plays or Corneille's *Horace;*

> Je rends grâces aux dieux de n'être pas Romain,
> Pour conserver encor quelque chose d'humain.[8]

Possibly Johnson was misled by the theatrical poseurs of the heroic plays into imagining that Demetrius and Leontius were true to life. His prologue exclaims,

> If no wild draught depart from reason's rules,
> Nor gods his heroes, nor his lovers fools:
> Intriguing wits! his artless plot forgive,
> And spare him, beauties! tho' his lovers live.
>
> (17-20)

The result was to desiccate his characters, just as Addison had done.

Dramatic personages are known to us only as they speak, and Johnson's are gravely handicapped by the

[7] See "The Mighty Moral of *Irene,*" in *From Sensibility to Romanticism,* ed. F. W. Hilles and Harold Bloom (New York, 1965), p. 91. With reference to Aspasia (her name means "well-pleasing"), Waingrow cites the seventieth *Rambler,* which identifies a minority among mankind "whose principles are so firmly fixed, whose conviction is so constantly present to their minds, and who have raised in themselves such ardent wishes for the approbation of God, and the happiness with which he has promised to reward obedience and perseverance, that they rise above all other cares and considerations, and uniformly examine every action and desire, by comparing it with the divine commands."

[8] *Horace,* lines 481-82. The speaker is Curiace, as valiant as the brothers Horace but less certain of his own infallibility.

pompous blank verse, laden with abstractions, that he puts into their mouths. Since he is celebrated as the champion of "generality," something needs to be said about this device as it appears in *Irene*, where it all but takes the place of imagery. Sometimes it is successful enough: "No more the glutted sabre thirsts for blood, / And weary cruelty remits her tortures" (i.i.9-10). But more often the relentless piling on of generalization has a diluting effect, as can be illustrated from two lines of Aspasia's. In the first, Johnson has hit upon an effective phrase, "futurity's untravell'd waste." But he is not content to stop there, and weakly elaborates: "Far as futurity's untravell'd waste / Lies open to conjecture's dubious ken" (iv.i.68-69).

Or consider a more extended example:

> CALI. Let prudence, ere the suit be farther urg'd,
>   Impartial weigh the pleasure with the danger,
>   A little longer, and she's thine for ever.
> DEMETRIUS. Prudence and love conspire in this
>   request,
>   Lest unacquainted with our bold attempt,
>   Surprize o'erwhelm her, and retard our flight.
>
> (iii.iii.8-13)

Here the characters borrow and develop each other's language. They see themselves as agents of eternal verities. Prudence and love act through them, whether in conflict, as Cali thinks, or in harmony, as Demetrius does. In each case the speaker is pointing out a material fact: Cali, that if Demetrius won't spoil everything by seeing Aspasia now, he will have her happily ever after; Demetrius, that prudence is really the ally of love rather than its enemy, since the whole plan may go awry if their sudden appearance should alarm Aspasia.

Elsewhere Johnson's use of this device succeeds in peopling the world with large and incalculable forces, which lie behind and dominate the activities in which they find their particular embodiment. But it is easy to see why he should have had trouble achieving this kind of effect throughout an entire play. He is not Euripides or Racine, and does not really imagine any mysterious power that operates through his characters; prudence, pleasure, and love, in the speech just quoted, are really nothing more than figures of speech. And this rhetorical device is better suited to dispassionate reflection than to spontaneous dialogue. It is inappropriate for Irene to say, when it seems that she will be tortured, "Stern Torture shakes his bloody scourge before me, / And Anguish gnashes on the fatal wheel" (ii.i.15-16).

Here, no doubt, the influence of *Cato* was especially baleful, as Johnson seems to have realized when he gave magisterial support to the view of his creature Dick Minim (*Idler* 60) that *Cato* was rather a poem than a play.

> About things on which the public thinks long it commonly attains to think right; and of *Cato* it has been not unjustly determined that it is rather a poem in dialogue than a drama, rather a succession of just sentiments in elegant language than a representation of natural affections, or of any state probable or possible in human life. . . . Of the agents we have no care: we consider not what they are doing, or what they are suffering; we wish only to know what they have to say. (*Life of Addison*, ii, 132)

A few lines later he delivers a judgment that may easily be applied to *Irene*: "Its success has introduced or confirmed among us the use of dialogue too declamatory, of unaffecting elegance, and chill philosophy." Mrs. Thrale recognized the affinity between Johnson's play and Addison's.

> Now though to move Terror & Pity those two throbbing Pulses of the Drama, be the first Thing

required in a Tragedy; there are others which are necessary to make it complete, as Sentiment Diction &c. 'Tis entertaining enough to observe the effect of each style separately—& we shall have Cato and Irene at one End; the Earl of Essex & George Barnwell at the other.[9]

Johnson's declaration is well known that "Addison speaks the language of poets, and Shakespeare, of men" (*Preface*, Yale *Works* VII, 84), but the remark just preceding it is equally noteworthy: "He knew how he should most please; and whether his practice is more agreeable to nature, or whether his example has prejudiced the nation, we still find that on our stage something must be done as well as said, and inactive declamation is very coldly heard, however musical or elegant, passionate or sublime." The term "prejudiced" suggests that there is nothing intrinsically wrong with a dramatic form that emphasizes this aspect in order to concentrate on the inner movement of mind and soul. When stage spectacle is reduced to a minimum, and likewise the illusion of the variousness of life that Johnson praised in Shakespeare, then a deeply psychological drama is possible, in which the long and carefully orchestrated speeches have the inner coherence and completeness of the lyric poem.

The question, then, is whether Johnson really achieves what the method demands, a subtle exposure of psychological development. Unhappily he does not. The psychology of his characters is too frontal, too ob-

[9] *Thraliana*, I, 248. She is quoting Young, who speaks in the *Conjectures on Original Composition* of "those two throbbing pulses of the drama, by which alone it is shown to live, *terror* and *pity*." *The Earl of Essex* was the title of several plays, notably one by John Banks (1681). But she may have meant the version by Henry Brooke (1761), in reference to which Johnson composed his parodic line, "Who drives fat oxen should himself be fat" (*Miscellanies*, I, 193).

119

vious, to bear the weight of this kind of drama. The writers of the heroic plays, much though they may have boasted of a scientific grasp of the "springs of human nature," found themselves creating incongruous worlds in which form and content were at variance. For the most part they preferred a sophisticated exploitation of this variance rather than a reexamination of the "heroic" basis of their drama, though in *All for Love* Dryden does seem to understand the kind of psychological study that the genre affords, and tries to adapt Shakespeare's most varied and colorful tragedy to this end, as if using a lens to focus a broad beam of light into a brilliant point.

Many writers had boasted, like Johnson in his prologue to *Irene*, that by means of simplicity in language and stage spectacle they were reforming the neoclassical play from the excesses of heroic drama. But the danger was that the earnestly neoclassical dramatist would retain the long speeches without either heroic vitality or Racinian subtlety, and treat them as methodical lectures. The deepest difficulty in *Irene* is that the characters, except intermittently, have no human existence. Naturally they emit speeches that refer to the progress of the action, but beyond this it is remarkable how seldom they express any sentiment with which Johnson would not agree. Even more remarkable is the rarity of any speech that carries real emotional force. The exception proves the rule when Aspasia has a vision of the harem as infected by a truly Johnsonian melancholy:

> Soon shall the dire seraglio's horrid gates
> Close like th' eternal bars of death upon thee,
> Immur'd, and buried in perpetual sloth,
> That gloomy slumber of the stagnant soul; . . .
> There wear the tedious hours of life away,

Beneath each curse of unrelenting Heav'n,
Despair, and slav'ry, solitude, and guilt.

(III.viii.79-87)

This isolated moment of genuine feeling derives from
a private preoccupation of the author, to whom, with
the sole exception of the words "seraglio" and "slav'ry,"
the lines would perfectly apply. This is even clearer in
the manuscript sketch: "Melancholly broods or pours
her influence oer the stagnant soul. The gloom of idle-
ness" (Yale *Poems*, p. 165).

Johnson was apparently far from sure how he ought
to represent emotion in dramatic verse, and surprisingly he ended by imitating the excesses of the heroic
drama. One may be disconcerted to find Gibbon cen-
suring a speech in *Irene* for "the extravagance of the
rant" (ch. 68, VII, 187, n. 74), but the stricture is just. We
can get near the heart of Johnson's difficulties as
a dramatist if we look at a passage where Abdalla
grows angry at Cali's sententiousness, and rebukes him
with a truly Johnsonian sententiousness of his own:

Hast thou grown old amidst the croud of courts,
And turn'd th' instructive page of human life,
To cant, at last, of reason to a lover? (III.i.32-34)

From this measured language he modulates a few lines
later into mere rant. To Cali's reasonable inquiry, "But
why this sudden warmth?" he replies,

Because I love:

Because my slighted passion burns in vain!
Why roars the lioness distress'd by hunger?
Why foam the swelling waves when tempests rise?
Why shakes the ground, when subterraneous fires
Fierce through the bursting caverns rend their way?

(48-53)

121

When he wants to express violent passion Johnson apparently finds no medium available except the old heroic fustian. Only thus can he execute the design sketched in the outline for one of his scenes: "Dem. raves on Aspasia" (Yale *Poems*, p. 222).

In an unabashedly heroic extravagance like *The Conquest of Granada*, or even in Congreve's *Mourning Bride*, from which Johnson echoes a bombastic passage, such language would seem ordinary if not tame. Everything depends on context and implication. The point is not simply that Johnson descends into bathos, but that he must be presumed to do so with his eyes open. Having examined the popular drama of recent decades, he concludes that if he wishes to represent emotion he must do it in this manner. The Johnson we know in Boswell's *Life* spoke vehemently about damnation, but we do not imagine that he was likely to cry out as Irene does, "Unutterable anguish! Guilt and Despair!"[10]

---

[10] v.ix.49-50. Nicoll (pp. 74-75) lists a dozen such passages from a long series of plays, of which these will serve as examples: "Damnation! Hell and Furies! Flames and Tortures!" (R. Hurst's *The Roman Maid*, 1724); "Hell and Confusion!" (Rowe's *Ulysses*, 1705); "Hell and Confusion, Horror and Despair!" (Havard's *Scanderbeg*, 1733).

Cali's line, "Why foam the swelling waves when tempests rise?" (III.i.51), seems to echo the penultimate line of the following passage in *The Mourning Bride*, which is worth quoting as an example of what Johnson could find in a reasonably philosophical tragedy that was distinguished for the excellence of its verse. Zara has just come upon a headless corpse, which she mistakes for that of the man she loves.

> Ha! prostrate! bloody! headless! O—start Eyes,
> Split Heart, burst ev'ry Vein, at this dire Object:
> At once dissolve and flow; meet Blood with Blood;
> Dash your encountering Streams, with mutual Violence,
> 'Till Surges roll, and foaming Billows rise,
> And curl their Crimson Heads, to kiss the Clouds!
>
> (v.ii.162-67)

122

Irene exhibits yet another relic of the heroic drama in its curious emphasis on love. One may surmise a biographical explanation—Bronson suggests that Aspasia resembles Elizabeth Porter, and that the play is "Johnson's marriage offering" (p. 137)—but the central role of love derives mainly from the usage of Restoration drama. As in so many of those plays, it is represented as a motivating force for the entire action. Indeed, it seems to be largely in order to rescue Aspasia that Demetrius sets out to save his country. In a rare moment of human weakness when he pauses to say farewell to his lady, he defends himself in these terms:

> Reproach not, Greece, a lover's fond delays,
> Nor think thy cause neglected while I gaze,
> New force, new courage, from each glance I gain,
> And find our passions not infus'd in vain.
>
> (III.xi.19-22)

The rhyming couplets which Johnson reserves for the end of each act increase the resemblance here to the language of the heroic plays. Even Demetrius' association of love with liberty is wholly conventional: Nicoll lists a series of plays in which this was the principal theme, including Charles Johnson's aptly titled *Love and Liberty* (1709). The hero of Martyn's *Timoleon* (1730), for instance, "burns with Liberty, and Love" (Nicoll, p. 63).

The famous passage in the *Preface to Shakespeare* deserves to be quoted at some length.

> Upon every other stage the universal agent is love, by whose power all good and evil is distributed, and every action quickened or retarded. To bring a lover, a lady and a rival into the fable; . . . to make them meet in rapture and part in agony; to fill their mouths with hyperbolical joy and out-

123

rageous sorrow; to distress them as nothing human ever was distressed; to deliver them as nothing human ever was delivered, is the business of a modern dramatist. For this, probability is violated, life is misrepresented, and language is depraved. But love is only one of many passions, and as it has no great influence upon the sum of life, it has little operation in the dramas of a poet, who caught his ideas from the living world, and exhibited only what he saw before him.   (Yale *Works* VII, 63)

As a description of Shakespeare, this looks absurd: one might wonder if Johnson had forgotten Juliet, Desdemona, Cleopatra, and the heroines of the comedies. But this opinion—which was by no means original with Johnson[11]—is perfectly justified in the sense in which he meant it. He knew very well that love is present in Shakespeare; it is present as it is in life, rather than in accordance with the conventions of a peculiarly systematized form of drama. Shakespeare "caught his ideas from the living world," not from previous dramatists. Johnson caught the ideas of his own play from other plays, and he is virtually describing *Irene* when he calls love the universal agent in most drama. He has dutifully brought a lover, a lady, and a rival into his fable, they meet in rapture and part in agony, they give voice to hyperbolical sentiments, and on their behalf language is depraved.

Johnson's subject is a religious crisis that occurs at the moment when a mighty civilization falls. He has

[11] Hooker (I, 438-39) gives a summary of such statements. Warton had taken a similar position in his *Essay on the Writings and Genius of Pope* (1756), which Johnson had reviewed: "One would imagine, from the the practice of our modern play-wrights, that love was the only passion, capable of producing any great calamities in human life." "LEAR and MACBETH are . . . striking instances what interesting tragedies may be written, without having recourse to a love-story" (4th edn. [1782], I, 272, 275).

had the wisdom to preserve Irene—as earlier plays on the subject had not—from romantic entanglements, but he has nonetheless introduced the love affair (if so pure a passion can be called by so immodest a name) of Demetrius and Aspasia. And he is obliged to frolic incongruously in the language of gallantry. Quite apart from the Greek characters, Mahomet himself knows how to say that he receives virgins from "Each realm where beauty turns the graceful shape, / Swells the fair breast or animates the glance" (i.iv.13-14). This was worked up from the manuscript note, "Each region where beauty shed her influence, turns the shape, swells the breast or animates the eye sends the fairest" (Yale *Poems*, p. 128). One is reminded of the phrases from *Sweets of Sin* that emerge from time to time in the mind of Leopold Bloom.

That some such love-plot was obligatory is suggested by the *Critical Review*'s approval in 1771 of Cumberland's version of *Timon of Athens*: "This is certainly no injudicious alteration of the original piece, which is deficient in respect of such a female character as claims any connection with the fable, or may in the least deserve the compassion of the audience." Whether Johnson knew it or not, his two heroines were descended from a standard Restoration convention in which one was virtuous and the other lustful, like Almeria and Zara in *The Mourning Bride*. The convention achieved permanency by the type-casting of Mrs. Bracegirdle and Mrs. Barry in a score of such roles, and perhaps reflects a conception of two basic extremes of female psychology.[12] In this sense Johnson's innovation is to make the Mrs. Barry figure less lustful, as he tries to develop her religious struggle. But for whatever reasons he introduced the love-plot, its effect is to deflect

[12] I owe this observation to Eric Rothstein, *Restoration Tragedy* (Madison, 1967), pp. 141-44. The review of Cumberland is in the *Critical Review*, 32 (1771), 470.

attention from the potentially tragic elements of the play and to focus it on a conventional and not especially interesting amatory theme.

None of the matters which we have been discussing encourages much confidence in Johnson's understanding of drama, much less of tragedy. For the present study their main significance is to suggest that when he set out to write a tragedy his energies were directed in seriously unproductive directions. We may now address ourselves more directly to the larger themes of the play and consider what tragic possibilities they may contain.

As Waingrow observes, a good deal is made of the problem of means and ends. "Be virtuous ends pursued by virtuous means," Aspasia sternly warns her lover, "Nor think th' intention sanctifies the deed" (III.viii.58-59). The speech is quoted in a passionately favorable review in the *Gentleman's Magazine* with the comment, "The sophistry of the maxim, *it is lawful to do evil that good may come,* is finely exposed."[13] Aspasia comes to see that Greece cannot be saved without enlisting the help of Cali, and Cali is a traitor, even though his treachery is directed toward the bitter enemy of Christianity and Greece.

Here, then, is a moral and political theme of great interest: good and evil are inextricably involved with each other, and we cannot attain one without implicating ourselves in the other. It is a central theme in *Hamlet*. But how central is it in *Irene?* There are at least two reasons why we reflect very little upon it during the actual course of the play. The first, perhaps accidentally from the point of view of Johnson's design, is that the rescue of Aspasia rather than of Greece always appears to be the true subject. Of Greece, except as a dis-

[13] *Gentleman's Magazine*, 19 (1749), 80. One would like to know how direct a hand Johnson may have had in this highly flattering review.

embodied name, we know nothing whatever, except that Avarice had prevented it from making any effort in its own defense (I.i). The contrast between Greek Liberty—another abstraction—and the Turkish menace has hardly been demonstrated.

There is a further reason why Aspasia's moral qualms do not distress us as much as they might. How monstrous, really, is Cali Bassa? From the Greek point of view he is doing exactly the right thing, and he never betrays any great depths of depravity. Even his acquiescence in Abdalla's plan to poison Demetrius is forced upon him as the only way to save the plot from collapsing. When Abdalla puts forward a naked might-makes-right doctrine as his title to Aspasia, Cali protests, "Yet in the use of pow'r remember justice" (III.iv.10). Abdalla retorts, "Can then th' assassin lift his treach'rous hand / Against his king, and cry, Remember justice?" I do not see why not. We know that Cali is out of favor with Mahomet for having preferred the rule of his wiser and more humane father, and he has described the present state of affairs in the language of a patriot: "Such are the woes when arbitrary pow'r, / And lawless passion, hold the sword of justice" (I.ii.53-54). He applies to Abdalla exactly the same standard as to the realm in general: power alone does not make justice. Of course his behavior toward Mahomet remains treacherous, but not in a way that seems appalling. I do not deny that this theme is present in *Irene*, but only that it has the prominence—whatever Johnson intended—that we might wish it did.

We may now turn to the theme of apostasy, in which if anywhere the moral and emotional heart of the play will be found. This was a quite ambitious choice of subject, requiring great skill to make it succeed; William Popple remarked in 1735 (in connection with Steele's *Christian Hero*) that the English theater "seems not to approve of a RELIGIOUS DISTRESS for *Tragedy*." But Johnson apparently could not decide how he ought to handle the subject, and ended by muddling it. Waingrow even makes the surprising suggestion that he has "taken pains to eliminate a religious conflict," the argument being that Irene's motives for deserting Christianity are "either base or falsely rationalized," and thus incapable of dramatizing a true choice between religions.[14] The point about her motives for embracing Mohammedanism is true enough; moreover, her adherence to Christianity is equally pleasure-oriented. Against Mahomet's early promises of regal delights she protests, "Must I for these renounce the hope of Heav'n, / Immortal crowns and fulness of enjoyment?" (ii.vii.13-14). Contrariwise the version of Christianity invoked by Aspasia is based (like Johnson's own) almost entirely on fear.[15] The opposite of a salutary fear, then, is Irene's thoughtlessly complacent hope. Religion for her is only an instrument for obtaining personal rewards and satisfactions. In this sense her choice of Mohammedanism is certainly calculating and base.

But that does not for a moment change Johnson's assumption that apostasy itself is evil. When Cali betrays his country, the act is treacherous regardless of what might be said in favor of his motives, and when Irene betrays her religion, the baseness of her motives only makes the action more contemptible. Moreover, it is hard to see how Johnson could have managed the theme if Irene had favored Islam from any kind of spiritual conviction. A play that countenanced such a heroine would, if it accepted Johnson's moral assumptions, be a very harsh and repellent one. In a note on *I Henry IV* he defends the principle of the holy war on the grounds that the Mohammedans are committed "to

[14] Popple, *The Prompter*, no. 29 (18 Feb. 1735). (Most of the theatrical *Prompters* are by Aaron Hill, but those signed "P" are by Popple.) Waingrow, p. 82.

[15] Bronson makes this point: *Johnson Agonistes*, p. 132.

extirpate by the sword all other religions . . . and only lying in wait till opportunity shall promise them success" (Yale *Works*, VII, 455).

For whatever reason, Johnson evades the problem by avoiding any connected argument on religious principles, and treats the question as one of allegiance to a power whose claims are taken for granted. Accordingly he presents Christianity, like Greece, simply as a uniform fact, an abstract noun whose particular attributes are never examined. It happens that one reason for the fall of the Eastern Empire was its hostility to Latin Christendom,[16] but Johnson must ignore the issue, since the simplicity of Irene's choice would be confused if the Christianity which she abandons should exhibit signs of schism and internal doubt.

Yet there seems no question that Johnson felt deeply about apostasy, and intended to ground his play upon it. In the brief *Life of Hughes* he regrets that the poet was persuaded to revise his original design for the popular *Siege of Damascus*: "He had made Phocyas apostatize from his religion; after which the abhorrence of Eudocia would have been reasonable, his misery would have been just, and the horrors of his repentance exemplary" (*Lives*, II, 163). This remark is interesting, because Phocyas seems sufficiently base even as Hughes presents him, betraying his city in order to avenge his rejection as a suitor by Eudocia's father. Her abhorrence when she learns what he has done is wholly understandable. One senses how strongly Johnson felt about the apostasy theme. *The Siege of Damascus*, indeed, anticipates (rather crudely) a number of his preoccupations, and it is easy to suppose that he was interested in it. "Guilt" is often applied to Phocyas' treason,

[16] According to Gibbon, "The first minister of the empire, the great duke, was heard to declare that he had rather behold, in Constantinople, the turban of Mahomet than the pope's tiara or a cardinal's hat" (ch. 68, VII, 177).

and some vestiges of the abandoned theme suggest how closely Hughes, like Johnson, connected treason with apostasy. The conflict of ends and means is also present: Eudocia (like Aspasia) exclaims when Phocyas protests that he has saved Damascus by betraying it, "Safe? free? O no!—Life, Freedom, every Good / Turns to a Curse, if sought by wicked Means" (iv.ii, p. 48).[17] The clumsiness with which Hughes handles the religious issue helps to clarify the dangers which Johnson avoided when he played it down. Hughes' Moslems are treacherous, blood-thirsty brutes who use their faith as a mere excuse for rape and pillage. The one humane leader among them is virtually a crypto-Christian:

> O Power Supreme,
> That mad'st my Heart, and know'st its inmost Frame!
> If yet I err, O lead me into Truth,
> Or pardon unknown Error!   (v.ii, p. 64)

Johnson's Mahomet is neither bloodthirsty nor ripe for conversion, and it is well to avoid involving him in religious disputation.

If the apostasy theme seems weak or ill-developed in *Irene*, the explanation is probably biographical. Bronson has a penetrating discussion of Johnson's unwillingness to permit even the slightest conviction to arguments in its favor (pp. 131-35). But in any case there is plenty of evidence that we are supposed to consider it important. Thus Mustapha, the most philosophical of the Turks, expresses contempt for Irene's decision even before she has made it, and accurately

17 My references are to the first edition (1720). In regard to the revision which Johnson mentions, Thomas Davies says that Cibber "by his sole authority" forced Hughes to alter the original in which Phocyas turns Moslem: "Colley, with his usual confidence, declared that the audience would not bear a hero who could change his religion" (*Memoirs of the Life of David Garrick* [1780], I, 209-10).

explains her motivation: "Heav'n will contemn the mercenary fervour, / Which love of greatness, not of truth, inflames" (I.iii.26-27). Mahomet himself, immediately after achieving the amorous conquest toward which his whole energy has been directed, comes forward *solus* to deliver a parallel verdict:

> Ambition was her crime, but meaner folly
> Dooms me to loath at once, and doat on falshood,
> And idolize th' apostate I contemn.   (IV.vii.9-11)

This is a little curious: the Turks, who want to subject all the world to their creed and are willing to use the sword to do it, despise Irene for apostasy from the Christian faith. And this is represented as a sin allied to the deepest depravity of soul, embracing other sins not obviously related to it. Mustapha tells Irene that the Sultan "knows how near apostacy to treason" (v.vii.21). The connection is made clearer when, after her death, Mahomet consoles himself for the loss of her great beauty: "So shone the first apostate" (v.xi.11). For there is a remarkably frequent attempt to associate Irene's fall with that of Satan himself, as if she were recapitulating his treachery to God. Something similar is true of Cali, with whose mental struggle she has much in common. He extols Ambition as an admirable passion (III.i), and it is clear that it dominates his life; he is first mentioned in the play as "tir'd of slav'ry, tho' the highest slave" (I.i.113), exactly as Milton's Satan impiously rejects his subordinate rank. So also Aspasia, after Irene has unashamedly celebrated Ambition as "the stamp, impress'd by Heav'n / To mark the noblest minds," predicts that she will soon realize her true condition, "Curst as the tyrant of th' infernal realms, / With gloomy state and agonizing pomp" (III.viii.111-12, 134-35). Curiously, this exchange was omitted when *Irene* was performed. The associations with the fallen angels are noticed by a writer in the *Gentleman's Magazine* in 1762, commenting on Johnson's alterations from the historical Irene and especially on her apostasy, "from which he has drawn the most useful moral lessons, having introduced a striking contrast between her and *Aspasia,* another Christian virgin, who, like *Abdiel,* in spite of persuasion and example, retains her integrity."[18]

During the course of the play an important key word, *guilt,* is repeated some twenty times. Apart from the personal reasons why Johnson should dwell on this idea, there is a striking anticipation in one of his sources, Charles Goring's *Irene; or the Fair Greek,* in which a brother of Irene commits suicide "Rather than live in my Apostate Guilt."[19] Likewise Aspasia warns, "Will not th' apostate feel the pangs of guilt, / And wish too late for innocence and peace?" (III.viii.132-33). Most of the uses of *guilt* carry this religious connotation, but others suggest a political one, reinforcing the connection between apostasy and treachery. As Mustapha says of the scheming Cali,

> How guilt once harbour'd in the conscious breast,
> Intimidates the brave, degrades the great.

[18] Observations appended to "The STORY of IRENE. From VERTOT's History of the Knights of MALTA," *Gentleman's Magazine,* 32 (1762), p. 619. This writer sees *Irene* as "a remarkable instance, that the best-written and most instructive plays are not the most successful in the representation, and that business and bustle, the shifting of scenes and the *feu de theatre,* are essential on the *English* stage." My authority for the statement that the Aspasia-Irene exchange was cut in performance is the account in the *Gentleman's Magazine,* 19 (1749), p. 80, which quotes both speeches in the course of lengthy excerpts from the play. Its omission need not have any special significance, for, as Johnson says in a note to *Richard II,* "Nothing is more frequent among dramatick writers, than to shorten their dialogues for the stage" (Yale *Works,* VII, 432).

[19] Cited by Bronson, *Johnson Agonistes,* p. 107.

> See Cali, dread of kings, and pride of armies,
> By treason, levell'd with the dregs of men.
>
> (IV.viii.14-17)

For Irene the two meanings coalesce. She has betrayed her country and her faith to gain the glory promised by Mahomet, and in return she is fated, by a series of mischances, to seem to have conspired against him. He therefore accuses her of a guilt that is not actually hers; but in fact she is more deeply guilty, since she has tried to buy his clemency by betraying her Greek friends. "Who charges guilt on me?" she demands of Mahomet, and receives the stern reply,

> Who charges guilt?
> Ask of thy heart; attend the voice of conscience—
> Who charges guilt! (v.vii.6-8)

That this theme is meant to be prominent, incidentally, can be supported by evidence from Johnson's own time. The *Gentleman's Magazine* review, commenting on Irene's "unutterable anguish! Guilt and Despair!" remarks "How strongly is such a life recommended, as secures a peaceful resignation in the hour of death, by the terrors thus expressed as the consequence of guilt by *Irene!*" And in 1760 Johnson's friend Murphy described in verse how ". . . Fair IRENE sees, alas! too late / Her innocence exchang'd for guilty state."[20]

Insofar as Irene genuinely exhibits this guilt, she is undoubtedly a tragic figure. Her soliloquy near the end of the play sounds an authentically tragic note as she watches the "happy bark" that bears the Greeks to safety,

> While I, not yet familiar to my crimes,
> Recoil from thought, and shudder at myself.

[20] *Gentleman's Magazine*, 19 (1749), 80; Murphy, *A Poetical Epistle to Samuel Johnson*, quoted by Boswell in the *Life*, I, 355.

How am I chang'd! How lately did Irene
Fly from the busy pleasures of her sex,
Well pleas'd to search the treasures of remembrance,
And live her guiltless moments o'er anew!

(v.vi.11-16)

In addition to the sense of ineradicable guilt, there is
the feeling of loss of what was formerly hers, and indeed of her better self. Aspiring to great glory, she has
betrayed not merely some external entity, whether
Greece or Religion, but also her own nature, and has
cut herself off from her fellow man. It is a tragic course
closely analogous to those of Macbeth and Doctor
Faustus, as well as to the Satan of *Paradise Lost*. Helen
Gardner has called this pattern the tragedy of
exclusion.[21]

Yet this theme is not as visible as it should be when
one actually reads the play. Partly this is because the
focus of interest is too strongly concentrated upon Demetrius and Aspasia, and we are made to see everything from their point of view. The obverse of Irene's
guilt is Aspasia's innocence. The summary of the play
in The *Gentleman's Magazine* insists upon the point:
"Thus *Aspasia*, whose heroic virtue and ardent piety
had refused the splendor of empire when offered as the
hire of guilt and apostasy, is delivered from slavery, and
preserved to possess the pleasures of conscious innocence in the arms of the man she loves" (p. 78). Irene's
death therefore seems entirely deserved, just as we accept Hamlet's attitude toward the deaths of Rosen-
crantz and Guildenstern: "Why, man, they did make
love to this employment." It is a case of simple poetic
justice. And this raises a larger and indeed fundamen-

[21] "Milton's Satan and the Theme of Damnation in Elizabethan
Tragedy," *Essays and Studies*, I (1948), 46-66. The essay is reprinted as "The Tragedy of Damnation" in *Elizabethan Drama:
Modern Essays in Criticism*, ed. R. J. Kaufmann (New York,
1961), 320-41.

tal question, that of the "mighty moral" (Prologue, 8) which the play was intended to enforce.

In the Prologue Johnson promises to show "what anguish racks the guilty breast," and accordingly Mustapha, in the final speech of the play, explains what has happened:

> So sure the fall of greatness rais'd on crimes,
> So fix'd the justice of all-conscious Heav'n.
> When haughty Guilt exults with impious Joy,
> Mistake shall blast, or accident destroy;
> Weak man with erring rage may throw the dart,
> But Heav'n shall guide it to the guilty heart.
>
> (v.xiii.10-15)

From the accidents and mistakes of human affairs the unalterable pattern of Providence emerges. In the first draft Johnson emphasizes the relation of guilt to punishment: "And that Heav'ns justice proceeds thr[ough] dark paths. Laborious maze—imputed guilt—Angels gaze Tickel" (Yale *Poems*, p. 228). The reference is to Tickell's *On the Death of Addison*, "the long laborious maze / Of Heaven's decrees, where wond'ring angels gaze." The "dart" is aimed in mockery of man's feeble attempts to prosecute his own designs, as in *The Vanity of Human Wishes* where "Fate wings with ev'ry wish th' afflictive dart" (15). It is the own-petard principle expounded by Horatio at the end of *Hamlet*:

> So shall you hear
> Of carnal, bloody, and unnatural acts;
> Of accidental judgments, casual slaughters;
> Of deaths put on by cunning and forced cause;
> And, in this upshot, purposes mistook
> Fall'n on th' inventors' heads.

But if Ophelia lies in her ignoble grave, and Hamlet's body is borne like a soldier to the stage, Demetrius and Aspasia have time to attempt a last expostulation with

Irene and then to make good their escape: "A galley waits us, and the winds invite" (v.v.52). The Prologue exhorts us to learn not only what happens to Guilt, but also "how Heav'n supports the virtuous mind" (9). Purposes may have been mistook, but only the guilty suffer. We are shown a providential universe in which everything happens for the best, and the fall of Greece and of Irene are both lost in the moral gratulation of the ending. The play has turned out to be an extended cautionary tale, recommending virtue in preference to treachery and guilt. Johnson the moralist has overwhelmed Johnson the tragedian, and everything that one can put forward to illustrate the tragic dimension of *Irene* has the hollow ring of specious demonstration.

Meanwhile the aesthetic liabilities remain, the feebleness of the characterization and the turgid bumble of the verse. Of these, at least, we can suspect that Johnson later was fully conscious. Over and over again he criticizes plays in terms that apply very accurately to his own. The speeches in *Comus*, for example, "have not the spriteliness of a dialogue animated by reciprocal contention, but seem rather declamations deliberately composed and formally repeated on a moral question. . . . It is a drama in the epick style, inelegantly splendid, and tediously instructive" (*Life of Milton*, i, 168-69). Thomson was ill-qualified for tragedy because "It does not appear that he had much sense of the pathetick, and his diffusive and descriptive style produced declamation rather than dialogue" (*Life of Thomson*, iii, 293). In his frequent praise of Shakespeare as the poet of Nature and the master of the pathetic, we recognize Johnson's homage to a genius who could give life to dramatic creations as he himself could not. Even *Julius Caesar* can be seen as "somewhat cold and unaffecting, compared with some other of Shakespeare's plays," and it may not be fanciful to think of *Irene* when Johnson suggests that "his adherence to the real story, and to

136

Roman manners, seems to have impeded the natural vigour of his genius" (Yale *Works*, VIII, 836).

Johnson looked back on his play with the humility of a proud man who is not too proud to learn from his mistakes. "Men in highest dignity," Milton observed in the preface to *Samson Agonistes*, "have labour'd not a little to be thought able to compose a Tragedy." Johnson did not succeed and he knew it. But surprisingly, as the quotations in the foregoing paragraph may suggest, he totally failed to perceive why this was so. What he must originally have conceived was a drama of ideas, but instead of designing an action in which ratiocinative dialogue could be appropriate, and instead of providing characters who could plausibly speak it, he followed the example of *Cato* in forcing his moral ideas into a plot that emphasizes suspense and intrigue. We have seen how carefully he developed these elements, but the suspense he tried to attain was of a mechanical kind (will the characters succeed in their scheme or be betrayed?) when the moral suspense of Irene's conversion ought to have been at the center. The love-plot adds further distraction, and in such a framework Johnson's moral ideas inevitably seem extraneous. His characters must desist from the action demanded by the structure of the play, and must disregard the passions which are supposed to be driving them, in order to expound doctrines which, to make matters worse, are dull.

Need Johnson have failed? I do not say that he could have achieved a true *drama* of ideas like Schiller's *Wallenstein*, where moral and philosophical issues rise out of a human (and dramatic) predicament. But another kind of model was available. Instead of irrelevantly condemning *Comus* for its lack of sprightly dialogue, he might have perceived that it would have been a far better guide than *Cato*. And when he objects to *Cato* in almost the same terms, it is clear that he has not really reflected on the difference between the two. One senses a rueful backward glance when he writes in 1758, "The art of dramatic disposition, the contexture of the scenes, the opposition of characters, the involution of the plot, the expedients of suspension, and the stratagems of surprize, are to be learned by practice; and it is cruel to discourage a poet for ever, because he has not from genius what only experience can bestow" (*Idler* 25). The truth is that *Irene* is undramatic not because the characters talk too much, or because more should have been done with the expedients of suspension and the stratagems of surprise, but rather because the drama itself is misplaced, and centers on a not very fascinating action instead of on the intellectual and moral issues that really matter to the author.

If only he had found an appropriate form, he might well have succeeded. The actor James Quin, famous for his grave dignity, made a popular success of *Comus*.[22] And such a realization might have saved Johnson from trying to write tragedy at all. If, as seems probable, he was incapable of giving fair treatment to the temptations of apostasy, then the tragic depths of his story could never have found adequate expression, and it would have been far better to settle for reflective solemnity. Moreover, to rescue such a production from lugubriousness, and to draw upon his strong ironic sense, something like a philosophical romance might have been ideal. In *Rasselas* one feels that Johnson had at last found the genre and the style that eluded him when he struggled over *Irene*.

[22] See the account given by Bertram Joseph in *The Tragic Actor* (New York, 1959), pp. 78-79.

CHAPTER 6

The Vanity of Human Wishes

AMONG Johnson's noncritical works the two which have continued to enjoy the greatest esteem are *The Vanity of Human Wishes* and *Rasselas*. The first is a formal "imitation" of a classical satire and the second is rich in gently satirical effects, but both are often described as having an affinity with tragedy. In my view *Rasselas*, despite its inconclusive conclusion and its exposure of the perpetual frustration of human desires, succeeds in resolving tragic, comic, and satiric elements into a perspective of harmony and detachment. And although to many readers it may seem darker than this, its tragic elements are finally too tenuous and ambiguous to repay extended treatment here.

The case is quite different with *The Vanity of Human Wishes*, in which Johnson achieves what Ian Jack (adapting a phrase of Dryden's) has called "tragical satire."[1] The poem has been the subject of so many excellent critical discussions that a comprehensive analysis here would be neither necessary nor useful. My purpose is a more limited one: to investigate what is meant by the tragic quality which critics have consistently found in it, and to try to see what relation this quality may have to the satiric elements which it also contains.

The Vanity of Human Wishes is offered as an imitation of the tenth satire of Juvenal, in the specialized sense of "imitation" as it is defined in the *Dictionary*: "A method of translating looser than paraphrase, in

---

[1] Dryden's phrase is applied to Juvenal in *A Discourse Concerning the Original and Progress of Satire* (Watson, II, 140), and used by Jack in his chapter on *The Vanity of Human Wishes* in *Augustan Satire* (Oxford, 1945).

which modern examples and illustrations are used for ancient, or domestick for foreign." The poet, then, will show his skill in adapting suitable modern instances to the argument of his model. Johnson does not imply any significant alteration of tone and implication: that would detract from the success of the imitation, "which pleases when the thoughts are unexpectedly applicable and the parallels lucky" (*Life of Pope*, III, 176). The greatest difficulty of the imitator will be in preserving fidelity to the original:

> The man of learning may be sometimes surprised and delighted by an unexpected parallel; but the comparison requires knowledge of the original, which will likewise often detect strained applications. Between Roman images and English manners there will be an irreconcileable dissimilitude, and the work will be generally uncouth and party-coloured; neither original nor translated, neither ancient nor modern.   (*Ibid.*, p. 247.)

Juvenal's tenth satire had already been translated by Dryden, whose version was reasonably faithful to the literal sense of the original but seemed open to criticism for its prevailing tone. This poem, in particular, was considered sufficiently solemn to serve as a magazine of materials for preachers.[2] Thus Johnson's opinion of Dryden's version, and his decision to enter into

---

[2] Dennis saw in Juvenal "the violent Emotions and vehement Style of Tragedy"; Dryden said that "Juvenal excels in the tragical satire," and noted that Bishop Burnet recommended this poem in particular, together with those of Persius, as "the store-houses and magazines of moral virtues." Jack, who mentions these passages, observes that Juvenal's tenth satire was used as a quarry by Christian writers throughout the Middle Ages (*Augustan Satire*, pp. 102-103, 136). The quotations are from Dennis, *To Matthew Prior, Esq; Upon the Roman Satirists* (Hooker, II, 219), and Dryden, *Discourse Concerning the Original and Progress of Satire* (Watson, II, 140, 123).

competition with it, were based on well-accepted assumptions.

> The general character of this translation will be given when it is said to preserve the wit, but to want the dignity of the original. The peculiarity of Juvenal is a mixture of gaiety and stateliness, of pointed sentences, and declamatory grandeur. . . . It is therefore perhaps possible to give a better representation of that great satirist, even in those parts which Dryden himself has translated, some passages excepted, which will never be excelled.
>
> *(Life of Dryden,* i, 447.)

Let us pause, then, to see what we can surmise about Johnson's conception of his task. He had to furnish modern instances in place of Roman ones, while preserving a fairly strict fidelity to their effect in the original; and he had to capture the tone of his model, which comprised two quite different aspects, wit and grandeur. To Juvenal he applies the term "that great satirist," and we are certainly not led to suppose that the poem, though declamatory and weighty, is anything other than a satire. He intended, we may suppose, to "imitate" that quality in Juvenal which has been called "a vehement and burning passion, like the 'saeva indignatio' of Swift."[3]

Yet the difference between his poem and Juvenal's is so striking, particularly in this matter of tone, that it has led a series of modern critics to deny its satiric intention. The Roman poet mercilessly exposes the result of intemperate desire and belittles his subjects with cruel caricature. Johnson, on the contrary, shows a deep sympathy for the common fate of man, and quite early in the poem suggests a radical divergence from Juvenal's attitude. Democritus, according to the original, "laughs

[3] W. Y. Sellar and J. P. Postgate, "Juvenal," in the *Encyclopaedia Britannica,* 11th ed.

141

at all the Vulgar Cares and Fears; / At their vain Triumphs, and their vainer Tears" (Dryden's version, 79-80). In the same passage in Johnson the emphasis is wholly different: "All aid the farce, and all thy mirth maintain, / Whose joys are causeless, or whose griefs are vain" (67-68). There would seem to be an implied exception of genuine suffering, which is not "vain" and is therefore not included in the "farce." And later in the poem there are two passages of more or less autobiographical content, the descriptions of the scholar and of innocent old age, that illustrate the point.[4]

The neoclassical writers who called Juvenal "tragical" were principally alluding to the technical matter of his elevated style, or in Dennis's words "the violent Emotions and vehement Style of Tragedy."[5] But a number of modern critics have found tragedy, in its metaphysical sense, in *The Vanity of Human Wishes,* in consonance with Walter Scott's remark that its "deep and pathetic morality . . . has often extracted tears from those whose eyes wander dry over pages professedly sentimental."[6] From various excellent discussions of this kind, that of Mary Lascelles may be chosen as exemplary. Her conclusion is that Juvenal employs a satiric irony to expose the distance between our pretensions and our powers, while Johnson regards the human condition with a deeper kind of tragic irony. Thus, "Johnson's response to the man who plays high and loses all is the Shakespearean—that is, the tragic—re-

[4] For the autobiographical element, see the notes in the Yale *Poems* on lines 135-64 and 291-98. These passages diverge more than most from the original; the twenty lines that allude to Johnson's mother (291-310) are developed from six lines in the Latin (240-45). According to Mrs. Thrale, "When Dr. Johnson read his own satire, in which the life of a scholar is painted, . . . he burst into a passion of tears one day" (*Miscellanies*, I, 180).

[5] See n. 2, above.

[6] *Lives of the Novelists,* chapter on Johnson (Everyman ed., p. 164).

sponse"; and again, "The awe and pity with which Johnson contemplates the spectacle of human unfulfilment makes of *The Vanity of Human Wishes* a great tragic poem."[7]

Miss Lascelles' position suggests the approach of what we may call the tragic school of interpreters, which has been to emphasize the portraits, especially those of Wolsey and Charles XII. In Juvenal the fall of Sejanus, for example, is full of circumstantial detail, which is intended to focus the reader's attention on the fickleness and hypocrisy of the people who first supported and then reviled him (as in Ben Jonson's *Sejanus*). Johnson presents his Wolsey with far greater dignity, and with only the briefest allusion to the hostility of the former sycophants (four lines, to Juvenal's twenty-five). The passage ends in a generalized allusion to Shakespeare's *Henry VIII*, with Wolsey seeking "the refuge of monastic rest" (118) and reproaching the broken faith of kings. It is very much like the outline of a tragedy.

This kind of interpretation compels us to recognize that parts of the poem, at least, are either not satiric at all, or satiric in a very peculiar way. The point is best illustrated in the often-noticed disparity between Juvenal's Hannibal and Johnson's Charles XII of Sweden. Johnson was well aware of the antiheroic convention in Augustan satire, as for example in Prior's ballad on the taking of Namur or Swift's satirical elegy on Marlborough; in a way he draws upon it in the terrible lines,

[7] "Johnson and Juvenal," in *New Light on Dr. Johnson*, ed. F. W. Hilles (New Haven, 1959), pp. 52, 55. The earliest expression of this view seems to have been Francis G. Schoff's "Johnson on Juvenal," *Notes and Queries*, 198 (1953), 293-96. Another treatment of the two poets is that of Henry Gifford, "*The Vanity of Human Wishes*," *Review of English Studies*, n.s. 6 (1955), 157-65, who concludes that "it is the tragic sense of life that informs Johnson's poem," which deals with "the mystery of human existence."

143

"From Marlb'rough's eyes the streams of dotage flow, /
And Swift expires a driv'ler and a show" (317-18), with
the deep irony of compelling Swift and the man he
hated to share the closed unity of a couplet, just as they
have had to share the fate of man. But he is often interested in effects of a very different kind. Dryden renders
Juvenal's account of Hannibal fairly literally in lines
like these:

> A Sign-Post Dawber wou'd disdain to paint
> The one Ey'd Heroe on his Elephant....
> Go, climb the rugged *Alps*, Ambitious Fool,
> To please the Boys, and be a Theme at School.
> (254-55, 271-72)

The sarcasm is brutally unforgiving. For Johnson the
subject aroused more solemn emotions.

> The death of great men is not always proportioned
> to the lustre of their lives. Hannibal, says Juvenal,
> did not perish by a javelin or a sword; the slaugh-
> ters of Cannae were revenged by a ring. The death
> of Pope was imputed by some of his friends to a
> silver saucepan, in which it was his delight to heat
> potted lampreys.   (*Life of Pope*, III, 200)

Johnson perceives the ironies in the situation, but in
Pope's case his reference is mild and humane, with its
pleasant use of the phrase "it was his delight." And he
transformed Juvenal's Hannibal into the great portrait
of Charles XII of Sweden.

> His fall was destin'd to a barren strand,
> A petty fortress, and a dubious hand;
> He left the name, at which the world grew pale,
> To point a moral, or adorn a tale.   (219-22)

It is Johnson, not schoolboys, whose moral is pointed
and whose tale is adorned.

Further analysis of the passage would demonstrate that Charles, though he exhibits definite limitations of vision and perhaps even of humanity, is heroic in the sense that figures in Augustan satire seldom are. He is an overreacher, he is deluded, but he is certainly not ignoble. But can we go further, and claim that he is genuinely tragic? Eliot remarked that "these thirty-two lines compose a paragraph which is, in itself, quite perfect in form: the rising curve of ambition, the sudden calamity, and the slow decline and degradation."[8] The effect seems to be that of a miniature tragedy, and Johnson actually contemplated writing one on this subject.[9]

Against such a view at least three objections can be raised. One is that the tragedy, if it exists at all, is only potentially present, since the story is not especially particularized. Johnson's characters are really emblematic figures, as indeed the transposition of Roman and modern examples would suggest; they are the agents or representatives of abstract forces that are larger than any individual, however great. Thus we see Wolsey, "Law in his voice, and fortune in his hand" (100), and thus Charles XII, "Unconquer'd lord of pleasure and of pain" (196). What we have is more like the prospectus for a tragedy than the tragedy itself, and Charles is present mainly in order to support a thesis. Moreover, the shapely form which Eliot describes suggests something quite different from the quality of most political tragedies, which might be characterized in the words

[8] "Johnson as Critic and Poet," in *On Poetry and Poets* (London, 1957), p. 180. In an earlier essay Eliot praised the "just inevitable sequence of *barren, petty,* and *dubious*" in lines 219-20 (introduction to the Haslewood edition of Johnson's satires, 1930, reprinted in the *Pelican Guide to English Literature,* IV, 271). The collations with the rough draft in the Yale *Poems* show that Johnson achieved this effect only by careful reworking: both the "petty fortress" and the "dubious hand" began as "nameless."

[9] See his letter to John Taylor, 10 Aug. 1742 (*Letters,* I, 23).

of Bacon's essay "Of Great Place": "The standing is slippery; and the regress is either a downfall, or at least an eclipse." For Johnson the rise and fall of great men seems a relatively slow and stately process, like the waxing and waning of the moon, or growth and decay. In tragedy it is perhaps more like mountain-climbing: immense skill expended in the face of ever-present danger, and the stroke of disaster coming like a sudden blow.

A related objection is that the simple *de casibus* exemplum, while it is fundamental to the idea of the tragic, is (considered simply in itself) an inadequate basis for tragedy as the artistic imitation of an action. Modern criticism would not care to accept as tragic all of the stories related by Chaucer's Monk, and in fact the type, depending on its treatment, need not be tragic at all. Humpty Dumpty is a *de casibus* figure. If the Charles XII passage is tragic, it must be so by virtue of its imaginative presentation, however brief (as I have argued in opposition to Joyce, or at any rate Stephen Dedalus, in Chapter 1).

Finally, an even more fundamental objection may be advanced: that a tragic interpretation of Charles XII is a wilful misreading of Johnson's intention, which is satiric. Howard D. Weinbrot, approaching the poem from a formal analysis of Augustan satire, inverts the values of the tragic school and regards it as an assault on human pride. Thus Charles is seen as "super-human but inhuman," held up as an example to avoid, not to admire or sympathize with.[10] Such a view is a useful corrective to the notion that we have any clear—much less any intimate—understanding of Charles' feelings, but it does not really disprove the possibility of tragic emotion. Many tragic heroes are inhuman in their

---

[10] "*The Vanity of Human Wishes* and the Satiric Structure," ch. 8 of *The Formal Strain: Studies in Augustan Imitation and Satire* (Chicago, 1969).

146

greatness, arrive at a fate which is both appropriate and effected by their own actions, and do not necessarily "learn" from their fall.

A fully satiric treatment of Charles is implied in a brief allusion in the *Essay on Man*:

> Heroes are much the same, the point's agreed,
> From Macedonia's madman to the Swede;
> The whole strange purpose of their lives, to find
> Or make, an enemy of all mankind!
> Not one looks backward, onward still he goes,
> Yet ne'er looks forward farther than his nose.
>
> (IV. 219-24)

When Johnson quoted these lines from memory, Boswell objected to "Yet ne'er looks forward farther than his nose" as being low. Johnson replied, "Sir, it is intended to be low: it is satire. The expression is debased, to debase the character" (*Life*, v, 83). And in *Adventurer* 99, where he defends "projectors" from the unthinking derision of the Augustan satirists, he describes Charles XII as one of those true projectors whose ambitions should be regarded with revulsion.

> I cannot conceive, why he that has burnt cities, and wasted nations, and filled the world with horror and desolation, should be more kindly regarded by mankind, than he that died in the rudiments of wickedness; why he that accomplished mischief should be glorious, and he that only endeavoured it should be criminal: I would wish Caesar and Catiline, Xerxes and Alexander, Charles and Peter, huddled together in obscurity or detestation.

For whatever reason, he did not choose, four years earlier, to present Charles in this light in *The Vanity of Human Wishes*.

But considerations like these should not lead us to suppose that the poem is altogether remote from satire.

147

One may imagine that Johnson knew he was ignoring much of Juvenal's sarcastic acerbity, and that he was transforming passages of vivid (not to say grotesque) particularity into something much more solemn and general. But it is quite another matter to believe that he intended the poem to be essentially unsatiric, or, what is more important, that it would actually convey that impression to us if we were not reading selectively. It is clear that the tragic school, from Scott to Miss Lascelles, have been responding to something that really exists in *The Vanity of Human Wishes*. But in so doing they have not given full weight to another equally real aspect, which led Joseph Warton to write, "The imitations of Horace by Pope, and of Juvenal by Johnson, are preferable to their originals in the appositeness of their examples and in the poignancy of their ridicule."[11] For this one-sidedness of emphasis the comparison with Juvenal is partly to blame. The difference between Johnson's version and its model is so apparent that critics have been inclined to regard it as one of kind rather than degree. And their approach, emphasizing as it does the great set-piece portraits, is likely to neglect other passages which have considerable poetic merit and are essential to the structure of the poem.

Here, however, we must ask what kind of structure *The Vanity of Human Wishes* may reasonably be said to have. Early in the poem Johnson follows Juvenal quite closely, and appears to recommend the example of jesting Democritus. Later he departs a good deal from his source and for much of the time, at least, evokes a mood which has been called tragic. What, then, should we make of Democritus? One critic concludes that he has been "unsuitably" retained; another takes the somewhat desperate course of declaring *The*

11 *The Adventurer*, no. 133 (12 Feb. 1754).

Vanity a failure, which abruptly drops its mocking program and attempts a treatment quite unsuited to its subject.[12] But another possibility all but forces itself upon us: that Johnson has attempted to do more than one thing in this poem, to join both the satiric and the tragic modes in a larger whole.

To take this approach need not imply an especially high claim for the "unity" of the poem, or an assertion that it embodies some kind of symbolic *concordia discors*. Indeed, I shall urge that the terms of the argument explicitly deny the possibility of reconciling its discordant elements, except by escaping them entirely in the way proposed by the ending of the poem. If I am right, then Johnson is making a virtue of his tendency, which Geoffrey Tillotson has noticed, to conduct an argument rather erratically through a series of quite independent paragraphs. Or, looking at it in another way, Johnson obeys the principle of organization by accretion which Ralph Cohen finds in the Augustan mode: the verse paragraphs are carefully shaped within themselves, but assembled in the larger structure with an additive rather than an organic effect.[13] In either case, one cannot claim too subtle an interrelation of parts. *The Vanity of Human Wishes*, even more than Juvenal's tenth satire, is a very miscellaneous poem. One could easily fabricate reasons to explain why Johnson expands one passage or contracts another, but perhaps it is wisest to assume that he has a right to be simply idiosyncratic in these matters. To take a relatively trivial example, there is no obvious reason why he should substitute modern parallels for all but one of Juvenal's por-

[12] Gifford, *"The Vanity of Human Wishes,"* p. 158; Patrick O'Flaherty, "Johnson as Satirist: A New Look at *The Vanity of Human Wishes,*" *English Literary History*, 34 (1967), 78-91.

[13] Tillotson, *Augustan Poetic Diction* (London, 1964), p. 135; Cohen, "The Augustan Mode in English Poetry," *Eighteenth Century Studies*, 1 (1967), 15.

traits, retaining Xerxes (though adding "the bold Ba-varian" as well). I am tempted to believe simply that the passage had a special imaginative fascination for him. We know that he alluded to it later, on two quite different occasions, and that a couplet from it was his favorite in all of his poetry.[14]

Let us return, at this point, to the lines, "From Marlb'rough's eyes the streams of dotage flow, / And Swift expires a driv'ler and a show" (317-18). This couplet is the only direct reference to Juvenal's Swiftian disgust at the impotence of old age, which he mocks with a vehement obscenity that the Loeb translator feels obliged to omit and Dryden to render more witty and less explicit:

> The limber Nerve, in vain provok'd to rise,
> Inglorious from the Field of Battel flies:
> Poor Feeble Dotard, how cou'd he advance
> With his Blew-head-piece, and his broken Lance?
>
> (Dryden, 328-31; in Juvenal, 204-209)

Dryden if anything softens Juvenal's revulsion in the lines,

> The Skull and Forehead one Bald Barren plain;
> And Gums unarm'd to Mumble Meat in vain:
> Besides th' Eternal Drivel, that supplies
> The dropping Beard, from Nostrils, Mouth, and Eyes.
>
> (318-21)

To compare these lines with Johnson's treatment of old age may easily lead us to call his version tragic, but we should not forget that the prevailing tone of the pas-

---

[14] For these references, see the notes in the Yale *Poems* to lines 232 and 239-40. Johnson of course retains a number of less extended classical references, though often with considerable condensation; thus "the rapid Greek" (179) is all that remains of Juvenal's six lines on Alexander (168-73).

sage is satiric as much as sympathetic. The lines inspired by Johnson's aged mother (291-310), in which
Nature at last "bids afflicted worth retire to peace,"
have frequently been mentioned as if they were the en-
tirety of the section. But in fact they are an expansion
of Juvenal's brief reference to the sorrows of age *even
when* it is not contemptible; and they are preceded by
lines which correspond perfectly to Warton's opinion
of the poignancy of Johnson's ridicule. The dotard loses
the pleasures of the senses, and "shuns to know, / That
life protracted is protracted woe" (257-58)—a sentence
which is often quoted, and justly so, as a typically Johnsonian statement about the life of man. Thus far we
may presume that Johnson intends a degree of sympathy; we all feel a kind of horror when we consider
that "Time hovers o'er, impatient to destroy, / And
shuts up all the passages of joy" (259-60). As he so often
does, Johnson universalizes the condition by attributing
it to a force, *Time*, to which we are all in bondage, and
gives it point and immediacy by the brilliant stroke of
personification: Time is *impatient* to destroy.

The old man, then, is tedious to himself, and with
this we may easily sympathize. On the other hand, we
must do justice to the epigrammatic skill with which
Johnson depicts another aspect of his condition: he is
tedious to others, and insofar as it is worth their while
to humor him, he encourages moral debasement of a
particularly despicable kind.

But everlasting dictates croud his tongue,
Perversely grave, or positively wrong.
The still returning tale, and ling'ring jest,
Perplex the fawning niece and pamper'd guest,
While growing hopes scarce awe the gath'ring sneer,
And scarce a legacy can bribe to hear;
The watchful guests still hint the last offence,

151

The daughter's petulance, the son's expence,
Improve his heady rage with treach'rous skill,
And mould his passions till they make his will.

(273-82)

From the loathsome old man—loathsome morally, not
just physically—the emphasis shifts to the predatory
heirs, whose skill in fawning is "perplexed" by the ram-
bling confusion of his stories and jests. He has become
so appalling that even a legacy is barely reward
enough for their attentions. And at last, tyrannical
though he is, he becomes the victim and they the
agents, as they "hint," "improve," and "mould" his feelings, until—with a neat pun—"they make his will."
Johnson has often been praised for the strength and
vitality of his verbs, but his adjectives and participles
as well show a peculiarly Augustan accuracy of implication. The tale is "still returning"—the listeners perceive with despair that, like fate, it looms once again
into view; the jest is "ling'ring," as it stumbles labori-
ously through its familiar course. And the sycophants'
role forbids them to deflect the tale and the jest; on the
contrary, they are obliged to welcome them with every
sign of delight.

Thus far, I have suggested that *The Vanity of Human
Wishes* contains two predominant modes, those of
satiric attack and tragic sympathy. Sometimes they alternate; sometimes they appear more intimately joined.
But it is not necessary to claim that they are reconciled
in any profound way, for, as I have intimated, Johnson
denies the possibility of real reconciliation. The overtly
religious conclusion to the poem does not emerge
logically from it, but is supplied, as if from outside, as
the only possible escape from its dilemmas. We have
been given a series of impressions of human life, producing emotions which are varied and perhaps even
contradictory. Just as in the final sentence of *Rasselas*,

152

we are offered no means of finding stability amid the vicissitudes of life, but are advised instead to redirect our attention to "the choice of eternity" (*Rasselas*, ch. 47).

The radical difference between Juvenal's ending and Johnson's has often been noticed. The Roman poet recommends the Stoic posture which Johnson so often criticized as inhuman, and far from endorsing the efficacy of prayer, instructs his reader to concede as little as possible to the gods.

> Yet, not to rob the Priests of pious Gain,
> That Altars be not wholly built in vain;
> Forgive the Gods the rest, and stand confin'd
> To Health of Body, and Content of Mind:
> A Soul, that can securely Death defie,
> And count it Nature's Priviledge, to Dye.
>
> (Dryden, 546-51)

Mens sana in corpore sano: this is the answer to both of the themes of Juvenal's satire, the vanity of ambition (for power, wealth, and so on), and the final disillusionment with life itself. Johnson would probably agree with the former ("the wisest justice on the banks of Trent," 124), but his answer to the latter is the reverse of Juvenal's: only "celestial wisdom," acting for a benevolent God, can make "the happiness she does not find" (367-68).

In this sense *The Vanity of Human Wishes* is not only didactic, but actually homiletic. If I were to guess at Johnson's conception of his relation to Juvenal, I would surmise that he wanted us to be struck by precisely this difference between the two poems. While admiring the aptness of his modern parallels and the weighty solemnity of his language, we will have noticed how much less mocking his version is, and how a tragic feeling keeps breaking in upon the satire, though never wholly displacing it. We know from Johnson's many discus-

153

sions of Stoicism that he cannot have regarded Juvenal's answer as in any sense adequate, so that it deserves the criticism of the *Rambler*: "The folly of human wishes and persuits has always been a standing subject of mirth and declamation, and has been ridiculed and lamented from age to age; till perhaps the fruitless repetition of complaints and censures may be justly numbered among the subjects of censure and complaint" (*Rambler* 66). Mere censure, mere mirth and declamation, are "fruitless"; Johnson's method is to lead us through the stages of the Roman poet's argument, and then to show that religion reveals a conclusion of which Juvenal had not the slightest intimation. Thus I suggest that he intended his Christian ending as a kind of tour de force, answering the despair of the classical poet with the truth of revelation, and making the happiness he could not find.

The title which Johnson gave his imitation suggests this correction of classical by means of Biblical wisdom. We are meant to think of Ecclesiastes, to which he often alluded in his sermons and periodical writings.[15]

> The numerous miseries of human life have extorted in all ages an universal complaint. The wisest of men [Solomon] terminated all his experiments in search of happiness, by the mournful confession, that "all is vanity"; and the antient patriarchs lamented, that "the days of their pilgrimage were few and evil."　　　　　(*Adventurer* 120)

[15] In *Rasselas* Johnson seems to have followed an exegetical tradition in which Ecclesiastes is seen as recommending a judicious enjoyment of the things of this world: see Thomas R. Preston, "The Biblical Context of Johnson's *Rasselas*," *PMLA*, 84 (1969), 274-81. In *The Vanity of Human Wishes*, however, and in most of Johnson's passing references to Ecclesiastes, the possible satisfactions of the present are rejected in a much more thoroughgoing way.

To dwell upon the miseries of life would be useless, and indeed cruel, if it did not perform the essential service of distracting man from the illusory pleasures of this world and impelling him to fix his attention on eternity.

> Some have endeavoured to engage us in the contemplation of the evils of life for a very wise and good end. They have proposed, by laying before us the uncertainty of prosperity, the vanity of pleasure, and the inquietudes of power, the difficult attainment of most earthly blessings, and the short duration of them all, to divert our thoughts from the glittering follies and tempting delusions that surround us, to an inquiry after more certain and permanent felicity.
>
> (Sermon V, 1825 Works, IX, 331)

In particular, this "inquiry" involves a redirection of two of man's most fundamental passions, those of hope and fear. In his sermon on the text, "I have seen all the works that are done under the sun; and behold, all is vanity and vexation of spirit" (Ecclesiastes 1 : 14), Johnson says that Solomon "had taken a survey of all the gradations of human life," just as *The Vanity of Human Wishes* begins with observation surveying mankind; and Solomon reached a similar conclusion, that "the history of mankind is little else than a narrative of designs which have failed, and hopes that have been disappointed" (Sermon 12, 1825 *Works*, IX, 396, 398). Before undertaking his "survey," Johnson asks,

> Then say how hope and fear, desire and hate,
> O'erspread with snares the clouded maze of fate,
> Where wav'ring man, betray'd by vent'rous pride,
> To tread the dreary paths without a guide,
> As treach'rous phantoms in the mist delude,
> Shuns fancied ills, or chases airy good.   (5-10)

155

If man is indeed "without a guide"—Johnson takes for granted the inadequacy of Juvenal's *mens sana* in this regard—then the catalogue of human folly and misery must compel us to raise the question again, in even more pessimistic terms.

> Where then shall Hope and Fear their objects find?
> Must dull Suspence corrupt the stagnant mind?
> Must helpless man, in ignorance sedate,
> Roll darkling down the torrent of his fate?
>
> (343-46)

In the first published edition the final line read "Swim darkling down the current of his fate"; the revision forcibly enhances the idea of utter helplessness.

Hope and *Fear* are not the vague, indefinite terms that they have become today, but denote a view of the human condition that Johnson believes to be both psychologically and theologically true. First of all, these emotions are an inseparable part of life; as Imlac found, not even the Happy Valley could empower him to "bid farewell to hope and fear" (*Rasselas*, ch. 12). But more importantly, empiricist psychology defines them as a sort of double mainspring of human life. "Every man is conscious," Johnson writes in a sermon, "that he neither performs, nor forbears any thing upon any other motive than the prospect, either of an immediate gratification, or a distant reward" (Sermon 14, *Works*, IX, 414). The answer to the vanity of human wishes, then, is to redirect these basic drives in the right way. "To live religiously, is to walk, not by sight, but by faith; to act in confidence of things unseen, in hope of future recompense, and in fear of future punishment" (Sermon 10, *Works*, IX, 380). Thus Aspasia's eloquence briefly impels Irene to recognize the emptiness of "The glitt'ring vanities of empty greatness, / The hopes and fears, the joys and pains of life." Aspasia seizes the hint, and urges her friend, "Let nobler hopes

156

and juster fears succeed" (*Irene*, 11.i.6-9). Only in
heaven will hope and fear cease to be necessary.[16]

In effect, *The Vanity of Human Wishes* counsels a
Boethian withdrawal from the inevitable disappointments and sorrows of the temporal world. It warns
against subservience to "delusive Fortune" (75), and
urges the lesson of the passage from Boethius which
Johnson translated for the 1752 edition of the *Rambler*
(repeating his use of the word "darkling"):

> O Thou whose pow'r o'er moving worlds presides,
> Whose voice created, and whose wisdom guides,
> On darkling man in pure effulgence shine,
> And chear the clouded mind with light divine.
> 'Tis thine alone to calm the pious breast
> With silent confidence and holy rest:
> From thee, great God, we spring, to thee we tend,
> Path, motive, guide, original, and end.
>
> (Motto to *Rambler* 7, Yale *Poems*, p. 243)

It is now time to draw back a little from the poem,
and to ask whether it does in fact convey the impression
which, if my argument is correct, Johnson intended that
it should. Is Ian Jack right in seeing an "almost medie-
val" pessimism in the *contemptus mundi* tradition?[17]
Does the poem genuinely escape the tragic (and the

---

[16] Under *faith* in the *Dictionary* Johnson quotes Prior's lines
from "Charity: A Paraphrase on the Thirteenth Chapter of the
First Epistle to the Corinthians": "Then *faith* shall fail, and holy
hope shall die; / One lost in certainty, and one in joy." In the
Life of Prior he calls this poem "eminently beautiful" (*Lives*, II,
205). I owe the reference to Chester F. Chapin, *The Religious
Thought of Samuel Johnson* (Ann Arbor, 1968), p. 75. For a
fuller discussion of Johnson's uses of *hope* and *fear*, and a defense of the rewards-and-punishments argument against critics
like C. S. Lewis who despise it as "theological hedonism," see
Paul Kent Alkon, *Samuel Johnson and Moral Discipline* (Evans-
ton, Ill., 1967), pp. 53-64 and 167-77.

[17] *Augustan Satire*, p. 145.

satiric) by refusing to be bound by transitory hopes and fears, in the way that *Antony and Cleopatra*—to take an extrareligious example—seems to escape from the confines of tragedy?

> 'Tis paltry to be Caesar:
> Not being Fortune, he's but Fortune's knave,
> A minister of her will.
>
> (*Antony and Cleopatra*, v.ii.2-4)

These are questions which every reader must answer for himself. For my own part, I am inclined to think that even in this poem the moralist never quite suppresses the man. As Gray wrote in the lines which Johnson singled out for particular admiration,

> For who to dumb Forgetfulness a prey,
> This pleasing anxious being e'er resign'd,
> Left the warm precincts of the cheerful day,
> Nor cast one longing ling'ring look behind?

And, retreating still further from the poem, it is possible to distinguish between the meaning it is intended to enforce and the meaning we give it if we cannot share Johnson's religious premises. Like Pascal, he wins through to his knowledge of a higher truth by exposing the sickening inadequacy of any temporal truth; but for many readers today this is a conclusion which may be imaginatively understood but not shared. In this case, the main body of the poem may take on a different appearance, and become something much closer to tragedy than Johnson designed it to be. Nor is such an interpretation an anachronistic, twentieth-century misreading. To illustrate my meaning I cannot do better than to quote the following passage from F. M. Cornford's brilliant study of Thucydides' *History* as a tragic drama:

Elpis had not to the Greek the associations which Christianity has given to "Hope"; she is not a vir-

tue, but a dangerous passion. The future is dark
and uncertain, and although rational foresight
(*gnóme*) can see a little way into the gloom, Fortune, or Fate, or Providence, is an incalculable factor which at any moment may reverse the purposes
and defeat the designs of man. Elpis is the passion
which deludes man to count on the future as if he
could perfectly control it; and thus she is a
phase of infatuate pride, a temptress who besets
prosperity.[18]

Man in this sense is, we may say, condemned indeed to
"tread the dreary paths without a guide" (8), he is indeed the helpless victim of delusive Fortune, but to
know these things is not to be able to escape them.

Such reflections as these may help to explain why the
"tragic" elements of *The Vanity of Human Wishes* have
so often been admired, and indeed interpreted as setting the tone of the poem as a whole. But although it is
idle to ask that our aesthetic response be governed by
the presumed intention of the writer, it may yet be true
that Johnson intended the poem to have an effect that
was neither tragic nor satirical, moving beyond both
into a larger and more comprehensive vision. It should
be emphasized that no absolute statement of value is intended in a phrase like "larger and more comprehensive vision." A work which draws upon tragedy and
satire at once may lack the intensity and penetration of
either kind at its best, and may seem more discursive
than imaginative. May it not also seem peculiarly
Johnsonian?

[18] *Thucydides Mythistoricus* (London, 1907), pp. 167-68. (The
objections of classical scholars to Cornford's views on the historical causes of the Peloponnesian War do not affect my use of
his argument here.)

III. JOHNSON'S CRITICISM
OF TRAGEDY

CHAPTER 7

A Johnsonian Theory of Tragedy

1. Introductory

AN ATTEMPT to reconstruct Johnson's ideas about tragedy involves doing what he never did himself; his critical writing is seldom directed to the distinctive qualities of specific literary kinds.[1] For the most part it seems intended as impartial description of authors and works in the tradition of Addison's papers on *Paradise Lost*, and as such sets Johnson apart both from theorists like Dennis and from self-apologists like Dryden.

Committed though he was to the way of thinking that we commonly call neoclassical, Johnson was little enamored of many of its doctrines. As W. R. Keast suggests in "The Theoretical Foundations of Johnson's Criticism," he transferred his interest from the artifact to the relation between author and audience.[2] Yet rather surprisingly he showed small enthusiasm for the psychological criticism that was being undertaken in his own day. He may have praised Burke or Kames, but it would be hard to prove that beyond brief allusions, like Imlac's Burkean remarks in his "Dissertation upon Poetry" (*Rasselas*, ch. 10), Johnson ever really tried to assimilate the psychological theories of the new aesthe-

[1] W. R. Keast says that "the absence in his theory of any save a rather general account of literary effects, such as are common alike to all forms of the art," is his most serious defect as a critic ("Johnson's Criticism of the Metaphysical Poets," *English Literary History*, 17 [1950], 70). J. H. Hagstrum lists a number of "attempts at generic criticism"—of pastorals, epitaphs, and so on —and concludes that "Johnson's heart was not in them" (*Samuel Johnson's Literary Criticism* [Chicago, 1952], p. 33).

[2] Keast's essay appears in *Critics and Criticism*, ed. R. S. Crane (Chicago, 1953), pp. 389-407.

ticians, much less their investigation into the analogies between the different arts or their abstract discussions of general qualities like the sublime, the beautiful, the romantic, or the picturesque. If he was not entirely old-fashioned, he was not much attracted by the new fashions.

To someone more in sympathy with the new trend, Johnson could even appear an intellectual lightweight. Such at least is the opinion of Thomas Twining, a distinguished editor of the *Poetics*, who wrote in the year of Johnson's death: "Johnson's mind is fettered with prejudices civil, poetical, political, religious, and even superstitious. As a reasoner he is nothing; he has not the least tincture of the *esprit philosophique* upon any subject." Twining continues with an attack, not untypical of educated opinion at the end of the century, on Johnson's qualifications to talk about poetry: "He is not a poet, nor has any taste for what is properly called poetry; for imagination, enthusiasm, &c. His poetry—I mean what he esteems such—is only good sense put into good metre. . . . The general taste and feelings of the most poetical people, of the best poets, are against him."[3] By the end of his life Johnson was consciously a reactionary, defending an old-fashioned view of literature against the new poetical people, and refusing to concede that the fashionable "philosophy" was the appropriate arena of debate. But he was a reactionary without a committed faith in the complications of the older system, and in some ways he occupies a position of isolation between two great eras of criticism. This of course is one way of saying that he was massively individual and self-confident, but it also helps to explain

[3] Letter to his brother Richard, 3 May 1784, in *Recreations and Studies of a Country Clergyman of the Eighteenth Century, Being Selections from the Correspondence of the Rev. Thomas Twining, M.A.* (London, 1882), pp. 119-20.

the naggingly contentious quality of some of his most
famous pronouncements.

2. A Johnsonian Theory

"The two kinds of dramatick poetry," Johnson wrote
in *Rambler* 125, should be "defined only by their effects
upon the mind." For a priori rules he had little use; one
such rule, the number of speakers allowed in classical
drama, he described elsewhere with pleasant irony:
"The antients, remembering that the tragedy was at
first pronounced only by one, durst not for some time
venture beyond two; at last when custom and impunity
had made them daring, they extended their liberty to
the admission of three, but restrained themselves by a
critical edict from further exorbitance" (*Rambler* 156).

Johnson's own definition of tragedy in the *Dictionary*
has been quoted in Chapter 2: "A dramatick representation of a serious action." "Tragedy," he tells us in
the *Preface*, "was not in those times a poem of more
general dignity or elevation than comedy; it required
only a calamitous conclusion, with which the common
criticism of that age was satisfied, whatever lighter
pleasure it afforded in its progress" (Yale *Works*, VII,
68). In one sense this is a plea for the heroic stature of
tragedy, as against plays which "by changing the catastrophe, were tragedies to-day and comedies to-mor-
row." But in another sense it leaves open the possibility
that a tragedy, so long as it is dignified and elevated,
can have a happy ending.

In these two words *dignity* and *elevation* we come
close to Johnson's basic requirements for tragedy, requirements which no doubt were deliberately vague.
Dryden had written in Neander's peroration, responding to the charge that rhyme is unnatural,

I answer you, therefore, by distinguishing betwixt
what is nearest to the nature of comedy, which is

165

the imitation of common persons and ordinary
speaking, and what is nearest the nature of a serious play: this last is indeed the representation of
nature, but 'tis nature wrought up to an higher
pitch. The plot, the characters, the wit, the passions, the descriptions, are all exalted above the
level of common converse, as high as the imagination of the poet can carry them with proportion to
verisimility.   (Watson, I, 86-87)

"With proportion to verisimility": the phrase suggests
a crucial problem in Johnson's criticism, the relation between art and life (which will be postponed until the
next chapter). While he largely repudiated Dryden's
neoclassical assumption about comedy (as in *Rambler*
125), he seems always to have accepted the necessity for
"that exaltation above common life, which in tragick or
heroick writings often reconciles us to bold flights and
daring figures" (*Rambler* 37).

There is a curious note of doubt here—we have to be
reconciled to the daring figures—which was not present in Dryden's account, but which pervades all of
Johnson's treatments of the subject. The problem is
acutely posed in a review in the *Gentleman's Magazine*,
probably by Johnson, of a now-forgotten play: "The
language, though it is measured, is scarcely elevated
into poetry; but as all dialogue in verse is a deviation
from nature, this defect, however it may derogate from
its merit as a poem, could not much lessen its effect
upon the spectators."[4] Tragedy must be elevated, but
elevation is a deviation from nature.

---

[4] Review of Macnamara Morgan's *Philoclea* in the *Gentleman's Magazine*, 24 (1754), p. 84. For the attribution to Johnson,
see D. J. Greene, "Was Johnson Theatrical Critic of the *Gentleman's Magazine?*" *Review of English Studies*, n.s. 3 (1952), 161.
It is supported by Arthur Sherbo, "Samuel Johnson and the
Gentleman's Magazine, 1750-1755," in *Johnsonian Studies*, ed.
Magdi Wahba (Cairo, 1962), pp. 147-48.

One of Johnson's not very frequent uses of the word *tragical*, with the same connotations of suspicion and doubt, occurs in his description of a speech of Richard III: "There is in this, as in many of our authour's speeches of passion, something very trifling, and something very striking. Richard's debate, whether he should quarrel with himself, is too long continued, but the subsequent exaggeration of his crimes is truly tragical" (note to v.iii.177, p. 631).[5] Exaggeration is evidently acceptable in tragedy, and seems to be contrasted with the "trifling" for which Johnson so often reproached Shakespeare. But at the same time the playwright is constantly in danger of overwriting.

> His declamations or set speeches are commonly cold and weak, for his power was the power of nature; when he endeavoured, like other tragick writers, to catch opportunities of amplification, and instead of inquiring what the occasion demanded, to show how much his stores of knowledge could supply, he seldom escapes without the pity or resentment of his reader. *(Preface,* p. 73)

As often as this subject arises, the pejorative note is heard. Characters in comedy, Johnson says, are allowed by Horace "to raise their language in the transports of anger to the turgid vehemence of tragedy" (*Rambler* 152). Turgidity is not a quality which he admires. We recall the difficulties he had with the language of *Irene.*

As the *Dictionary* definition suggests, a tragedy for Johnson is simply a serious play. In *Rambler* 156 he takes the traditional view that "the design of tragedy is to instruct by moving the passions," which serious but untragic drama is perfectly capable of doing, and when he mentions "the tragick passions" (*Rambler* 98)

[5] All references to Johnson on Shakespeare are to the Yale *Works,* vols. VII and VIII. As the volumes are page-numbered consecutively, they are not separately cited.

he means simply the grand passions as opposed to "little civilities and ceremonious delicacies." His definition of tragedy is so wide that it includes much that a more limited one would not and yet excludes as well much that is now thought central to the form. Prince Hal, we are told, is "the hero both of the comick and tragick part" of the *Henry IV* plays, and a little later Johnson speaks of "the tragick scenes of *Henry IV* and *V*" (Yale *Works*, vii, 523, and viii, 611-12). The most remarkable statement of this kind is the declaration that Congreve's comedies have "in some degree, the operation of tragedies: they surprise rather than divert, and raise admiration oftener than merriment" (*Life of Congreve*, ii, 228).

For Johnson tragedy and comedy are not comprehensive visions of life so much as different selections from life. I have argued in Chapter 4 that his "tragic sense" is only part of a balanced attitude toward the varieties of human experience, some of which arouse solemn but not tragic reflections, and others irony or humor. This idea of selection is present in his account of the origin of the dramatic form, where Shakespeare is praised for a less thoroughgoing division of kinds than most playwrights have followed.

> Shakespeare's plays are not in the rigorous and critical sense either tragedies or comedies, but compositions of a distinct kind; exhibiting the real state of sublunary nature, which partakes of good and evil, joy and sorrow, mingled with endless variety of proportion and innumerable modes of combination. . . .
>
> Out of this chaos of mingled purposes and casualties the ancient poets, according to the laws which custom had prescribed, selected some the crimes of men, and some their absurdities; some the momentous vicissitudes of life, and some the lighter occurrences; some the terrours of distress,

and some the gayeties of prosperity. Thus rose the two modes of imitation, known by the names of tragedy and comedy, compositions intended to promote different ends by contrary means.

(Preface, p. 66)

By implication the ends need not really be so different. Johnson prefers a reflection of "the real state of sublunary nature" to the genres which traditionally focus and intensify one or another aspect of experience. And if "in the rigorous and critical sense" Shakespeare's plays are therefore neither tragedies nor comedies, one may suspect that, even in a larger sense, Johnson's admiration for them excludes their specifically tragic and comic aspects. To this question the next chapter will largely be directed.

One comes away with the impression that Johnson defines tragedy in a quite external way. It is dignified, it employs elevated language, it does not allow the use of excessively comic scenes (*Rambler* 125), and when comedy is successfully introduced (as in Shakespeare) the result may be excellent but is no longer tragedy. What Johnson manifestly lacks is a sense of the inner force of a genre, in appreciation of which we can call *Twelfth Night* a masterpiece of comedy or *King Lear* of tragedy. When he does briefly mention the characteristic issues of tragedy, it is as a catalogue of traditional subjects: "the fall of greatness, the danger of innocence, or the crosses of love" (*Preface,* p. 74).

I am not of course arguing that Johnson should have foreseen the tendency of modern criticism, but even in historical context two serious limitations are apparent. The first is that his own awareness of the tragic elements in life, as in the account of "poor Peyton" which was discussed in Chapter 4, is richer and more interesting than the assumptions he holds about tragedy as a genre. And secondly, as the evidence in Chapter 3

169

was designed to show, critics of Johnson's own time and earlier were capable of very penetrating remarks about tragedy. Consider this passage from Rowe:

> To these I might add, that incomparable Character of *Shylock* the *Jew*, in *The Merchant of Venice*; but tho' we have seen that Play Receiv'd and Acted as a Comedy, and the Part of the *Jew* perform'd by an Excellent Comedian [Dogget in Granville's version, 1701], yet I cannot but think it was design'd Tragically by the Author. There appears in it such a deadly Spirit of Revenge, such a savage Fierceness and Fellness, and such a bloody designation of Cruelty and Mischief, as cannot agree either with the Stile or Characters of Comedy.
>
> (Nichol Smith, p. 11)

Here "tragically" is supported by reference to the nature or quality of emotion in the play, and awkward as it is Rowe's discussion suggests a real insight into its contradictory nature. The same is not true of Johnson's perfunctory assessment: "Of *The Merchant of Venice* the stile is even and easy, with few peculiarities of dicton, or anomalies of construction. The comick part raises laughter, and the serious fixes expectation" (p. 241).

But Johnson said in *Rambler* 125 that comedy and tragedy should be defined by their effects on the mind. Are there any indications that he seriously pursues this line of thinking? There is his dismissal of Mrs. Montagu's *Essay on Shakespeare*—"No, Sir, there is no real criticism in it: none shewing the beauty of thought, as formed on the workings of the human heart"—which leads to a fuller statement later in the same conversation:

> We have an example of true criticism in Burke's "Essay on the Sublime and Beautiful;" and, if I

recollect, there is also Du Bos; and Bouhours, who shews all beauty to depend on truth. There is no great merit in telling how many plays have ghosts in them, and how this ghost is better than that. You must shew how terrour is impressed on the human heart.   (*Life*, II, 88, 90)

Here clearly is half, at least, of the Aristotelian formula of pity-and-fear, a formula which was mentioned in passing in the last sentence of *Rambler* 125. The terms also appear, strangely disguised by Johnsonian terminology, in the *Preface*, when we are told of Shakespeare's intentions "to sink [his audience] in dejection, and mollify them with tender emotions" (p. 74). "Dejection" does not at once suggest "fear," but appears in the second definition of the word in the *Dictionary*: "Awe; dejection of mind at the presence of any person or thing."

Yet in Johnson's criticism of actual tragedies one looks in vain for analysis of "how terrour is impressed on the human heart." And despite the much-agitated prominence of catharsis as a subject for criticism, he has only one direct discussion of it, and that in response to an application by Boswell.

I introduced Aristotle's doctrine in his "Art of Poetry," of "*the kátharsis ton pathemáton*, the purging of the passions," as the purpose of tragedy. "But how are the passions to be purged by terrour and pity?" (said I, with an assumed air of ignorance, to incite him to talk, for which it was often necessary to employ some address). JOHNSON. "Why, Sir, you are to consider what is the meaning of purging in the original sense. It is to expel impurities from the human body. The mind is subject to the same imperfection. The passions are the great movers of human actions; but they are mixed

171

with such impurities, that it is necessary they should be purged or refined by means of terrour and pity. For instance, ambition is a noble passion; but by seeing upon the stage, that a man who is so excessively ambitious as to raise himself by injustice, is punished, we are terrified at the fatal consequences of such a passion. In the same manner a certain degree of resentment is necessary; but if we see that a man carries it too far, we pity the object of it, and are taught to moderate that passion."

(*Life*, III, 39)

While Boswell makes the somewhat uncharacteristic admission that "my record upon this occasion does great injustice to Johnson's expression," we may assume that he has gotten it more or less right (especially as he was only assuming an air of ignorance).

The main thing to notice is that Johnson adopts the old homeopathic view of catharsis, invoked by Milton in the preface to *Samson Agonistes* ("for so in Physic things of melancholic hue and quality are us'd against melancholy") and expounded by Dacier in terms very close to Johnson's own: "Tragedy is a true Medicine, which Purges the Passions. Since it teaches, the Ambitious to Moderate his Ambition; the Wicked, to Fear God; the Passionate, to restrain his Anger, &c. but 'tis a very agreeable Medicine, and works only by Pleasure."[6] Johnson, like Dacier, uses the medicinal metaphor to support a highly intellectual position. Tragedy, that is, teaches us in a literal sense, rather than by some mysterious moral purification of the passions. We learn from examples to avoid behavior that will lead to no good. This may not be a very profound conception of tragedy, but on Johnson's behalf one may urge not merely that it was an old and honorable tradition, but also that he really didn't care very much about it. He

[6] *Aristotle's Art of Poetry* (London, 1705), p. 80.

defined catharsis because Boswell asked him to define it. In any case he would scarcely commend the contemporary theories that advocated the excitation of passion for its own sake. "Rational" is one of his most honorific terms. The two nonmedical illustrations for *cathartick* in the *Dictionary* are interesting in this regard:

> Lustrations and *catharticks* of the mind were sought for, and all endeavour used to calm and regulate the fury of the passions. *Decay of Piety.*
>
> Plato has called mathematical demonstrations the *catharticks* or purgatives of the soul. *Addison.*[7]

It may well be that Aristotle meant something quite immediate and physical by "catharsis" (as the passage on cathartic music in Book VIII of the *Politics* suggests), and the sentimental school of aesthetics would have been glad to accept such a view, but Johnson was always hostile to any account of art as powerfully arousing the passions. Boswell said that when he introduced the topic of music,

> I told him, that it affected me to such a degree, as often to agitate my nerves painfully, producing in my mind alternate sensations of pathetick dejection, so that I was ready to shed tears; and of daring resolution, so that I was inclined to rush into the thickest part of the battle. "Sir, (said he,) I should never hear it, if it made me such a fool."
>
> (*Life*, III, 197)

In tragedy Johnson was not at all interested in the sensation of one's own benevolence; even Hume had no use

---

[7] Johnson is quoting *The Causes of the Decay of Christian Piety*, "written by the Author of *The Whole Duty of Man*" (1667). Boswell records that he used the book during the Hebridean tour (*Life*, V, 227). The Addison reference is to *Spectator* 507. There is no entry for *catharsis* in the *Dictionary*, and nothing of interest under *purge* or *purgation*.

173

for the excesses of the view that sympathy is always pleasurable, for if that were so "an Hospital would be a more entertaining Place than a Ball." Johnson's nearest affinities might have been with his contemporary Lessing, who was writing that tragedy is "the school of the moral world," and that "purification rests in nothing else than in the transformation of passions into virtuous habits."[8]

At any rate Johnson was profoundly at odds with contemporary thinking about the pleasure aroused by tragedy, and held to something very like the old Lucretian or Stoic emphasis on the consciousness of our own safety.

> It will be asked, how the drama moves. . . . The reflection that strikes the heart is not, that the evils before us are real evils, but that they are evils to which we ourselves may be exposed. If there be any fallacy [i.e., "delusion"], it is not that we fancy the players, but that we fancy ourselves unhappy for a moment; but we rather lament the possibility than suppose the presence of misery, as a mother weeps over her babe, when she remembers that death may take it from her. The delight of tragedy proceeds from our consciousness of fiction; if we thought murder and treasons real, they would please no more. (*Preface*, p. 78)

One of the first adversaries to rise up against this famous passage was William Kenrick, who postulated a kind of involuntary empathy with the suffering of the characters, and refused to accept an intellectual basis for what is primarily an emotional experience: "The understanding enters into a compact, as it were, to keep

---

[8] Hume, letter to Adam Smith, 28 July 1759, in *Letters*, ed. J.Y.T. Greig (Oxford, 1932), I, 313. Lessing, *Hamburg Dramaturgy* (1769), trans. Helen Zimmern (New York, 1962), nos. 2 and 78, pp. 8, 193.

holiday."[9] The note of rationality constantly recurs in Johnson's allusions to the subject, as in a *Rambler* which quotes Addison's phrase "the cathartics or purgatives of the soul" in a context of "truth and reason": "We are directed by what tokens to discover the favourable moment at which the heart is disposed for the operation of truth and reason, with what address to administer and with what vehicles to disguise 'the catharticks of the soul' " (*Rambler* 87).

While Johnson always praised the "pathetic" in tragedy, remarks like these suggest a fear of emotionalism which is related to the idea that plays ought to deliver their moral lessons clearly and directly, and perhaps also to the conviction that the stage itself is irrelevant to drama: "A play read, affects the mind like a play acted" (*Preface*, p. 79). In his remark about terror being impressed on the human heart, Johnson alludes to plays that "have ghosts in them." Both Boswell and Mrs. Thrale recorded that when he was a small boy he was so frightened by the ghost scene in *Hamlet* that he hurried to the door of his father's shop "that he might see folks about him."[10] This scene seems to have been a crucial one for eighteenth-century audiences, despite the neoclassical assumption that ghosts could only be admired through a kind of indulgence in old-fashioned plays. As William Richardson described it in the language of the sublime, "The ghost of Hamlet, even in nations where philosophy flourishes, and in periods the least addicted to superstition, will for ever terrify and appal. . . . The imagination left to her own inventions,

[9] *Monthly Review*, 33 (1765), 376. Between the two installments of his review Kenrick began a long crusade against Johnson, which became virtually pathological, by publishing the first of a series of attacks. The editor, Griffiths, indignantly denounced Kenrick's book in the December number (pp. 457-67), and Kenrick's contributions to the *Monthly* ceased.

[10] The quotation is from *Thraliana*, I, 161. For Boswell's version, see the *Life*, I, 70.

overwhelmed with obscurity, travels far into the regions of terror, into the abysses of fiery and unfathomable darkness." The "start" of Hamlet when he first sees the ghost was a traditional feature of stage performance, and by all accounts was brought to perfection by Garrick.[11] Yet when Boswell demanded, "Would you not, sir, start as Mr. Garrick does, if you saw a ghost?" Johnson replied, "I hope not. If I did, I should frighten the ghost." This was not simply facetiousness, for he had just maintained that "the action of all players in tragedy is bad. It should be a man's study to repress those signs of emotion and passion, as they are called" (*Life*, v, 38).

Johnson's attitude here is important because it suggests not only that he was impatient with genre, which caused him to neglect some important elements of tragedy, but also that he lacked totally that passion for stage-plays, for the whole business of assembling a theatrically effective production and of arranging to have human beings act it out, which has seized so many of the people who have written interestingly about the drama. In the *Preface* he has the confidence to declare that the spectators "come to hear a certain number of lines recited with just gesture and elegant modulation" (p. 77), and a little later he deplores the influence of the "shows and bustle" in Shakespeare's plays:

> Those to whom our authour's labours were exhibited had more skill in pomps or processions than in poetical language, and perhaps wanted some

[11] Richardson, "Essay II: Of the Character of Hamlet," in *Essays on Some of Shakespeare's Dramatic Characters* (1774; 5th ed., 1798), pp. 96-97 and 97-98. Aaron Hill describes how Hamlet "*starts back*, a Step or two, and expresses his Amazement" (*The Prompter*, no. 100, 24 Oct. 1735). For an account of Garrick's celebrated "starts," of which this seems to have been his most wonderful, see Bertram Joseph, *The Tragic Actor* (New York, 1959), p. 110 and plate 10.

visible and discriminated events, as comments on the dialogue. He knew how he should most please; and whether his practice is more agreeable to nature, or whether his example has prejudiced the nation, we still find that on our stage something must be done as well as said, and inactive declamation is very coldly heard, however musical or elegant, passionate or sublime.   (*Preface*, pp. 83-84)

Calling a play "a book recited," he grants that comedy may benefit from performance, but denies this advantage to tragedy: "What voice or what gesture can hope to add dignity or force to the soliloquy of *Cato*" (p. 79). Rather oddly he has taken his example from the very play which is later said to communicate no hope and fear to the heart (p. 84), a point noted by the *Critical Review*, which went on to praise the "feelings unknown to reading" which Booth excited in the role of Othello.[12]

3. Domestic Tragedy

So far this chapter has been largely negative, dealing with the vagueness and inadequacy of Johnson's definition of tragedy, his unconcern for whatever lights the theory of catharsis might have afforded him, and his hostility to drama as it appears on the stage. Let us now consider what aspects of tragedy did matter to him, and what positive aspects of his appreciation can be distinguished.

[12] "We agree with Mr. Johnson, that the soliloquy in Cato is not to be meliorated by action. We think, however, the editor to be defective in precision, when he brings his example from Addison instead of Shakespeare. . . . When Othello catches Iago by the throat, that inimitable actor's [Booth's] voice went through all the scale of rage, first choaked, low and tremulous, then rising by just gradations; but when it came to a climax, or what we may call the diapason of passion, his modulations brought forth feelings unknown to reading" (*Critical Review*, 20 [1765], 331).

The central note is sounded in a letter from which we have already quoted, describing a visit to Lichfield and the meditation on mortality which it aroused: "What is nearest us, touches us most. The passions rise higher at domestick than at imperial tragedies" (*Letters*, I, 240). While in important ways Johnson's notion of "domestic" differed from the bourgeois drama which attained such popularity during his lifetime, it owes much to the impulse which gave birth to that drama. The lamentable inadequacy of most of these plays, together with their echoes in later melodrama, encourage us to dismiss out of hand what Coleridge called "the trick of making tragedy-heroes and heroines out of shopkeepers and barmaids."[13]

We have already discussed Johnson's sense of domestic tragedy, which may be opposed to the traditional divison of tragedy and comedy by social class. That the latter was by no means extinct is illustrated by Goldsmith's account of the proper subjects for the two genres:

> When Tragedy exhibits to us some Great Man fallen from his height, and struggling with want and adversity, we feel his situation in the same manner as we suppose he himself must feel, and our pity is increased in proportion to the height from whence he fell. . . . While we melt for Belisarius, we scarce give halfpence to the Beggar who ac-

[13] Notes on *Lear* in *Shakespearean Criticism*, ed. T. M. Raysor (London, 1960), I, 54. Elsewhere Coleridge betrays a kind of snobbery in speaking of unheroic characters: the Greek tragedians, he says, did not "condescend in tragedy to wheedle away the applause of the spectators, by representing before them facsimiles of their own mean selves in all their existing meanness, or to work on the sluggish sympathies by a pathos not a whit more respectable than the maudlin tears of drunkenness" (*Biographia Literaria*, ed. J. Shawcross [Oxford, 1907], ch. 17, II, 33).

costs us in the street. The one has our pity; the other our contempt.[14]

Domestic drama, whatever its sentimental excesses, was intended to broaden the range of literary response. Theorists stopped saying that we are moved by the misfortunes of great men because they are great, and began to say that we are moved by the misfortunes of men like ourselves because they are like ourselves. As Arthur Murphy saw it, looking back from the start of the next century, "Lillo seems to be the first, who made the distress of domestic life as interesting as the events that have attended heroes and unfortunate kings. His tragedy of *George Barnwell* is well known, and *Fatal Curiosity* has scenes that go to the inmost feelings of the heart."[15]

But however deeply Johnson sympathized with human suffering, he never showed the slightest interest in the "domestic tragedy" of his own day, except for a lukewarm commendation of Moore's *Gamester* in a review attributed to him.[16] His treatment of the theme is interesting because instead of bringing ordinary people

[14] "An Essay on the Theatre; or, A Comparison between Laughing and Sentimental Comedy" (1773), in *Collected Works*, ed. Arthur Friedman (Oxford, 1966), III, 211.

[15] *The Life of David Garrick* (1801), I, 232.

[16] The review begins, "This tragedy is written in prose after the manner of *George Barnwell*," continues with a full synopsis, and concludes: "This is the dramatic action or plot of the *Gamester*, which, if it is not worked up with the pomp, the force, and the elegance of poetry is yet heighten'd with many tender incidents, and, as the dialect is perfectly colloquial, it probably produced a greater effect upon the majority of the audience than if it had been decorated with beauties which they cannot miss, at the expence of that plainness without which they cannot understand" (*Gentleman's Magazine*, 23 [1753], 59, 61). For the attribution, see D. J. Greene's article cited in n. 4 above.

179

up to the level of tragedy—though in his account of actual people like "poor Peyton" he may indeed do that —he attempts instead to bring the heroes of tragedy down to the level of ordinary people. The consequences of such an approach for his understanding of Shakespeare are so crucial that they must be reserved for the next chapter, but at present it will be useful to examine the basis of his assumptions. And this is to be found not in his ideas about drama but in his theory of biography, the part of literature which he told Boswell he loved most (*Life*, I, 425).

In *Rambler* 60 he specifically contrasts biography with more comprehensive histories and "imperial tragedy," which are said to lack the most fundamental of all literary requirements, the power to interest the reader.

> It is not easy for the most artful writer to give us an interest in happiness or misery, which we think ourselves never likely to feel, and with which we have never yet been made acquainted. Histories of the downfal of kingdoms, and revolutions of empires, are read with great tranquillity; the imperial tragedy pleases common auditors only by its pomp of ornament, and grandeur of ideas.

One remembers the elevated language which Johnson saw as characteristic of tragedy and which pervades the imperial tragedy *Irene*. ("Grandeur of ideas," incidentally, need not imply that tragedy concerns itself with mighty themes; "idea" in the *Dictionary* is defined only as "mental imagination," and is illustrated by examples which use it in this restricted sense.)

That the revolutions of empires are really so very boring one may excusably doubt, but Johnson's point is that our emotions are quickened chiefly by the sense of contact with other human beings. As he had said in an earlier essay,

180

Though the world is crowded with scenes of calamity, we look upon the general mass of wretchedness with very little regard, and fix our eyes upon the state of particular persons, whom the eminence of their qualities marks out from the multitude; as, in reading an account of a battle, we seldom reflect on the vulgar heaps of slaughter, but follow the hero, with our whole attention, through all the varieties of his fortune, without a thought of the thousands that are falling round him.

(*Rambler* 19)

The heroes are clearly enough distinguished by "the eminence of their qualities," and in discussing Johnson's sensitivity to domestic tragedy I suggested that he would not have supposed that an elaborate work of art could or should be built upon it. But just as exceptional people need not be confined to stations of high rank, so also heroes and princes are intelligible to the common reader only as he can perceive in them feelings like his own.

In other words, Johnson is concerned as usual with the principle which he states in the same *Rambler*, that "what is of most use is of most value." Or as this criterion is amplified in *Idler* 84, his other extended essay on biography, "Between falsehood and useless truth there is little difference. As gold which he cannot spend will make no man rich, so knowledge which he cannot apply will make no man wise." The result of this view is suspicion of literature that dwells on the heroic, not just because it is remote from life as we know it, but because it involves an artificial exaggeration of the heroic at the expense of the human. "He that recounts the life of another, commonly dwells most upon conspicuous events, lessens the familiarity of his tale to increase its dignity, shews his favourite at a distance decorated and magnified like the ancient actors in their tragick dress,

181

and endeavours to hide the man that he may produce a hero" (*Idler* 84).

Now, all of this, fruitful as it may be for an understanding of biography, implies a serious limitation in Johnson's conception of tragedy. The elevation and distancing in the Greek tragic characters is for Johnson *ipso facto* a defect. If the biographer is not to "lessen the familiarity of his tale to increase its dignity," what are we to think of that species of drama which, in Johnson's own estimation, is principally defined by its dignity and elevation? One begins to realize just how radical he thought the gulf to be between Shakespeare and all other dramatists, and how much his warmest praise of Shakespeare carries within it an implied rejection of much that is usually believed to be central to tragedy.

> It was observed of the ancient schools of declamation, that the more diligently they were frequented, the more was the student disqualified for the world, because he found nothing there which he should ever meet in any other place. The same remark may be applied to every stage but that of Shakespeare. The theatre, when it is under any other direction, is peopled by such characters as were never seen, conversing in a language which was never heard, upon topicks which will never arise in the commerce of mankind. (*Preface*, p. 63)

This is strong language, and expresses a disapproval—one might almost say contempt—for most of the drama which the world has agreed to admire.

Still it is important to emphasize that Johnson does not deny the significance of greatness, or endorse the tragedy of the little man as the direction which the art should take. In the *Dictionary* he defines "domestick" from its Latin root as "belonging to the house; not relating to things publick." Aristotle, after all, had said that the best tragedies were those that exploited the relationships within families, and in this sense Richmond Lattimore can call the *Agamemnon* "first of all, a domestic tragedy."[17] But it does mean that Johnson is indifferent or even hostile to important elements of many great tragedies which present an exceptional man in an exceptional situation, revealing a humanity that is fuller and greater than our own. One need not suppose that this is the only possible form of tragedy to realize that when Johnson does admire such a work—let us say *King Lear*—the criticism which results will betray misreading and distortion.

4. Some Tragedies and Tragedians

Before turning to Johnson's criticism of Shakespeare, where these and other problems can be explored in earnest, we may briefly consider such haphazard evidence as survives about his attitude toward specific tragedians and their works, including his remarkably Aristotelian attack on *Samson Agonistes*.

First of all, let us see what can be deduced about Johnson's understanding of Greek tragedy. His familiarity with the language was certainly adequate, and Mrs. Thrale tells how he once confounded a visitor who thought to triumph over his supposed weakness in Greek (*Miscellanies*, I, 183-84). As for tragedy, Boswell tells us that Johnson read Euripides at Oxford, and again in the last year of his life (*Life*, I, 70; IV, 311). Here and there one finds other indications of acquaintance with some of the plays,[18] but they are pretty sparse. About a sixth of the quotations and allusions in

[17] *Poetics*, ch. 14; Lattimore, introduction to his translation of the *Oresteia* (Chicago, 1953), p. 9. Johnson says that in *Aureng-Zebe* "the dialogue is often domestick, and therefore susceptible of sentiments accommodated to familiar incidents" (*Life of Dryden*, I, 360-61). Similarly, "The story of the Odyssey is interesting, as a great part of it is domestick" (*Life*, IV, 219).

[18] Johnson supported a point about the antiquity of "armorial bearings" by citing Euripides (*Life*, II, 179); Boswell quotes a

183

the *Rambler*, mostly from memory, are from Greek writers (almost half are from classical Latin), but these are mainly from the Greek Anthology, Plutarch, or other sources of aphoristic statement. And although Greek tragedy is rich in such material, Johnson alludes to it only five times in all of the *Ramblers*.[19] In addition to these not very striking references, there is a passage from the *Medea* which he admired enough to translate three times (once as a parody of a contemporary translation and once into Latin), a speech in which the Nurse laments that poets have never been able to soothe human suffering (Yale *Poems*, pp. 303-305). But this is only an instance of his fondness for quoting a passage for its own sake, often without reference to context, as in the case of some lines from Virgil about mortality whose specific application is the breeding of cattle (*Life*, II, 129). When Richard Cumberland sought Johnson's views on the Greek dramatists, "he candidly acknowledged that his studies had not lain amongst them"; and Joseph Warton claimed to have heard him make the remarkable admission that "he never had read a Greek Tragedy in his Life."[20]

---

note from his diary, "Legi primum actum Troadum" ["Read the first act of the *Troades*"] (*Life*, II, 263).

[19] My authority for the relative distribution of *Rambler* allusions is W. J. Bate's introduction, where the point is made that they are a valuable source of information about what elements of Johnson's reading came most readily to mind (Yale *Works*, III, xxxii). There are no references to Aeschylus, only one to Sophocles (the motto to *Rambler* 111, a brief tag from the *Oedipus*), and four to Euripides. Of these two are vague allusions (*Ramblers* 18 and 86, the latter to "one of the old poets"), one is a motto from the *Medea* to *Rambler* 45, and the fourth is a motto from the *Phoenissiae* to *Rambler* 67. In his other essays there is even less: passing allusions to Sophocles and Euripides in *Idlers* 66 and 68, and *Adventurer* 58; and a motto for *Idler* 89, misattributed to Euripides in the first edition but actually from Aulus Gellius.

[20] Cumberland, *Memoirs* (1807), I, 361; he also reported this

We may fairly conclude, then, that while Johnson sometimes read Greek tragedy (or at least Euripides), it did not occupy a very important place in his imagination. Like most of his contemporaries he judged it by exactly the same standards as he applied to modern drama, and inevitably found it wanting. "It could only be by long prejudice and the bigotry of learning that Milton could prefer the ancient tragedies with their encumbrance of a chorus to the exhibitions of the French and English stages" (*Life of Milton*, I, 188-89). When he did concede that historical differences should be taken into account, as when he told Langton that lacking "the lights of a latter age" the Greek dramatists could not be compared with Shakespeare, he immediately proceeded to make his habitual point that "the machinery of the Pagans is uninteresting to us: when a Goddess appears in Homer or Virgil, we grow weary; still more so in the Grecian tragedies, as in that kind of composition a nearer approach to Nature is intended" (*Life*, IV, 16).

This contempt for mythology is of course closely related to Johnson's criterion of fidelity to life, and ensures a radical inability to see the point of classical tragedy. It is not simply that he cannot conceive of human and superhuman characters occupying the same stage, although that is part of it: "In the *Prometheus* of Aeschylus we see Violence and Strength, and in the *Alcestis* of Euripides we see Death, brought upon the stage, all as active persons of the drama; but no prece-

conversation to Boswell (*Life*, IV, 384-85). On 30 March 1790 Warton wrote to Boswell, "I know not whether you would like to mention [Boswell did not] that Johnson once owned to me, knowing how enthusiastically fond I was of the Greek Tragedies, that he never had read a Greek Tragedy in his Life" (*The Correspondence and Other Papers of James Boswell Relating to the Making of the Life of Johnson*, ed. Marshall Waingrow [New York, 1969], p. 312). No doubt Johnson was teasing Warton, but the exaggeration may be less than one might have supposed.

dents can justify absurdity" (*Life of Milton*, i, 185). What is really involved is an inability to conceive of myth as anything more substantial than casual decoration. The fine passage about the pheonix at the end of *Samson Agonistes*, for example, "is so evidently contrary to reason and nature, that it ought never to be mentioned but as a fable in any serious poem" (*Rambler* 140). In consequence Johnson could dismiss out of hand Edmund Smith's *Phaedra and Hippolitus*, and would doubtless have dismissed Racine's *Phèdre* or Euripides' *Hippolytus* as well:

> The fable is mythological, a story which we are accustomed to reject as false, and the manners are so distant from our own that we know them not from sympathy, but by study: the ignorant do not understand the action, the learned reject it as a school-boy's tale; *incredulus odi*. What I cannot for a moment believe, I cannot for a moment behold with interest or anxiety. (*Life of Smith*, ii, 16)

This literalism of the imagination, if it allowed Johnson to see certain aspects of Shakespeare with unusual clarity, rendered him exceptionally unfit to understand most of the greatest tragedies of the world.

Finally, we do have a Johnsonian discussion of a Greek drama, a curious account of the *Oedipus* written as the preface for a translation by his friend Thomas Maurice (1780). In conversation he once told Joseph Cradock that "Oedipus was a poor miserable man, subjected to the greatest distress, without any degree of culpability of his own" (*Miscellanies*, ii, 62). In the preface for Maurice he could not speak so strongly against the play, and had moreover to emphasize its didactic value, so that his discussion follows a tortuous and even self-contradictory course. At the start Oedipus' innocence is urged, with the necessary reference to the mysteriousness of providence (somewhat as in the Dryden/ Lee version):

> The subject is a nation labouring under calamities of the most dreadful and portentous kind; and the leading character is a wise and mighty prince, expiating by his punishment the involuntary crimes of which those calamities were the effect. The design is of the most interesting and important nature, to inculcate a due moderation in our passions, and an implicit obedience to that providence of which the decrees are equally unknown and irresistable. (Hazen, p. 140)

After an encomium of the brilliantly managed plot, however, Johnson turns about and takes the opposite tack, adopting the explanation of which Dennis was the leading proponent:

> The principal objection to this tragedy is, that the punishment of Oedipus is much more than adequate to his crimes. . . . In vindication of Sophocles, it must be considered that the conduct of Oedipus is by no means so irreproachable as some have contended: for though his public character is delineated as that of a good king, anxious for the welfare of his subjects, and ardent in his endeavours to appease the gods by incense and supplication, yet we find him in private life choleric, haughty, inquisitive; impatient of controul, and impetuous in resentment. His character, even as a king, is not free from the imputation of imprudence, and our opinion of his piety is greatly invalidated by his contemptuous treatment of the wise, the benevolent, the sacred Tiresias.
> (Pp. 140-41)

Like many before him Johnson goes on to make the best defense that can be made—we pity Oedipus because

187

he suffers more than he deserves, but because he deserves *some* suffering we are not indignant—if it is assumed that Sophocles means to uphold the perfect goodness of something resembling a Christian providence.

But Johnson is not really committed to this defense, for as the remark to Cradock suggests he does recognize the monstrous inequity of Oedipus' fate, without for a moment suspecting that this could be the very point of the tragedy; in a modern writer's words, "The interrogations by which Oedipus exposes the truth about himself have a sublime impersonal malignity such as a series of forced moves at chess would impart if the game possessed tragic relevance to life."[21] And so Johnson, despite his role as mouthpiece for the well-meaning translator, washes his hands of the whole business by betraying his usual disgust with anachronism: "That his crimes and punishment still seem disproportionate [he had just been arguing that they don't], is not to be imputed as a fault to Sophocles, who proceeded only on the antient and popular notion of Destiny; which we know to have been the basis of Pagan theology" (p. 141). If that "theology" has been exploded, so much the worse for the tragedy which takes it for granted. That the *Oedipus* might be engaged in exploring the inhuman cruelty of a technically "just" universe does not occur to Johnson, and if it did he would certainly repudiate such an exploration as a proper subject for tragedy.

Scattered and disappointing as his remarks on Greek tragedy may be, they represent Johnson's only contact with any body of tragic drama other than that of Shakespeare and of Dryden and his successors. While various notes in the Shakespeare edition indicate that he had looked at other Elizabethan plays, he never says any-

[21] John Jones, *On Aristotle and Greek Tragedy* (London, 1962), p. 201.

188

thing that would suggest a real acquaintance with Marlowe, Webster, or even the great Restoration favorite Fletcher. And despite his wide reading in French literature, references to Corneille and Racine are perfunctory and usually dismissive: "Corneille is to Shakespeare as a clipped Hedge to a Forest" (*Thraliana*, I, 165).

But when we come to drama closer to his own time, Johnson is both better informed and, not surprisingly, more acute in his judgments. Here as always three main requirements for tragedy are in force: (1) it must be serious; (2) it must be "pathetic," in the sense of moving the emotions of the audience; (3) it must be moral, instructing even as it delights. What I wish to emphasize here is that these are requirements *for tragedy*, and that Johnson is quite surprisingly capable of relaxing them when other kinds of drama are in question. We may postpone a discussion of his views on comedy until we come to his famous ranking of Shakespeare's comedies above the tragedies, and look instead at what he says about the heroic drama of the Restoration, a species of literature which by convention at least was classified as tragedy.

One might surmise that Johnson's didactic tendency would arouse his indignation at the character of Almanzor in Dryden's *Conquest of Granada*, a swaggering bully whose way of life is deftly parodied in Buckingham's *Rehearsal*:

> Others may bost a single man to kill;
> But I, the blood of thousands daily spill.
> Let petty Kings the names of Parties know:
> Where e'er I come, I slay both friend and foe.

To the objection, "But, Mr. *Bayes*, I thought your *Heroes* had ever been men of great humanity and justice," the Dryden-figure replies, "Yes, they have been so; but for my part, I prefer that one quality of singly beating of whole Armies above all your moral virtues put together, I gad."[22] Johnson was perfectly aware of all this, but he was also willing not to judge an almost comically extravagant kind of play as he would a serious tragedy, and he has left us one of the finest of all appreciations of the heroic drama.

> The two parts of *The Conquest of Granada* are written with a seeming determination to glut the publick with dramatick wonders; to exhibit in its highest elevation a theatrical meteor of incredible love and impossible valour, and to leave no room for a wilder flight to the extravagance of posterity. All the rays of romantick heat, whether amorous or warlike, glow in Almanzor by a kind of concentration. He is above all laws; he is exempt from all restraints; he ranges the world at will, and governs wherever he appears. He fights without enquiring the cause, and loves in spite of the obligations of justice, of rejection by his mistress, and of prohibition from the dead. Yet the scenes are, for the most part, delightful; they exhibit a kind of illustrious depravity and majestick madness: such as, if it is sometimes despised, is often reverenced, and in which the ridiculous is mingled with the astonishing. (*Life of Dryden*, I, 348-49)

Interestingly enough, Johnson is much more severe upon *All for Love*, which in our own day is often put forward as the most successful Restoration tragedy. "It has one fault equal to many, though rather moral than critical, that by admitting the romantick omnipotence of Love, he has recommended as laudable and worthy of imitation that conduct which through all ages the good have censured as vicious, and the bad despised as foolish" (*Life of Dryden*, I, 361). It would appear that

---

[22] *The Rehearsal*, ed. Montague Summers (Stratford-upon-Avon, 1914), v.i, p. 69, and iv.i, p. 48.

190

he is willing to accept the playful exuberance of the heroic drama on its own terms, much as he accepted *The Beggar's Opera* and doubted that "any man was ever made a rogue by being present at its representation" (*Life*, II, 367). *All for Love* must be judged more severely because it proposes to be a serious representation of life and to furnish examples for our conduct. It proposes these things simply because it *is* a tragedy; as we have seen, Johnson regarded them as fundamental to the genre. There is no doubt that he considered such an achievement to be more important, as well as more difficult, than the achievement of *The Conquest of Granada*. His praise of that play, generous though it is, carries submerged implications that although the heroic drama is enjoyable, it is in important ways seriously inadequate. Dryden's success in this kind of writing may in the end be judged to be success in the second-best.

> We do not always know our own motives. I am not certain whether it was not rather the difficulty which he found in exhibiting the genuine operations of the heart than a servile submission to an injudicious audience that filled his plays with false magnificence. . . . Sentences were readier at his call than images; he could more easily fill the ear with some splendid novelty than awaken those ideas that slumber in the heart.
>
> (*Life of Dryden*, I, 458-59)

Johnson's longest extended piece of dramatic criticism is a pair of *Rambler*s (139 and 140) on *Samson Agonistes*, the first devoted to its structure, and the second, which need not detain us now, to "the sentiments." In *Rambler* 139 Johnson rests his argument on a confident invocation of Aristotle such as appears nowhere else in his works. "It is required by Aristotle to the perfection of a tragedy, and is equally necessary to every other species of regular composition, that it should

191

have a beginning, a middle, and an end." As the essay goes on the dogmatic tone grows stronger; "the rule laid down by this great critick" becomes "this law of poetical architecture," and before long Johnson is referring to "the indispensable laws of Aristotelian criticism," though the unity of action is the only one which he is concerned to discuss. And his conclusion, after a survey of the play, is quite fervently negative.

> This is undoubtedly a just and regular catastrophe, and the poem, therefore, has a beginning and an end which Aristotle himself could not have disapproved; but it must be allowed to want a middle, since nothing passes between the first act and the last, that either hastens or delays the death of Sampson. The whole drama, if its superfluities were cut off, would scarcely fill a single act; yet this is the tragedy which ignorance has admired, and bigotry applauded.

Let us leave aside the question of Johnson's hostility to Milton. Rancorous as it may have been, it did not prevent him from paying warm tribute in the *Life of Milton* to the structure of *Paradise Lost*, even while reaffirming his view that in *Samson* "the intermediate parts have neither cause nor consequence, neither hasten nor retard the catastrophe" (*Lives*, I, 189). Let us grant also that Milton, by his proud belief that he had written a Greek tragedy, left himself open to be judged on Aristotelian grounds. And furthermore, let us remember that in regard to Shakespeare, at least, Johnson conceived the Aristotelian "beginning, middle and end" loosely enough to say that apart from the histories "he has well enough preserved the unity of action" (*Preface*, p. 75). Yet when every allowance has been made, the fact stands that Johnson has no idea of what kind of work Milton has written. And this fact recalls the grave miscalculation that lay behind the failure of

192

Irene: the assumption that a play must necessarily engage its characters in an elaborate structure of activity, and that a work in which characters speak but are not so occupied must be an unsuccessful play.

Today we think chiefly of the tragic implications of *Samson*: the great hero rendered impotent through his own folly, eyeless in Gaza, and then rising all at once to a triumphant victory, but at the price of his own death; we may think as well of Milton himself, blind and thwarted in his hopes for his country. That such an appreciation was possible in the eighteenth century is shown by Cumberland's answer to Johnson in the *Observer* (no. 76) in 1788, which emphasizes the fact that the unity and development of *Samson* are psychological, and by analogy with several Greek tragedies indicates an awareness of its tragic dimension:

> Of the character I may say in few words, that Samson possesses all the terrific majesty of Prometheus chained, the mysterious distress of Oedipus, and the pitiable wretchedness of Philoctetes. His properties, like those of the first, are something above human; his misfortunes, like those of the second, are derivable from the displeasure of heaven, and involved in oracles; his condition, like that of the last, is the most abject which human nature can be reduced to from a state of dignity and splendour.

But Johnson is determined to measure the play against a standard by which it will certainly be found wanting. Even though he sees that the interviews with Manoah, Delilah, and Harapha may "tend to animate or exasperate Samson," he persists in looking for the characteristics of the well-made play. In this he deserves the rebuke of Dryden's Lisideius, " 'Tis a great mistake in us to believe the French present no part of the action on the stage: every alteration or crossing of a design, every new-sprung passion, and turn of it, is a part of the action, and much the noblest, except we conceive nothing to be action till they come to blows" (*Of Dramatic Poesy*, Watson, I, 52).

Among more recent plays, the only ones which excited Johnson's admiration were the she-tragedies of Rowe. He calls *The Fair Penitent* "one of the most pleasing tragedies on the stage . . . for there is scarcely any work of any poet at once so interesting by the fable and so delightful by the language" (*Life of Rowe*, II, 67). As one would expect the quality Johnson admires is Rowe's pathos. *Jane Shore*, "consisting chiefly of domestick scenes and private distress, lays hold upon the heart" (p. 69). To Mrs. Thrale and Hannah More he as much as admitted that he wept at the death of Jane Shore (*Miscellanies*, I, 283-84, and II, 196-97).

But this affection did not extend so far as to produce an unqualified admiration for Rowe's plays, and Johnson expressly rejected the notion of Rowe as Shakespeare redivivus. "In what he thought himself an imitator of Shakespeare it is not easy to conceive. The numbers, the diction, the sentiments, and the conduct, every thing in which imitation can consist, are remote in the utmost degree from the manner of Shakespeare" (*Life of Rowe*, II, 69). Where Rowe does receive comparison with Shakespeare, it is to his disadvantage: Shakespeare "has speeches, perhaps sometimes scenes, which have all the delicacy of Rowe, without his effeminacy" (*Preface*, p. 91). And as for his works in general, "I know not that there can be found in his plays any deep search into nature, any accurate discriminations of kindred qualities, or nice display of passion in its progress; all is general and undefined" (*Life of Rowe*, II, 76). In the case of Otway, whose name was so often coupled with Rowe's and whom Dick Minim credited with "uncommon powers of moving the passions" (*Idler* 60), Johnson was perfunctory. All he says about *Venice Preserved*, for instance, is that it is "a

194

tragedy, which still continues to be one of the favourites of the publick, notwithstanding the want of morality in the original design, and the despicable scenes of vile comedy with which he has diversified his tragick action" (*Life of Otway*, I, 245-46).

Finally, there is a series of reviews in the *Gentleman's Magazine* during the early 1750's which are almost certainly by Johnson, and one of these, of William Mason's *Elfrida* in 1752, gives expression to so many of his preoccupations about drama—and is so little known —that it is worth quoting at some length.[23] Mason, remembered today largely through his association with Gray, was a fashionably intellectual poet who strove to emulate Greek tragedy despite the disadvantages thereby incurred from the point of view of the English stage. His *Caractacus*, which Johnson used to ridicule in a coffeehouse "for the diversion of himself and of chance comers-in" (*Miscellanies*, I, 169), was actually translated *into Greek* by a certain George Henry Glasse, and in that form praised by Burney. This was the man who gave *Elfrida*, based on a British legend, to an ungrateful public. As the *Monthly Review* explained,

> *Elfrida* was not intended for the stage. Mr. *Mason* did not chuse to sink his plan to that level to which it must have been lower'd, in order to secure its success before an *English* audience; who would scarcely have relished its want of incidents, and of the usual variety of characters: deficiencies which are amply compensated for, to the judicious reader, by the introduction of the *chorus*.[24]

[23] For the attribution to Johnson, see the articles by Greene and Sherbo cited in n. 4 above. The review appears in the *Gentleman's Magazine*, 22 (1752), 224-27. A brief account of an anonymous *Remarks on Mr. Mason's Elfrida* (p. 243) is also very likely by Johnson.

[24] *Monthly Review*, 6 (1752), 387. This highly laudatory review is one of the few pieces whose author is not indicated in

A play not intended for the stage, lacking incidents and variety, but counterbalanced by the presence of a chorus: one can foresee what Johnson will say.

Elfrida is prefaced by five pompous letters in which, as Johnson says, Mason "discovers great veneration for antiquity, he uses the words *Nature* and *Aristotle* synonymously, and talks much of *simplicity of fable, chastised judgment, pure poetry* and *pure passion*." After a brief dismemberment of each of these terms—"It is difficult to discover by what power of the mind *judgment* is to be *chastised*, tho' *fancy* may be properly represented as chastised by *judgment*"—Johnson launches a frontal attack on the ancient drama, and challenges the idea that Aristotle's authority should carry any more weight in literature than in science and philosophy.

> When science first dawned after a long night of ignorance and superstition, it is easy to conceive why great regard was paid to *antiquity*. As no improvements had been made in any branch of literature for many centuries, the world was become rude and barbarous; the taste of mankind was universally vitiated, and genius could derive no assistance but from those who lived before the period of intellectual darkness commenced. But after learning has been not only revived but improved, after genius has again formed the taste, and criticism regulated the judgment, the same fondness for antiquity is ridiculous; nor is it more absurd to prefer the philosophy of *Aristotle* to that

Griffiths' set (see Nangle's index to the first series, p. 155). It is largely given over to quotation from Mason's prefatory letters and to two of the choral odes; I suspect complicity between the reviewer and Mason. Glasse's Greek version of *Caractacus* was approvingly and learnedly reviewed by Burney in the *Monthly Review*, 69 (1783), 500-509.

of *Newton*, than to prefer his rudiments to the more perfect plan of the modern drama. (P. 224)

One begins to suspect that in *Rambler* 139, written only a year previously, Johnson had disguised his contempt for Aristotelian theory in order to use it as a stick to beat Milton with. Here he says that Mason "commends the *Agonistes* of *Milton*, as being a *perfect model of genuine nature, and ancient simplicity,* tho' it is extremely defective even by the rules of *Aristotle,* and does not forcibly excite either pity or terror" (p. 224).

The bulk of Mason's prefatory letters is given over to the subject of the chorus, on his management of which he is eager to congratulate himself. Anyone who has taken the trouble to read *Elfrida* will agree with Johnson that Mason's chorus is hopelessly boring and inept, and indeed Gray did his best to argue his friend out of using it.[25] Johnson's criticism is based, as usual, on his assumption that the stage must be a naturalistic mirror of life. "If tragedy is perfect in proportion as it is an imitation of nature, and exhibits some great event as it is supposed really to have happened, whatever is foreign to that event ought to be excluded from tragedy, and whatever is out of nature is an offence against the highest law." In his zeal to prove that the effect of the chorus is "to render the drama totally different from life," he even endorses something like the theory of illusion or delusion which he mocks in the *Preface.*[26]

[25] Letter to Mason, ca. Dec. 1751, in *Correspondence of Thomas Gray,* ed. Paget Toynbee and Leonard Whibley (Oxford, 1935), I, 358, 359.

[26] "Whenever this *Chorus* is present, the power of fancy is at an end, the hero and the palace vanish, and the theatre and the actors rush upon the mind. To connect these women with the action, to introduce them speaking to the persons of the drama, and interested in the event, is therefore to counterwork all that can be effected by the most vigorous imagination, and the soundest

After a somewhat surprising attack on moralism when delivered in precepts rather than embodied in action, Johnson at last proceeds to a synopsis of the play and to the citation of various poetical passages, which he solemnly recommends to "those who are capable of that pleasure which arises from poetical imagery and expression" (p. 227). Mrs. Thrale indeed understood him to say that *Elfrida* was "too exquisitely pretty" to make fun of (*Miscellanies,* I, 169), but Boswell's account is more plausible:

> BOSWELL. "Surely, Sir, Mr. Mason's 'Elfrida' is a fine poem: at least you will allow there are some good passages in it." JOHNSON. "There are now and then some good imitations of Milton's bad manner." (*Life,* II, 335)

From such evidence as we have been able to assemble, we may conclude that Johnson's interest in tragedy was not vast. His esteem for the Greeks was qualified at best, and apart from Shakespeare and to some extent Rowe there was no modern tragedian whom he much admired. Thus the author of *Irene* did not sustain a lively concern for the development of the branch of literature in which he had first hoped to make his name. That he did not regard tragedy in his own time as a very prepossessing genre is suggested by the lady who tells the Rambler that she has passed "the superfluities of time, which the diversions of the town left upon my hands, in turning over a large collection of tragedies and romances"; these are said to contain a number of sentiments "common to all authors of this class" (*Rambler* 46). The review of *Elfrida* indicates Johnson's hostility to the more pretentious or experimental kinds of

---

judgment. It is to render the drama totally different from life, and to diffuse those ideas through the whole representation, which in the modern tragedy are only excited between the acts" (p. 224).

contemporary tragedy; his nearly total indifference to the humbler variety may be judged from his inability to read more than a page of a play which his friend Murphy had asked him to criticize (*Miscellanies*, I, 332), and from Dr. Maxwell's anecdote which, in its balanced judiciousness, carries the true Johnsonian ring: "Speaking of Arthur Murphy, whom he very much loved, 'I don't know (said he,) that Arthur can be classed with the very first dramatick writers; yet at present I doubt much whether we have any thing superiour to Arthur'" (*Life*, II, 127).

CHAPTER 8

Shakespeare

1. *Shakespeare as Tragic Artist*

MANY accounts survive of Johnson's imaginative response to Shakespearean tragedy, beginning with his boyhood fright at the ghost in *Hamlet*. A passage from his edition of Shakespeare is often quoted in which a description of the night in Dryden's *Conquest of Mexico* is contrasted with one in *Macbeth*:

> In the night of Dryden, all the disturbers of the world are laid asleep; in that of Shakespeare, nothing but sorcery, lust and murder, is awake. He that reads Dryden, finds himself lull'd with serenity, and disposed to solitude and contemplation. He that peruses Shakespeare, looks round alarmed, and starts to find himself alone.
>
> (II.i.49, pp. 769-70)[1]

Passages like this suggest an openness to some of the most terrible effects in Shakespearean tragedy, but the openness is often qualified by serious doubts as well. Of Desdemona's death Johnson writes, "I am glad that I have ended my revisal of this dreadful scene. It is not to be endured" (*Othello* v.ii.66, p. 1045). Of "the extrusion of Gloucester's eyes" in *King Lear* he says that it "seems an act too horrid to be endured in dramatick exhibition, and such as must always compel the mind to relieve its distress by incredulity" (p. 703).

---

[1] All references to Johnson on Shakespeare are to vols. VII and VIII of the Yale *Works*. As the volumes are consecutively page-numbered, they are not separately cited. Quotations from the Shakespeare commentary which are identified only by page number are taken from the "short strictures" at the ends of the plays.

These instances suggest two things: that Johnson was powerfully moved by some of the most terrible moments in the tragedies, and that he did not altogether approve of being moved in this way. Thus, paradoxically, a vivid awareness of what happens in the plays may contribute to a rejection of what is tragic in them. One may say further that while he often quoted Shakespeare in contexts of personal suffering, this tells us more about Johnson than about Shakespeare. The personal tone sometimes appears even in the notes to the plays: "Something like this, on less occasions, every breast has felt. Reflection and seriousness rush upon the mind upon the separation of a gay company, and especially after forced and unwilling merriment" (*Henry V*, IV.i.226, p. 553). There is the moving story of his quoting Macbeth's lines "Canst thou not minister to a mind diseas'd" to the doctor at his deathbed (*Life*, IV, 400-401), and there are the lines which he often repeated from *Measure for Measure*, "Ay, but to die and go we know not where; / To lie in cold obstruction and to rot" (*Miscellanies*, I, 439, and II, 69). The speech is highly applicable to Johnson's fear of death, especially in its physical aspect; Boswell in the Hebrides noticed "his horrour at dead men's bones" (*Life*, V, 327).

But even though Johnson was fond of applying Shakespearean passages to his own emotional needs, his considered view of the plays can almost be said to repudiate that emotional experience. In assessing his conception of Shakespeare's tragedies, one should probably take the word *rational* as the keynote, as in the program set out in 1756 in the "Proposals" for an edition: as the editor "hopes to leave his authour better understood, he wishes likewise to procure him more rational approbation" (p. 58). Johnson was not the man to praise the native woodnote warbler, and his Shakespeare is the poet of Nature because the plays are a

201

perfect mirror of life, not because Nature had endowed him with mysterious vatic powers.[2]

Those critics who regarded Shakespeare as a *lusus naturae* were at least spared the trouble of justifying a critical system that could not accommodate their most eminent author. Johnson on the other hand was always on the horns of a dilemma, obliged either to concede that his canons of criticism did not apply to Shakespeare, or to measure Shakespeare against them and find him wanting. Much of the unevenness of praise and blame in the *Preface* derives from this embarrassment, which he never faces openly.

On the few occasions when Johnson is willing to recognize that his critical principles and his intuitive appreciation do not always coincide, he is almost defiantly paradoxical.

> Works of imagination excel by their allurement and delight; by their power of attracting and detaining the attention. . . . By his proportion of this predomination I will consent that Dryden should be tried; of this, which, in opposition to reason, makes Ariosto the darling and the pride of Italy; of this, which, in defiance of criticism, continues Shakespeare the sovereign of the drama.
>
> (*Life of Dryden*, I, 454)

[2] In a note to Desdemona's speech just before she sings her willow song, Johnson recognizes at once the mental excitement that accompanies composition and the calculating judgment with which Shakespeare, like any writer, must have looked over what he had written. "This is perhaps the only insertion made in the latter editions which has improved the play. The rest seem to have been added for the sake of amplification or of ornament. When the imagination had subsided, and the mind was no longer agitated by the horror of the action, it became at leisure to look round for specious additions. This addition is natural. Desdemona can at first hardly forbear to sing the song; she endeavours to change her train of thoughts, but her imagination at last prevails, and she sings it" (*Othello* IV.iii.30, p. 1043).

This is noble praise, and yet praise of a curious kind. What is the use of procuring rational approbation for a writer who fascinates us in defiance of criticism and reason?

Exactly the same paradox appears in the *Preface*, where Johnson writes like Dryden or Dennis as the conscious beneficiary of an enlightened age, and explains the deficiency of Shakespeare's stories by reference to the immaturity of the national mind.

> Nations, like individuals, have their infancy. . . . Whatever is remote from common appearances is always welcome to vulgar, as to childish credulity; and of a country unenlightened by learning, the whole people is the vulgar. The study of those who then aspired to plebeian learning was laid out upon adventures, giants, dragons, and enchantments. *The Death of Arthur* was the favourite volume.
>
> The mind, which has feasted on the luxurious wonders of fiction, has no taste of the insipidity of truth. (P. 82)

The tone is almost that of Imlac's account of insanity, in which the mind "feasts on the luscious falsehood whenever she is offended with the bitterness of truth" (*Rasselas*, ch. 44), and in fact a phrase is repeated from *Rambler* 162, in which "Thrasybulus had . . . banquetted on flattery, till he could no longer bear the harshness of remonstrance or the insipidity of truth." Yet only a page later Johnson is eloquently admitting that this very quality is what compels the interest of even the most sophisticated reader of Shakespeare.

> His plots, whether historical or fabulous, are always crouded with incidents, by which the attention of a rude people was more easily caught than by sentiment or argumentation; and such is the

power of the marvellous even over those who despise it, that every man finds his mind more
strongly seized by the tragedies of Shakespeare
than of any other writer; others please us by particular speeches, but he always makes us anxious
for the event, and has perhaps excelled all but
Homer in securing the first purpose of a writer, by
exciting restless and unquenchable curiosity, and
compelling him that reads his work to read it
through.   (P. 83)

This, from the man who confessed to not reading books
through (*Life*, II, 226), and whose high praise of *Paradise Lost* ends with the admission that "none ever
wished it longer than it is" (*Life of Milton*, I, 183), is a
warm tribute indeed. And in a way Johnson's most outrageous censures proceed from it: he is afraid that the
reader will be so captivated that real faults will go
unnoticed.

But by what standard are they faults at all? The
Critical Review took it for granted that Johnson was
the agent of an outmoded Aristotelianism:

We cannot help thinking that Mr. Johnson has run
into the vulgar practice, by estimating the merits
of Shakespeare according to the rules of the
French academy, and the *little* English writers
who adopted them, as the criterions of *taste*. . . .
Shakespeare proceeds by storm. He knows nothing
of regular approaches to the fort of the human
heart. He effects his breach by the weight of his
metal, and makes his lodgment, though the enemy's
artillery is thundering round him from every bat-
tery of criticism, learning, and even probability.
He is invulnerable to them all, by that enchanted
armour in which the hand of heaven has cased him,
and on whose powerful influence reasoning, reflec-

tion, and observation, have always proved to be like the serpent's tongue licking the file.[3]

The curiously Shandean metaphor of the breach and the lodgment, with its faintly indecent connotations, is no doubt meant earnestly enough as a testimony to a power that simply defies the critical reason. The "regular approaches," indeed, are probably an ironic allusion to Johnson's own description in the *Drury Lane Prologue* of Ben Jonson, who "By regular approach essay'd the heart" (12).

While we may say that Johnson espoused a revisionist form of neoclassicism and that the reviewer was mistaken in his attempt to explain why the *Preface* so often seems ungenerous, it is nevertheless interesting that the criticism should be made at all. The tendency to exalt Shakespeare's characters and, more generally, his "beauties" had made criticism that dealt with plot or fable seem old-fashioned and misguided.[4] But on balance Johnson's interest in plot seems to have strengthened his criticism, not weakened it. He was never tempted to impose the more rigid neoclassical rules upon Shakespeare, and in the notes to the plays often reminds the reader that they "were written, and at first printed in one unbroken continuity, and ought now to

[3] *Critical Review*, 20 (1765), 321-22.

[4] In the 1750's Arthur Murphy hailed the new movement with an open attack on the old authority: "*Aristotle* was certainly mistaken when he called the Fable the Life and Soul of Tragedy; the Art of constructing the dramatic Story should always be subservient to the Exhibition of Character; our great *Shakespear* has breathed another Soul into Tragedy, which has found the Way of striking an Audience with Sentiment and Passion at the same Time" (*Gray's-Inn Journal* [1756], II, 267). Johnson at the same period was measuring *Samson Agonistes* against an Aristotelian rule; later he remarked that Shakespeare "has commonly what Aristotle requires, a beginning, a middle, and an end" (*Preface*, p. 75).

be exhibited with short pauses, interposed as often as the scene is changed, or any considerable time is required to pass. This method would at once quell a thousand absurdities" (*Preface*, p. 107). And his interest in the "fable" allows him to see *King Lear* not just as the portrait of grandeur and madness, but also as a brilliantly conceived action.

> There is perhaps no play which keeps the attention so strongly fixed; which so much agitates our passions and interests our curiosity. The artful involutions of distinct interests, the striking opposition of contrary characters, the sudden changes of fortune, and the quick succession of events, fill the mind with a perpetual tumult of indignation, pity, and hope. There is no scene which does not contribute to the aggravation of the distress or conduct of the action, and scarce a line which does not conduce to the progress of the scene. So powerful is the current of the poet's imagination, that the mind, which once ventures within it, is hurried irresistibly along.   (Pp. 702-703)

The real question here is not how fully Johnson embraced or modified some abstract conception of neoclassicism. What stands out finally is that he resolves every one of these questions by his own peculiar mode of measuring art against life. The subject is large enough to require a separate section and we shall return to it shortly. While Johnson's assumptions allow him great flexibility in regard to various "rules," they lead him to ignore some central features of tragedy. The point may be illustrated by his famous defense of the "mingled drama," which includes the attractive justification, "That this is a practice contrary to the rules of criticism will be readily allowed; but there is always an appeal open from criticism to nature" (*Preface*, p. 67).

If someone says that when tragedy includes comic scenes it becomes tragicomic and not tragic, no answer is possible, since the statement is true by definition. But the neoclassical dogmas were supposed to be founded on audience psychology (unity of place was necessary because of dramatic illusion, and so forth); and if he should instead assert that tragedy cannot include comic scenes because the spectators will rise up in revulsion, one may oppose empirical evidence to the contrary. As we are all admirers of the comic elements in Shakespearean tragedy, we are inclined to welcome Johnson as our ally against tiresomely restrictive criticism. Yet his defense of this practice is very odd indeed.

> Shakespeare's plays are not in the rigorous and critical sense either tragedies or comedies, but compositions of a distinct kind; exhibiting the real state of sublunary nature, which partakes of good and evil, joy and sorrow, mingled with endless variety of proportion and innumerable modes of combination; and expressing the course of the world, in which the loss of one is the gain of another; in which, at the same time, the reveller is hasting to his wine, and the mourner burying his friend; in which the malignity of one is sometimes defeated by the frolick of another; and many mischiefs and many benefits are done and hindered without design. . . . Almost all his plays are divided between serious and ludicrous characters, and, in the successive evolutions of the design, sometimes produce seriousness and sorrow, and sometimes levity and laughter. *(Preface, pp. 66, 67)*

If one cared to speculate about what cannot be known, it is conceivable that such an attitude may have characterized Shakespeare's own view of life; we are no longer encouraged to believe that his tragedies reflect a period of profound personal despair. Again, it is certainly true that his plays reflect more of the rich variousness of life than do those of any other dramatist (the inevitable analogy is with the novel). The tragedies develop in a more leisurely way, and seem at times less implacably disastrous, than those of more classical or neoclassical writers. Moreover, they usually give glimpses of a world where tragedy is not happening, and sometimes allow it to intrude briefly upon the very height of the tragic action, especially in the case of the comic characters to whom Johnson alludes: the grave-diggers in *Hamlet*, the clown who wishes Cleopatra joy of the worm.

Yet finally it is outrageous to claim that Shakespeare's plays, in a rigorous or in any other sense, are neither tragedies nor comedies. For what Johnson has really done is to suggest that all of them are equally the mirror of nature in its comprehensive sense, and to make light of the selection and shaping that they embody. Eloquent as his account of "the real state of sublunary nature" is, it describes Johnson's own ideal view of life much more than it does Shakespearean drama. If anything it brings to mind the solemn yet ironic tone of *Rasselas*; it recalls the balanced refusal to give in to tragic experience which is implied in Johnson's steadfast facing of life. But it carries with it significant difficulties for the understanding of dramatic tragedy.

2. *Art and Life*

The most serious modern attack on Johnson's qualifications as a critic is based on the ambiguity of his position between two great critical traditions. In René Wellek's influential analysis, Johnson succeeds neither in the neoclassical understanding of the work of art as objective "artifact" nor in the Romantic celebration of visionary truth, but demands instead truth of a literal and pedestrian kind, and cannot distinguish effectively

between art and life.[5] This is not the place to investigate the matter in detail, but one must certainly grant
that more than any other great critic Johnson distrusted
the power of art.

Against the pleasures of fiction, Johnson always up-
held the ideal of "truth," and maintained that the love
of it was inherent in human nature. In the *Life of Pope*,
according to Boswell's list of revisions, he first wrote
"the mind naturally loves truth" and then changed
"mind" to "heart" (*Life*, IV, 52); it is as much a matter
of instinct as of reason. As Mrs. Thrale observed,

> His veracity was indeed, from the most trivial to
> the most solemn occasions, strict, even to severity;
> he scorned to embellish a story with fictitious cir-
> cumstances, which (he used to say) took off from
> its real value. "A story (says Johnson) should be a
> specimen of life and manners; but if the surround-
> ing circumstances are false, as it is no more a rep-
> resentation of reality, it is no longer worthy our
> attention."   (*Miscellanies*, I, 347-48)

In a general way he is drawing upon a central neoclassical tradition, which may be found in Shaftesbury—
"Truth is the most powerful thing in the world, since
even fiction itself must be governed by it, and can only
please by its resemblance"—or earlier in the less Pla-
tonic Dryden: "That is not the best poesy which resembles notions of things that are not to things that are:
though the fancy may be great and the words flowing,
yet the soul is but half satisfied when there is not truth
in the foundation."[6] But in Johnson's hands this doc-

---

[5] *A History of Modern Criticism, 1750-1950*, I: *The Later
Eighteenth Century* (New Haven, 1955), 79.

[6] Shaftesbury, *A Letter Concerning Enthusiasm* (1707), par. 2,
in *Characteristics*, ed. J. M. Robertson (London, 1900), I, 6.
Dryden, *Defence of an Essay of Dramatic Poesy* (1668), Watson, I,
121.

trine becomes something much more rigidly allied to literal reality. His highest praise of Shakespeare's dialogue is that "it seems scarcely to claim the merit of fiction, but to have been gleaned by diligent selection out of common conversation, and common occurrences" (*Preface*, p. 63). In *Rambler* 151, on "the climacterics of the mind," he describes a taste for fiction as being peculiar to mental youth, and actually asserts that later on, during "the reign of judgment or reason," we are indifferent to "the painted vales of imagination" which offer a specious but inadequate imitation of truth.

The heart of Johnson's admiration of Shakespeare, so implicit in his criticism that he seldom goes out of his way to insist on it, is that improbable fiction is the easiest thing to write, while a really "just" picture of life requires the highest artistic powers. In the dedication which he wrote for Mrs. Lennox's *Shakespear Illustrated* (1753) he tacitly distinguishes Shakespeare's achievement from the "novels" and romances in which she had found the origin of many of his plots: "His works may be considered as a map of life, a faithful miniature of human transactions, and he that has read Shakespeare with attention, will perhaps find little new in the crouded world" (p. 49). And he goes on to observe not only that "his heroes are men," in contrast to the "phantoms" of most drama, but also that this excellence "has hitherto been unnoticed" (p. 49). That is to say, everyone has taken for granted something that is very remarkable indeed.

Rambler 156 had taken up the subject of Shakespeare's mingled drama before the *Preface* did, and, like Coleridge after him,[7] Johnson urged that Shake-

[7] "In Beaumont and Fletcher's tragedies the comic scenes are rarely so interfused amidst the tragic as to produce a unity of the tragic on the whole, without which the intermixture is a fault. In Shakespeare, this is always managed with transcendant skill. The Fool in *Lear* contributes in a very sensible manner

speare's success is that of a unique genius rather than the inevitable result of the tragicomic mode.

I do not however think it safe to judge of works of genius merely by the event. These resistless vicissitudes of the heart, this alternate prevalence of merriment and solemnity, may sometimes be more properly ascribed to the vigour of the writer than the justness of the design: and instead of vindicating tragi-comedy by the success of Shakespear, we ought perhaps to pay new honours to that transcendent and unbounded genius that could preside over the passions in sport.

If art were really indistinguishable from life, then any artist should be able to succeed best in tragicomedy, since he would be exhibiting the real state of sublunary nature. But Johnson in effect is saying that it is harder to imitate nature than to imitate abstractions, easier to obey the rules of tragedy or comedy than to work in a form that has no rules but depends on the genius of the writer to sustain it.

But if Johnson has a warm admiration for Shakespeare's art, it is true all the same that his admiration is founded on different reasons from those of most critics. Mrs. Thrale remarked that in the *Preface*, "While other critics expatiate on the creative powers and vivid imagination of that matchless poet, Dr. Johnson commends him for giving so just a representation of human manners" (*Miscellanies*, I, 313). When he does suggest that Shakespeare goes beyond Nature into some imaginary realm—

> Each change of many-colour'd life he drew,
> Exhausted worlds, and then imagin'd new:
> Existence saw him spurn her bounded reign,
> And panting Time toil'd after him in vain. . . .

---

to the tragic wildness of the whole drama" (*Table Talk and Omniana* [Oxford, 1917], pp. 251-52, 1 July 1833).

he means that he has still invented worlds analogous to our own: "His pow'rful strokes presiding truth impress'd" (*Drury Lane Prologue*, 3-7). And allowance must be made for the bombastic magniloquence appropriate to the occasion of the *Prologue*. When Garrick criticized the line, "And panting Time toil'd after him in vain," "Johnson exclaimed (smiling,) 'Prosaical rogues! next time I write, I'll make both time and space pant' " (*Life*, IV, 25).

While the notes to the plays, like the preface, are full of homage to the lifelike quality of Shakespeare's characters, dozens of notes could be assembled to show that Johnson was much less inclined than many critics of the next century to confuse art and life. He well knew that a dramatic character is the creature of the author, and exists or vanishes solely at his pleasure: see, for example, the account of the death of Falstaff (*Henry V* II.iii.22, p. 541) or of Mercutio, whose "wit, gaiety and courage, will always procure him friends that wish him a longer life; but his death is not precipitated, he has lived out the time allotted him in the construction of the play" (p. 956-57). A writer in the late Victorian tradition was actually able to complain that Johnson "seems to have regarded the Shakespearean characters as stage figures, not as real people."[8]

The real difficulty is not that Johnson sees Shakespeare's characters as too general or that he treats them as if they existed in real life, but rather that he uses them as material from which to illustrate the wisdom

[8] Charles F. Johnson, *Shakespeare and His Critics* (Boston, 1909), p. 116. The reader may like to see the example which supports this remarkable claim: "For instance, he says of our charming Viola, 'when she determines to seek service with the Duke Orsino, Viola is an excellent schemer, never at a loss.' As American college students say, 'We cannot stand for that.' Viola is a type of something most sacred to every man,—the maiden." A schemer is only a stage figure, a maiden is a real person.

of the Rambler. In other words, he often tends to forget (or at least undervalue) their role in a complex dramatic action, and to treat them as exemplary figures like those in his moral essays: Suspirius, Dick Shifter, and so forth. A speech in *Much Ado* provokes a long and very Johnsonian discussion of the effects of grief, with the conclusion, "Such was this writer's knowledge of the passions" (iii.i.68, p. 415). Or again, a speech by John of Gaunt receives the comment, "It is a matter of very melancholy consideration, that all human advantages confer more power of doing evil than good" (*Richard II*, i.iii.227, p. 431). Not to multiply examples, all of these notes are clearly offered as a form of instruction: Shakespeare's plays are the mirror of life, and Johnson means to enlarge our understanding of their excellence by pointing out how constantly they are confirmed by actual experience.

But of course the drawbacks to this mode of apprehending Shakespeare are at least as great as the advantages. Johnson is most out of his element in the romances, and in the comedies is likely to enforce requirements that have little relevance, as in his solemn objection to the plot of *Twelfth Night*: "The marriage of Olivia, and the succeeding perplexity, though well enough contrived to divert on the stage, wants credibility, and fails to produce the proper instruction required in the drama, as it exhibits no just picture of life" (p. 326). In the case of the tragedies, this predisposition is less obviously destructive, but there too it leads to real inadequacies of interpretation, since the plays are read as though they were naturalistic novels of a more or less didactic cast. Before the publication of the Shakespeare edition, a reviewer pointed out the imaginative failure in the elaborate account of witchcraft which had been written for the 1745 *Observations on Macbeth*. Johnson's assumption was that the witches can be condoned on the grounds that intelligent Elizabethans found "awful and affecting" superstitions which were subsequently "banished from the theatre to the nursery" (pp. 6, 3). "We will venture to say," the reviewer replied, "that the belief of witchcraft made no part of Shakespear's poetical creed, any more than it does that of many dramatic authors who have written since, even down to the author of Caractacus, who has introduced supernaturalism into that play."[9] Clearly it was an embarrassment to Johnson that *Macbeth* draws upon that supernaturalism which he had condemned in the ancient Greeks as beneath the contempt of a rational man: *incredulus odi*.

And more generally, one may say that his admiration for "nature" makes him insensitive to symbolic or thematic considerations which carry much of the tragic feeling. He cannot perhaps be blamed for not understanding the allusion to the Last Judgment in *King Lear*:

> KENT. Is this the promis'd end?
> EDGAR. Or image of that horror—
> ALBANY. Fall, and cease.
>
> These two exclamations are given to Edgar and Albany in the folio, to animate the dialogue, and employ all the persons on the stage, but they are very obscure.   (v.iii.263, p. 702)

But it seems a definite failure of imagination to reduce "When I love thee not, / Chaos is come again" to a naturalistic paraphrase: "When my love is for a moment suspended by suspicion, I have nothing in my mind but discord, tumult, perturbation, and confusion" (*Othello*, III.iii.92, p. 1030).

We may now consider two much-reprehended aspects of Johnson's criticism of Shakespeare: his appar-

[9] Review of *Anecdotes of Polite Literature*, which digresses into this mention of Johnson, in the *Critical Review*, 17 (1764), 441.

ent preference for the comedies over the tragedies, and his praise of what he calls "domestic tragedy." Invoking the support of the unpopular Rymer, he declares that Shakespeare's comedies reflect his "natural disposition," and implies that they surpass the tragedies (*Preface*, p. 69). One explanation for this remarkable opinion will be found in the idea of tragic elevation. As we have seen, Johnson assumes that it is the nature of tragedy to attempt an elevation above common life, which too often achieves nothing more than rhodomontade. Shakespeare is far from exempt from this criticism, and the drama that follows him is deformed by a "perpetual tumour of phrase" (*Rambler* 125); *tumour* means "affected pomp; false magnificence; puffy grandeur; swelling mien; unsubstantial greatness" (*Dictionary*). Comedy, on the other hand, is likely to avoid these dangers. It seems probable that Johnson's principle of fidelity to nature, understood as literal truth, leads him to have a special affection for the kind of drama that attempts no alterations or improvements upon life. Hazlitt, in trying to answer Johnson, recognizes this point while rejecting it: "That comedies should be written in a more easy and careless vein than tragedies, is but natural. This is only saying that a comedy is not so serious a thing as a tragedy."[10] For Johnson it is more realistic and in some sense more "true" than a tragedy. This is one reason why "familiar comedy is often more powerful on the theatre, than in the page; imperial tragedy is always less" (*Preface*, p. 79). Despising as he did the rant of tragic actors, it is easy to believe that he would prefer the silent interpretation of his own imagination to their histrionic posings.

Johnson believes so strongly that comedy is the most accurate mirror of life that he is willing to make extraordinary claims for its imperishability. It has always

[10] *The English Comic Writers*, The World's Classics (Oxford University Press, 1907), p. 36.

been a truism that wit does not last; as Horace Walpole perceptively wrote, comedy is concerned with the transitory hypocrisies and mannerisms that "have rendered man a fictitious animal."[11] Johnson, however, finds it necessary to insist that "real mirth must always be natural, and nature is uniform. Men have been wise in very different modes; but they have always laughed the same way" (*Life of Cowley*, I, 39-40). And this claim, quite likely remembered from Brumoy's *Dissertation upon the Greek Comedy* which Johnson translated in 1759,[12] is repeated in relation to Shakespeare.

> The force of his comick scenes has suffered little diminution from the changes made by a century and a half, in manners or in words. As his personages act upon principles arising from genuine passion, very little modified by particular forms, their pleasures and vexations are communicable to all times and to all places; they are natural, and therefore durable.   (*Preface*, pp. 69-70)

While other factors are doubtless involved, such as the less stringent moral demands which Johnson made upon comedy,[13] the essential point is its fidelity in re-

[11] "Thoughts on Comedy," written ca. 1775-76, published in Walpole's *Works* (1798), and reprinted in *Essays in Criticism*, 15 (1965), 165.

[12] According to Brumoy, "dissimulation, jealousy, policy, ambition, desire of dominion, and other interests and passions, are various without end, and take a thousand different forms in different situations of history; so that, as long as there is tragedy, there may be always novelty. . . . But the case is very different with avarice, trifling vanity, hypocrisy, and other vices, considered as ridiculous. . . . A miser, copied after nature, will always be the miser of Plautus or Molière; but a Nero, or a prince like Nero, will not always be the hero of Racine" (1825 *Works*, v, 408, 409, 410).

[13] In *Rambler* 125 he says that comedy should be defined simply as "such a dramatick representation of human life, as may excite mirth"; and years later he remarked of *She Stoops to Conquer*,

flecting life as men know it (which, as his censure of
Twelfth Night suggests, might be better satisfied by
Jonson than by Shakespeare). Of Congreve's *Old Bach-
elor* Johnson writes,

> Such a comedy written at such an age requires
> some consideration. As the lighter species of dra-
> matick poetry professes the imitation of common
> life, of real manners, and daily incidents, it appar-
> ently presupposes a familiar knowledge of many
> characters and exact observation of the passing
> world; the difficulty therefore is to conceive how
> this knowledge can be obtained by a boy.
>
> (*Life of Congreve*, II, 216)

One is tempted to deduce the contrary attributes of
tragedy: that it is elevated, generalized, imaginary,
bearing little resemblance to human life as we know it.

Just as he approved of Shakespeare's comedies, Johnson reserved his highest admiration for those aspects
of the tragedies that best answered his conception of
domestic tragedy, in the sense in which he defined it
when answering a minor critic in the *Gentleman's Magazine*: "By a *domestic* fable, he means a fable taken
from *common life*; not considering that persons who
are most elevated above common life, may be involved
in domestic distress, and consequently be the subjects
of a domestic fable."[14] In much the same way Steele had
emphasized the "domestic virtues" of Andromache in
Ambrose Philips' *Distrest Mother* (adapted from Racine's *Andromaque*), which he said were exhibited "in

---

"I know of no comedy for many years that has so much ex-
hilarated an audience, that has answered so much the great end
of comedy—making an audience merry" (*Life*, II, 233).

[14] The brief notice of "Remarks on Mr. Mason's *Elfrida*" appears in the *Gentleman's Magazine*, 22 (1752), 243, and is attributed to Johnson by Arthur Sherbo along with the review of
Elfrida itself (see Ch. 7, n. 4, above).

the most important Circumstances of a female Life, those of a Wife, a Widow, and a Mother" (*Spectator* 290).

While Johnson applies "domestic" in this sense to various Shakespearean plays, such as *Timon of Athens* (p. 745), the most remarkable instance occurs when he takes Arthur Murphy's side in a debate with Joseph Warton concerning the madness of Lear.

> It is disputed whether the predominant image in Lear's disordered mind be the loss of his kingdom or the cruelty of his daughters. Mr. Murphy, a very judicious critick, has evinced by induction of particular passages, that the cruelty of his daughters is the primary source of his distress, and that the loss of royalty affects him only as a secondary and subordinate evil; he observes with great justness, that Lear would move our compassion but little, did we not rather consider the injured father than the degraded king.   (pp. 704-705)

That Lear is compelled to learn his own humanity we all know, and he does come to call himself a very foolish, fond old man. But this emphasis of Johnson's, which was carried on by writers later in the century,[15] is mani-

---

[15] E.g., in a "Comparison of the Tragedy of the *Fair Penitent* by Rowe, and the *Fatal Dowry* by Massinger," in the *Gentleman's Magazine*, 52 (1782), 604: "The distress is domestick; and the personages of the drama are of such a level in life as to exclude no part of the audience, and no class of readers, from a sympathetick participation of their business and interests. . . . We admire the magnanimity of Tamerlane, and wonder at the unshaken virtue of Cato, but our tears gush for the lovely Isabella selling her husband's ring to procure bread for her child; and when the hoary head of Lear is driven out by the barbarity of those whom he had most obliged, *to bide the pelting of the pitiless storm*, what heart can keep its seat, or behold such a spectacle without anguish? The indignities sustained by the king are lost in our compassion for the sufferings of the father."

Or again, a reviewer trying to explain why *King Lear* "seems

festly only part of the truth. As an anonymous Gentleman cries out in the play, "A sight most pitiful in the
meanest wretch, / Past speaking of in a King!" (iv.vi.
205-206). Johnson's own veneration for the inherent
grandeur of kingship is obvious in the deliberately
courageous manliness—to us perhaps a little comic—
with which he carried out his interview with George
III. But as he prefers the common reader to what he
sometimes calls the bigotry of learning, so he wants art
to illuminate the experience that is common to all men,
not just to kings. He does not suggest that *King Lear*
could equally well have been written about a grocer,
but that it is about a man like us. Not many people
know what it is to lose a kingdom; everyone knows
what ingratitude in the family is like.

It goes without saying that however rightly Johnson
may have been reacting to the thrasonical excesses of
heroic drama, he was not sufficiently aware of the role
of the hero in Shakespeare. "Tragic heroes," as Northrop Frye has said, "are so much the highest points in
their human landscape that they seem the inevitable
conductors of the power about them, great trees more
likely to be struck by lightning than a clump of grass."[16]
Lear, like many tragic heroes, is not simply an enlarged
version of our common humanity, but an awesome and
mysterious figure incommensurate with ordinary experience. If we should be condemned to suffer in this
way we would be Gloucester, not Lear, just as we
would be Horatio and not Hamlet, Enobarbus and not
Antony.

Recent scholars have noted that Johnson, unlike most

---

not to have been a favourite play on its first appearance": "The
deficiencies of splendid exhibitions, or of preternatural beings,
could not perhaps be compensated by natural and unassuming
distress" (Review of Thomas Davies' *Dramatic Miscellanies* in
the *Critical Review*, 58 [1784], 58).

[16] *Anatomy of Criticism* (Princeton, 1957), p. 207.

eighteenth-century critics, is extremely reticent on the subject of the sublime in Shakespeare, a quality which he reserves for Milton, while Shakespeare is pre-eminently the master of the "pathetic."[17] Whether or not this implies a fear of uncontrolled (not to say tragic) emotion, it helps to explain why his most extravagant praise is directed to a scene in *Henry VIII*, a scene which some scholars attribute to Fletcher and which had already been admired by Rowe.[18]

> This scene is above any other part of Shakespeare's tragedies, and perhaps above any scene of any other poet, tender and pathetick, without gods, or furies, or poisons, or precipices, without the help of romantick circumstances, without improbable sallies of poetical lamentation, and without any throes of tumultuous misery.   (IV.ii.1, p. 653)

In succession Johnson seems to disparage the Greeks (gods and furies), *Hamlet* (poisons), and *King Lear* (precipices).

It is not hard to see why the scene in question has excited Johnson's enthusiasm. It deals with the Christian virtue of patience which he thought so important, and which indeed is personified in the name of Kathe-

---

[17] Arthur Sherbo notices the oddity of Johnson's silence on the sublime in Shakespeare (*Samuel Johnson, Editor of Shakespeare* [Urbana, 1956], p. 71). J. H. Hagstrum shows that Johnson saw Shakespeare as the exemplar of the pathetic, Milton of the sublime, and Pope of the beautiful, and makes a good case for Johnson's "emphasis on the tender and the pathetic in Shakespeare" as a means by which he can "dilute whatever violence appears in the plays" (*Samuel Johnson's Literary Criticism* [Chicago, 1952], p. 142). Johnson's treatment of the sublime in Milton, incidentally, owes more to Addison than to later aesthetic theorists.

[18] For a discussion of the attribution to Fletcher, see the introduction to J. C. Maxwell's edition (Cambridge, 1962). Rowe says that "the Distresses likewise of Queen *Katherine*, in this Play, are very movingly touch'd" (Nichol Smith, p. 17).

rine's attendant: "Patience, be near me still" (IV.ii.76).
And the scene opens with eighty lines on the career of
Wolsey which bear a close relation to the passage about
Wolsey in *The Vanity of Human Wishes,* and imply a
lesson which must have been highly attractive to
Johnson:

> His overthrow heap'd happiness upon him,
> For then, and not till then, he felt himself,
> And found the blessedness of being little;
> And to add greater honours to his age
> Than man could give him, he died fearing God.
>
> (IV.ii.64-68)

We are not required to concur in Johnson's enthusiasm,
but we may be grateful that he has given a specific example of the kind of tragedy which, in his view, does
what comedy can do, and exhibits the course of ordinary life with the tenderness and pathos that he valued
so much. These qualities are so important to him, in
fact, that he exalts the scene in which they appear
above those in any other tragedy by any other poet,
though he says that the rest of the play is such as a very
ordinary author could have written (p. 657).

3. Shakespeare's Language

To the foregoing discussion may be added some brief
remarks on Johnson's notorious attacks on Shakespeare's language, partly because it is hard to see how
great plays can be written badly, and partly because
once more, as the comment on "Chaos is come again"
may suggest, he is neglecting an important aspect of
tragedy. The issue is not really that Johnson condemns
various "faults" in Shakespeare's language—perhaps,
as Bradley suggested, some of them exist[19]—but that

---

[19] Bradley declared that the faults in Shakespeare's language
represent "a subject which later criticism has never fairly faced
and examined" (*Shakespearean Tragedy,* ch. 2, p. 73).

he gives the impression of misunderstanding what met-
apohorical language is all about.

Let us begin by considering the well-known attack
on Shakespeare's puns and wordplay, which by Johnson's time was already an overworked topic.[20] His censure is directed chiefly at what he considers the violation of proper dramatic speech, exactly as in the case
of his description of the "tumour, meanness, tedious-
ness, and obscurity" in the tragedies (*Preface*, p. 73).
The audience had thought it was watching the mirror
of life, and is suddenly repelled by an obvious display
of art.

> What he does best, he soon ceases to do. He is not
> long soft and pathetick without some idle conceit,
> or contemptible equivocation. He no sooner begins
> to move, than he counteracts himself; and terrour
> and pity, as they are rising in the mind, are
> checked and blasted by sudden frigidity.
>
> (*Preface*, p. 74)

> I wish these two lines could be honestly ejected.
> It is the fate of Shakespeare to counteract his own
> pathos. (*Othello* v.ii.21, p. 1045)

It is hard, in fact, to know on what grounds Johnson
thought that poetry was appropriate to drama, or why
Irene should not have been written in prose.

Thus Johnson's critical limitation is far more serious
than a distaste for puns, or even an inclination to detect
bombast where we fine great verse. He is of course not
unaware that poetry has its charms: "I suppose there

---

[20] See, e.g., Rowe in Nichol Smith, p. 13, and Dryden in the
Defence of the Epilogue (Watson, I, 179). George Colman in 1753
imagined a Temple of Fame where all the great authors commit
to the flames the defective parts of their works; "Shakespeare
carried to the altar a long string of puns, marked, 'The Taste
of the Age,' a small parcel of bombast, and a pretty large bundle
of incorrectness" (*Adventurer* 90, 15 Sept. 1753).

are few who do not feel themselves touched by poetical melody, and who will not confess that they are more or less moved by the same thoughts, as they are conveyed by different sounds, and more affected by the same words in one order, than in another" (*Rambler* 86). But his warmest praise for Shakespeare's language is aroused by the "ease and simplicity" with which the characters often talk, where the dialogue "seems scarcely to claim the merit of fiction" (*Preface*, p. 63). It is no wonder that he is so fond of the comedies, where he finds "a stile which never becomes obsolete, ... to be sought in the common intercourse of life, among those who speak only to be understood, without ambition of elegance" (p. 70). For elaborate metaphor Johnson has little use, and even less for poetry whose relevance to the action can only be indirect and symbolic. The wonderful "Full fathom five thy father lies" receives the casual and even contemptuous comment, "Ariel's lays, however seasonable and efficacious, must be allowed to be of no supernatural dignity or elegance, they express nothing great, nor reveal any thing above mortal discovery" (*Tempest* I.ii.396, p. 124).

Against the modern assumption that a poet is a man who, regardless of his beliefs or even delusions, is pre-eminently skilled in language, Johnson sees the poet as a man of comprehensive mental powers and great experience of life. To be sure Imlac says that the poet must "familiarize to himself every delicacy of speech, and grace of harmony" (*Rasselas*, ch. 10), but he spends the bulk of his discussion on the observation of nature and human affairs. And in *Rambler* 4 we are told of the old romances, "When a man had by practice gained some fluency of language, he had no further care than to retire to his closet, let loose his invention, and heat his mind with incredibilities; a book was thus produced without fear of criticism, without the toil of study, without knowledge of nature, or acquaintance with life."

Thus facility of language is the easiest and least important attribute of the writer. One might suspect that in Johnson's mind Shakespeare would have been just as good a dramatist if he had been a worse poet; except that the uncomfortable sense remains that Johnson already thinks him a bad one.

4. Didacticism

For the modern reader, the most serious of Johnson's limitations as a critic of Shakespeare is the recurring note of didacticism, of which the fullest expression occurs when he begins his survey of the "faults sufficient to obscure and overwhelm any other merit."

> His first defect is that to which may be imputed most of the evil in books or in men. He sacrifices virtue to convenience, and is so much more careful to please than to instruct, that he seems to write without any moral purpose. From his writings indeed a system of social duty may be selected, for he that thinks reasonably must think morally; but his precepts and axioms drop casually from him; he makes no just distribution of good or evil, nor is always careful to shew in the virtuous a disapprobation of the wicked; he carries his persons indifferently through right and wrong, and at the close dismisses them without further care, and leaves their examples to operate by chance. This fault the barbarity of his age cannot extenuate; for it is always a writer's duty to make the world better, and justice is a virtue independant on time or place. (*Preface*, p. 71)

Leaving aside the point about poetic justice, the crucial question is this: how explicitly did Johnson suppose that a work of art should convey its "moral purpose?"

That art ought to be instructive was so universal a faith in Johnson's time that some degree of didacticism, even in a critic who was not a professed moralist, would have been obligatory. Pope singled out Shakespearean *sententiae* for approbation, and Dryden, following Bossu, endorsed a simple-minded didactic program of one moral per play.[21] But Johnson's statement contains enough ambiguity to cause Kenrick to complain in bewilderment,

> If it be admitted, as our Editor actually admits, that a system of social duty may be selected from his writings, and that his precepts and axioms were virtuous; we may justly ask, whether they are less so for dropping casually from him? Must a writer be charged with making a sacrifice of virtue, because he does not professedly inculcate it? Is every writer *ex professo* a parson or a moral philosopher?[22]

The answer must be that Johnson is not always sure: sometimes it is enough that the drama enact a moral, at other times direct moral commentary is demanded. He does not abstract instructive sentences from the context as absurdly as Theobald—"I never read that excellent Passage in *Shakespear*, where the *King* counsels *Hamlet* to forget his *dead* Father, but I admire the Poet for his Eloquence, and the Justness of his Instruc-

[21] In his marginal indications of "beauties" in Shakespeare, Pope emphasized relatively nondramatic descriptive passages and *sententiae*; see John Butt's pamphlet *Pope's Taste in Shakespeare* (London, 1936). Dryden learned from Bossu "to make the moral of the work, that is, to lay down to yourself what that precept of morality shall be, which you would insinuate into the people; as namely Homer's (which I have copied in my *Conquest of Granada*) was that union preserves a commonwealth, and discord destroys it; Sophocles, in his *Oedipus*, that no man is to be accounted happy before his death" (*The Grounds of Criticism in Tragedy*, Watson, I, 248).

[22] *Monthly Review*, 33 (1765), 291.

tion"[23]—but in his own way he is guilty of comparable offences.

> DUKE.   Thy best of rest is sleep,
> And that thou oft provok'st; yet grosly fear'st
> Thy death, which is no more.

Here Dr. Warburton might have found a sentiment worthy of his animadversion. I cannot without indignation find Shakespeare saying, that "death is only sleep," lengthening out his exhortation by a sentence which in the Friar is impious, in the reasoner is foolish, and in the poet trite and vulgar.
> (*Measure for Measure* III.i.17, pp. 192-93)

Johnson is not exactly describing the entire play as a mouthpiece for its author, since he recognizes that the lines are spoken by the duke (in disguise as a friar) rather than by Shakespeare, but he is so offended by what the duke says that he does not stop to consider its place in the drama. These lines occur in a scene in which Claudio certainly prevails, both morally and imaginatively, in his refusal to believe that death is only sleep. Johnson's myopia is the more surprising since he was himself so fond of quoting Claudio's speech later in the same scene, "Ay, but to die, and go we know not where. . . ."

The fact is that Johnson's didacticism is not confined to "lapses" or "homiletical moments," as Hagstrum suggests and as we may well wish to believe.[24] And while in the review of Mason's *Elfrida* he seems to say that a

[23] *The Censor*, no. 54 (23 Feb. 1717).
[24] *Samuel Johnson's Literary Criticism*, pp. 72, 76. It is worth noting that Johnson's objection to the casualness of Shakespeare's moral precepts is directly anticipated in *Rambler* 29: "The antient poets are, indeed, by no means unexceptionable teachers of morality; their precepts are to be always considered as the sallies of a genius, intent rather upon giving pleasure than instruction, eager to take every advantage of insinuation, and pro-

work of art should convey its moral indirectly, rather than by explicit precepts,[25] it would be idle to pretend that he is any the less severe in demanding the indirect moral. No critic has given more impressive testimony than Johnson to the power of literature to fascinate and delight, but perhaps no critic was more concerned lest it lead the captivated reader astray. Many of the moral judgments about Shakespeare, indeed, must be seen as carefully emphasized lessons for the unsuspecting reader whom the story may have carried away.

These moral judgments, to be sure, are often perfectly appropriate to the plays in question, and only offend a modern sensibility by their tone or emphasis. Johnson is not being irrelevant when he comments on the prayer scene in *Hamlet*, "This speech, in which Hamlet, represented as a virtuous character, is not content with taking blood for blood, but contrives damnation for the man that he would punish, is too horrible to be read or to be uttered" (iii.iii.93, p. 990). The scene has become a crux of modern *Hamlet* criticism, and Johnson's is certainly the instinctive human reaction to it (whether or not scholarship may persuade us that it is not the

---

vided the passions can be engaged on its side, very little solicitous about the suffrage of reason." Johnson goes on to discuss the "reflections upon life" which may be separated out from their works and "treasured up" by the reader.

[25] "The mind is more affected by things than words, and incident and event become the vehicles of instruction, not by giving occasion to a *Chorus* to repeat moral sentences, but by the series in which they happen, and the causes by which they are produced. These are comprehended by every understanding, they strike every imagination, and are retained by every memory. The beauties of poetry are perceived but by few, and the aphorisms of philosophy are easily overlooked and forgotten; nor can he be supposed to have much knowledge of the human heart, who can seriously talk of *instructing* an audience *how to be affected*, and can believe that pity and terror will be regulated by the directions of a *Chorus*" (*Gentleman's Magazine*, 22 [1752], 224-25). For the attribution to Johnson, see Ch. 7, n. 4.

Elizabethan reaction). It is remarkable, incidentally, that Johnson sufficiently accepts the ethos of the play not to object to a plot founded on revenge, although one presumes that revenge was abhorrent to him.[26]

But it is probably true that the search for a usable "moral" leads Johnson to be lamentably reductive as often as it generates insight. The worst instance is the Rymerian statement that Iago is right to charge Desdemona with "deceit" against her father, and that the play teaches us to avoid "the imprudent generosity of disproportionate marriages" (*Othello* III.iii.210, pp. 1032-33). This claim, which Johnson repeated in conversation, is the more surprising when we consider that the concluding summary of *Othello* is one of his best, and that this seems to have been, with *Henry IV*, his favorite Shakespearean play.[27]

At issue, then, is the fact that Johnson's moralism is not simply applied negatively, to criticize Shakespeare for writing without a clear moral purpose; it also produces serious misreadings of plays or passages which he particularly admires, as may be illustrated from a history play that has affinities with tragedy. His notes to *Richard II* take no notice of the king's maudlin and

[26] One cannot be sure, since in the Hebrides he seemed to countenance the right of revenge if the state fails to secure justice for the injured party, which would apply well enough to Hamlet's case; but near the end of his life he speaks, as one would expect, of revenge as forbidden by Scripture (*Life*, v, 87-88, and IV, 211).

[27] Mrs. Thrale says that these two plays "had indeed no rivals in Johnson's favour." She especially remembers his admiration of "Iago's ingenious malice, and subtle revenge" (*Miscellanies*, I, 283). When Boswell, having elicited the definition of catharsis, proceeded to draw him out further by suggesting that *Othello* has no moral since "no man could resist the circumstances of suspicion which were artfully suggested to Othello's mind," Johnson replied, "In the first place, Sir, we learn from Othello this very useful moral, not to make an unequal match; in the second place, we learn not to yield too readily to suspicion" (*Life*, III, 40).

histrionic self-pity; Johnson wants a figure of Patience worthy of the *Rambler,* and accordingly he finds one.

> It seems to be the design of the poet to raise Richard to esteem in his fall, and consequently to interest the reader in his favour. He gives him only passive fortitude, the virtue of a confessor rather than of a king. In his prosperity we saw him imperious and oppressive, but in his distress he is wise, patient, and pious. (III.ii.93, p. 440)

> This sentiment is drawn from nature. Nothing is more offensive to a mind convinced that his distress is without a remedy, and preparing to submit quietly to irresistible calamity, than these petty and conjectured comforts which unskilful officiousness thinks it virtue to administer.
> (III.ii.207, pp. 441-42)

And when he characteristically condemns wordplay for counteracting "pathos," he fails to see that the speaker here is not Shakespeare but Richard, in whom such rhetorical showmanship is entirely in character.

> Shakespeare is very apt to deviate from the *pathetick* to the *ridiculous.* Had the speech of Richard ended at this line it had exhibited the natural language of submissive misery, conforming its intention to the present fortune, and calmly ending its purposes in death. (III.iii.156, p. 443)

Apparently Johnson never suspects that Richard has been self-dramatizing in the lines with which he thought the speech should end ("My large kingdom for a little grave, / A little little grave, an obscure grave") or that he is shortly to be at it again ("Down, down, I come; like glistering Phaeton"). And so he doggedly continues to reprove Shakespeare for "playing with sounds" (IV.i.194, p. 447) or for "childish prattle"

229

(v.i.46, p. 449), never noticing that it is Richard who plays with sounds.

Finally, we must consider the question of poetic justice, which is often invoked in the Shakespeare edition, but which a passage in the *Life of Addison* is supposed to have repudiated. "Little regard to poetical justice" is shown in *Hamlet,* for "the gratification which would arise from the destruction of an usurper and a murderer, is abated by the untimely death of Ophelia, the young, the beautiful, the harmless, and the pious" (p. 1011). Trying to find a "reason" for Juliet's fate, Johnson seizes on the lines, "I pray thee, leave me to myself to-night; / For I have need of many orisons," and comments, "Juliet plays most of her pranks under the appearance of religion; perhaps Shakespeare meant to punish her hypocrisy" (iv.iii.1, p. 953).

Shakespeare's plays are much concerned with the problem of justice, and a sense that justice has been outraged at the end of a tragedy is by no means inappropriate. What vitiates Johnson's kind of poetic justice is shown by his remark on *Measure for Measure* that "Angelo's crimes were such, as must sufficiently justify punishment, whether its end be to secure the innocent from wrong, or to deter guilt by example" (v.i.444, p. 213). Perhaps every reader feels the same way, but we must remember that the play is expressly concerned with the *human* justice by which, like Johnson, we may expect Angelo to be punished; and of course the absence of punishment is anything but a casual blunder in the plot. More fundamentally, such punishment, whether it does or does not occur, is wholly different from a poetic justice in which a character is said to be "punished" if he is poisoned, or run through by a sword, or destroyed by a fever.

Johnson's famous approbation of Tate's *Lear* is similarly based on a sense that the universe ought to be just, and that although the wicked often prosper in actual life, "I cannot easily be persuaded, that the observation of justice makes a play worse."

> Shakespeare has suffered the virtue of Cordelia to perish in a just cause, contrary to the natural ideas of justice, to the hope of the reader, and, what is yet more strange, to the faith of chronicles. . . . In the present case the publick has decided. Cordelia, from the time of Tate, has always retired with victory and felicity. And, if my sensations could add any thing to the general suffrage, I might relate, that I was many years ago so shocked by Cordelia's death, that I know not whether I ever endured to read again the last scenes of the play till I undertook to revise them as an editor. (P. 704)

This is an argument from the feelings of the audience—further evidence, by the way, that an emotional catharsis is not part of Johnson's theory—in which the "general suffrage" is corroborated by Johnson's own response. Yet the statement is not altogether dogmatic. Art may (though not must) improve upon life and satisfy our instinctive wish that virtue be rewarded; furthermore this is a play presumably based on actual history, and according to the chronicles virtue *was* rewarded. In any case Johnson accurately describes the mood which the ending of *King Lear* conveys, even though he is unwilling to approve of it. Thus in a way we can say that his response to the tragedy is an appropriate one, even if his conclusions are not.

My point is that this is not, in essence, an especially theoretical passage; nor are Johnson's remarks fifteen years later on *Cato* a theoretical recantation.

> Whatever pleasure there may be in seeing crimes punished and virtue rewarded, yet, since wickedness often prospers in real life, the poet is certainly at liberty to give it prosperity on the stage. For if

poetry has an imitation of reality, how are its laws
broken by exhibiting the world in its true form?
The stage may sometimes gratify our wishes; but,
if it be truly the *mirror of life*, it ought to shew us
sometimes what we are to expect.

(*Life of Addison*, II, 135)

In the first place, these remarks directly follow a quotation from Dennis, the great proponent of the view that
the poet must *always* reward and punish his personages
as God would do. In the second place, Johnson is discussing a play wholly different in kind from *King Lear*,
a play in whose heroic Roman ethic the death of Cato
is a kind of victory, a cause for exultation rather than
despair. Obviously no audience resented Cato's death
as they did Cordelia's, and Johnson could easily have
appealed to the common reader in both instances. The
general suffrage, it is fair to say, approved the absence
of poetic justice in *Cato*, just as it deplored it in the
original version of *King Lear*. And here as always Johnson's reasons for a critical position derive from moral
assumptions about the nature of life rather than from
aesthetic assumptions about the nature of tragedy.

Very likely "didacticism" is too crude a word to describe what disturbs us in this attitude of Johnson's.
What we are opposed to is not art with moral implications but the unsubtle, hortatory, Sunday-school kind
of lesson-finding that Johnson and many of his contemporaries often display. Yet if every overt instance of
moralizing were expunged from Johnson's works, his
understanding of tragedy would still be limited (for
reasons which do him honor as a man, if not as a critic).
One suspects that he never asked himself why tragedy,
to adopt the rough definition which he called inadequate, deals in unhappy endings. In refusing to see it
as a genre, and in persisting in his determination to
judge it by the standards of sublunary nature as we all

experience it, he fails to see that it brings forward and intensifies certain aspects of experience at the expense of others. If those very aspects were exceptionally prevalent in his own life, and if he constantly strove to master them, that would help to explain his resolute opposition to their full exploration in literature.

Johnson assumes the permanence and integrity of moral order. He cannot sympathize with those who must break it, and is always afraid that their transgressions will be made speciously attractive by art, as in his denunciation of *All for Love* for a fault "rather moral than critical" of recommending "that conduct which through all ages the good have censured as vicious, and the bad despised as foolish" (*Life of Dryden*, I, 361). In any case no man is equally fitted for all things. Just as a tragic sense of life may have been something which Johnson did not wish to possess, so also an understanding of literary tragedy may have been limited in him by the very qualities which, in other directions, contribute to his greatness.

5. *Johnson and the New Character Criticism*

As a critic Johnson seems isolated between two great traditions, the neoclassical and the romantic. In this section I should like to carry on an argument which was begun in Chapter 3, and to discuss the contribution of those critics who began to concentrate on the analysis of character. It is not their fault that we sometimes perceive in them the seeds of an over-elaborate character criticism; indeed, if we read them without prejudice, they display a depth of understanding of tragedy that can be equalled by no earlier critic. As a number of them were contemporaries of Johnson, and as there are occasional forays into character criticism in his edition of Shakespeare, it will be profitable to consider what he might have learned from them.

Like any other critical method, theirs had its faults

233

and its limitations, but its profound contribution was to get the criticism of drama off the dead center where it had rested since the sixteenth century. That the old Aristotelian dogmas had lost most of their conviction is obvious, but nothing very satisfactory had taken their place, and against the modified Aristotelianism of a critic like Johnson most people had nothing better to urge than a sense of nameless ineffable beauties that were somehow guaranteed by "feeling."[28] The character critics of course owed a great deal to this attitude, but it was their distinction to have something genuinely interesting to say. And by virtue of redirecting analysis in a new way, they enabled it to throw off some of the most inhibiting of the old assumptions without ever having to attack them directly.

Let us consider first of all *Richard III*, which was Garrick's first role and one of his greatest, and attracted a number of commentators. Johnson's notes on the play are briefer and less discursive than usual, and his conclusion is neither appreciative nor enlightening.

> This is one of the most celebrated of our authour's performances; yet I know not whether it has not happened to him as to others, to be praised most when praise is not most deserved. That this play has scenes noble in themselves, and very well contrived to strike in the exhibition, cannot be denied. But some parts are trifling, others shocking, and some improbable. (P. 632)

Against this admittedly perfunctory treatment, from which we at least deduce that Johnson did not care to

[28] The reviewer whom I have already quoted as condemning Johnson for obeying French rules declared, "Of all our sensations, *taste* is the most variable and uncertain. Shakespeare is to be tried by a more sure criterion, that of *feeling*, which is the same in all ages and all climates" (*Critical Review*, 20 [1765], 322).

say much about the play, we may set an essay by William Richardson, published in 1784.

> The whole tragedy is an exhibition of guilt, where abhorrence for the criminal is much stronger than our interest in the sufferers, or esteem for those, who, by accident rather than great exertion, promote his downfal. We are pleased, no doubt, with his punishment; but the display of his enormities, and their progress to this completion, are the chief objects of our attention.[29]

This treatment of Richard's "punishment" shows a real advance beyond the usual invocation of poetic justice. Richardson sees very well that while Richard's downfall is the appointed end of the play, it is *only* the end, and that the real interest lies elsewhere. He sees moreover that the characters who "promote his downfal" are by no means heroes counterbalancing Richard, as they might have been in a Restoration tragedy, and that our interest is concentrated almost entirely on a monster.

Reflections like these lead easily to the idea that *Richard III* is not a tragedy at all. If its chief effect is to fascinate us with the workings of "great intellectual ability employed for inhuman and perfidious purposes," as Richardson concludes (p. 204), then the usual implications of tragedy seem to be absent. I do not mean that Richardson says this; on the contrary, he accepts the play as a tragedy. But his analysis at least opens the way to such a view, while the older criticism simply cannot distinguish between the tragic dimension of *Richard III* and *Oedipus* or *King Lear*.

If our subject were not tragedy, much could be made of Maurice Morgann's brilliant essay on Falstaff; in-

---

[29] "Essay VI. On the Dramatic Character of Richard the Third," in *Essays on Some of Shakespeare's Dramatic Characters* (1784; 5th ed., 1798), p. 200.

stead we may turn to Joseph Warton's papers on *Lear*. We have already seen Johnson's only mention of them, his declaration in favor of Arthur Murphy on the question of Lear's madness.[30] The endorsement of Murphy's much weaker essays (both men, incidentally, were his friends) suggests that he views the matter simply as an argument as to which of two "passions" is stronger in Lear, his love of kingship or of his daughters. It is disappointing to find Johnson willing to see so complex a subject reduced to such simple terms.

Warton's papers in the *Adventurer*, on the other hand, are much more than this; they represent an extended and sensitive close reading which demonstrates an imaginative response to the play. He quotes almost all of the passages which recur in any modern account of *King Lear*, and often comments at sufficient length to show the quality of his understanding. Thus on the line "O me, my heart! my rising heart!—but down," he comments,

> By which single line, the inexpressible anguish of his mind, and the dreadful conflict of opposite passions with which it is agitated are more forcibly expressed than by the long and laboured speech, enumerating the causes of his anguish, that Rowe and other modern tragic writers would certainly have put into his mouth.[31]

Again and again he dwells on the implications of the simplest speeches, such as "I gave you all!" or "Wilt break my heart!" To give one final example, he shows

[30] *Gray's-Inn Journal*, no. 78 (13 April 1754). In no. 79 Murphy prints a letter (apparently a genuine one) from a correspondent who suggests, reasonably enough, that love of both crown and family may be simultaneously present; but in no. 81 he reiterates his own view.

[31] My quotations are from *Adventurers* 113 and 116 (4 Dec. and 15 Dec. 1753); the series is concluded in no. 122 (5 Jan. 1754).

a clear awareness of the thematic significance of Edgar's madness:

> The assumed madness of Edgar, and the real distraction of Lear, form a judicious contrast. Upon perceiving the nakedness and wretchedness of this figure, the poor king asks a question that I never could read without strong emotions of pity and admiration:
>
>> What! have his daughters brought him
>>   to this pass?
>> Could'st thou save nothing? Didst thou
>>   give them all?

For its time this is an exceptionally fine interpretation of *Lear*, not because Warton is a greater critic than Johnson, but because he is asking quite different questions of the play. Johnson's discussion (one of his longest) sensibly refutes Warton's claim that "the intervention of Edmund destroys the simplicity of the story" (p. 703), and indeed his strength, as has already been noticed, is in the analysis of plot. But the bulk of his comment is given over to an account of the barbarism of Lear's time (in order to excuse "improbability") and the defense of poetic justice that ends in the approval of Tate, a conclusion which was no longer obligatory, though most of his readers must have concurred with it.[32]

---

[32] To an adherent of the school of feeling Johnson's position is irreproachable: "Lear has derived little advantage from the efforts of those who endeavoured to remove its imperfections; but we still prefer the happy conclusion: reason opposes it, while the tortured feelings at once decide the contest" (review of Davies' *Dramatic Miscellanies* in the *Critical Review*, 58 [1784], 58-59). Murphy in the *Gray's-Inn Journal*, no. 81, had granted that an audience would prefer Tate's version, but hinted that Garrick ought to attempt the original, even if his genius would render it unbearably affecting.

Finally, the contrast between Johnson and this new criticism may be shown by reference to *Hamlet*. It is well known that the question why Hamlet delays was virtually ignored until the 1770's. Until then he seems to have been taken as a straightforward and heroic character who has to overcome certain obstacles (the question of the ghost's veracity; the strength and cunning of Claudius) before he can proceed to his revenge.[33] Johnson a few years earlier, while touching upon character analysis in some of his notes—"This idea of dotage encroaching upon wisdom, will solve all the phaenomena of the character of Polonius" (ii.ii.86, p. 974)—follows the older critics in assuming plot and structure to be foremost.

> The conduct is perhaps not wholly secure against objections. The action is indeed for the most part in continual progression, but there are some scenes which neither forward nor retard it. Of the feigned madness of Hamlet there appears no adequate cause, for he does nothing which he might not have done with the reputation of sanity. He plays the madman most, when he treats Ophelia with so much rudeness, which seems to be useless and wanton cruelty. (P. 1011)

Thus while "the pretended madness of Hamlet causes much mirth," there is no sufficient reason for it, and

[33] A detailed survey of the subject is provided by Paul S. Conklin, *A History of Hamlet Criticism, 1601-1821* (London, 1947). The first published analyses of this kind were Henry Mackenzie's "Criticism on the Character and Tragedy of Hamlet" in the *Mirror* (1770), in which the author of *The Man of Feeling* describes Hamlet as a man of feeling, and William Richardson's *Essay on the Character of Hamlet* (1774), which Bradley cites as a *terminus a quo* for his kind of criticism. Quite possibly Hamlet seemed more complicated to actors than he did to critics, for the elder Sheridan told Boswell in 1763 that Hamlet is "delicate and irresolute," and that much of his conduct is a rationalization of delay (*London Journal*, p. 235).

hence to some degree it is a defect in the play. Johnson does not inquire whether the "madness" might be a complication of real as well as artificial emotions, nor does he try to find a reason for the "useless and wanton cruelty" toward Ophelia.

As for the action in general,

> Hamlet is, through the whole play, rather an instrument than an agent. After he has, by the stratagem of the play, convicted the King, he makes no attempt to punish him, and his death is at last effected by an incident which Hamlet has no part in producing. . . .
>
> The poet is accused of having shewn little regard to poetical justice, and may be charged with equal neglect of poetical probability. The apparition left the regions of the dead to little purpose; the revenge which he demands is not obtained but by the death of him that was required to take it; and the gratification which would arise from the destruction of an usurper and a murderer, is abated by the untimely death of Ophelia, the young, the beautiful, the harmless, and the pious. (P. 1011)

This is accurate description of a vigorously commonsense kind, and does not attempt to go beyond description. Johnson looks for a straightforward revenge plot in which the hero shall press forward to his revenge, and when *Hamlet* is obviously different from this model he is perplexed but does not seek to explain. One does not feel that he has thought about the strange fatalism with which Hamlet returns from the sea voyage, the talk about the destiny that shapes our ends and the special providence in the fall of a sparrow. He does not consider that the play may be expressly concerned with the fact that justice, though it comes at last when Claudius is killed, comes very inefficiently from a hu-

239

man point of view. Least of all does he suspect that the failure of poetic justice and of probability itself may lie at the heart of the tragedy.

With Henry Mackenzie, on the other hand, we find ourselves presented with the kind of explanation that two centuries of subsequent criticism have made familiar; he tries to find reasons for what Johnson is content to dismiss as bungling.

> Had Shakespeare made Hamlet pursue his vengeance with a steady determined purpose, had he led him through difficulties arising from accidental causes, and not from the doubts and hesitation of his own mind, the anxiety of the spectator might have been highly raised; but it would have been anxiety for the event, not for the person. As it is, we feel not only the virtues, but the weaknesses of Hamlet, as our own; we see a man who, in other circumstances, would have exercised all the moral and social virtues, . . . placed in a situation in which even the amiable qualities of his mind serve but to aggravate his distress, and to perplex his conduct.[34]

William Richardson a few years later extended this line of thinking, expressly mentioning his desire "to remove some strong objections urged by Dr. Johnson against both the play, and the character." Hamlet's hesitation and scruples, in Richardson's view, "lead him at one time to indecision; and then betray him, by the self-condemning consciousness of such apparent imbecility, into acts of rash and inconsiderate violence."[35]

As it stands, this kind of analysis may not do much more than Johnson's to explore the metaphysical overtones of the action, but it does transfer the focus away

[34] *The Mirror*, no. 99 (18 April 1770).
[35] *Essay on Some of Shakespeare's Dramatic Characters*, pp. 138 and 119.

from the action considered as a chain of "probable" events, and toward the character whose complexity is reflected in an action far less orderly or intelligible than those of *All for Love* or *Cato* or *Irene*. In so doing, moreover, it opens up the imagination to deep currents of tragic feeling which the older criticism was at a loss to describe; and what we cannot put into words we have difficulty in recognizing. We see what we expect to see.

The greatest of all the paradoxes in Johnson's criticism of Shakespeare is that the moralist who insists on truth to real life feels so little attraction to the character criticism in which that disposition could have found ample fulfillment, and instead judges the plays by a moral and critical standard that vitiates his criticism. In asserting his moral views so strenuously, furthermore, Johnson may be seen as overcompensating for his own acute sense of the intoxicating charms of art. His contemptuous dismissal of romances in *Rambler* 4 has already been quoted; one of the *Dictionary* definitions of *romance* is "A lie; a fiction." Yet Johnson's warfare against escapist literature is in part motivated by his own continual temptation to indulge in literature in that way. In his boyhood, as Bishop Percy tells us, "he was immoderately fond of reading romances of chivalry, and he retained his fondness for them through life. . . . Yet I have heard him attribute to these extravagant fictions that unsettled turn of mind which prevented his ever fixing in any profession" (*Life*, I, 49). J. H. Hagstrum describes Johnson's "literary realism" as being "as much the imposition of a starkly necessary discipline by a highly imaginative and violently emotional man as it was an insight of plain common sense."[36] Many of the contradictory or baffling aspects of his Shakespeare criticism can only be explained—

[35] *Essays on Some of Shakespeare's Dramatic Characters*, pp. 138 and 119.

though not, of course, justified—by referring them to his biography; and curiously enough, they reflect precisely those elements in his personality that have led modern readers to regard him as a tragic figure, just as his moral essays are built upon a life of suffering but are intended to teach the conquest of tragedy.

CHAPTER 9

Conclusion

IN THE first chapter I offered only a very general account of "the tragic," and avoided any direct analysis of the distinction between that concept and tragedy considered as a literary form. Now that my study of Johnson is complete, it is time to discuss more rigorously the consequences of measuring his thought against modern theories of tragedy. If it seemed best to explore the implications of his terms before imposing ours, it is certainly possible that our own are in every sense more adequate than his.

Yet I would reiterate that "tragedy" is no single entity, but rather a term around which a quite exceptional number of ideas have accumulated; it represents a cultural tradition based on the one hand on a series of highly diverse literary masterpieces, and on the other on an evolving conception of tragic experience as a metaphysical phenomenon. There is, therefore, no single canonical theory against which Johnson can or should be judged, and to put forward any single theory in this book would be needlessly restrictive. It is nonetheless true that most modern writers on tragedy have much more in common with each other than they do with Johnson or Dryden or Dennis, and there may be some value in making explicit the nature of the gulf between eighteenth-century assumptions and more recent ones.

To begin with, there is a belief too widespread to be groundless that the idea of tragedy is intimately related to a dramatic form. If the Aristotelian terms of reversal and recognition (though not catharsis) have largely fallen out of favor, the notion persists that tragedy is not simply an attitude or a condition, but rather is significant only as it is embodied in an action. Moreover, such

243

an action is not confusing and disorganized as most actions in actual life tend to be; it is focused and clarified by art to make it both aesthetically satisfying and intellectually intelligible. The result is a shape having its own inner logic and driving force, as described for example by Susanne Langer:

> A dramatic act is a commitment. It creates a situation in which the agent or agents must necessarily make a further move; that is, it motivates a subsequent act (or acts). The situation, which is the completion of a given act, is already the impetus to another—as, in running, the footfall that catches our weight at the end of one bound already sends us forward to land on the other foot.[1]

To some extent Johnson recognizes this, as in his account of *King Lear*, in which "there is no scene which does not contribute to the aggravation of the distress or conduct of the action" (Yale *Works*, VIII, 703). But he probably has in mind something closer to the mechanical symmetry of the well-made play than the more philosophical sense of onrushing consequences that writers like Mrs. Langer suggest. And as we have seen, when Johnson most fully exhibits a sense of human tragedy he is talking about relatively static situations rather than about formally shaped actions.

In any case, modern accounts of tragedy assume a good deal more than simply a consecutive series of actions, however powerfully impelled. As an instance of the many elements which the term "tragedy" can be held to include, one may quote Robert B. Heilman:

> *Tragedy* should be used only to describe the situation in which the divided human being faces basic conflicts, perhaps rationally insoluble, of obliga-

---

[1] "The Tragic Rhythm," in *Feeling and Form* (New York, 1953), p. 355.

244

tions and passions; makes choices, for good or for evil; errs knowingly or involuntarily; accepts consequences; comes into a new, larger awareness; suffers or dies, yet with a larger wisdom.[2]

One can think of exceptions to many of these criteria, but if few tragedies satisfy all of them at once, it is still true that all can be substantiated in great tragedies. If the definition betrays the assumption that *Oedipus Tyrannus* and *King Lear* are paradigmatic works, it is none the worse for that. What I want to point out is how little of such a definition would have made sense to Johnson and his contemporaries. The notion of the "divided human being" was so new an idea for critics that even Hamlet was not interpreted in that light until the 1770's. The presence of "basic conflicts" would have been obvious enough, but not the possibility that they were "rationally insoluble"; on the contrary, tragedy taught us not to make avoidable mistakes. And any account of enlarged awareness or wisdom is lacking before essays like Warton's on *Lear*, which furthermore do not necessarily recognize it as an essential feature of tragedy.

One reason this is so is that a definition like Heilman's, however much it may depend on ideas about tragedy as a genre, derives at least as much from the conviction that tragedy has profound metaphysical implications. The point of the "larger awareness" and the "larger wisdom" is tersely embodied in the Aeschylean line, "We learn by suffering." Man may suffer until he is destroyed, he may struggle against evil and be conquered by it, but in some ultimate sense he learns deep truths about himself and his place in the universe. In a phrase which one often sees, tragedy teaches us what it means to be human.

[2] "Tragedy and Melodrama," *Texas Quarterly*, 3 (Summer 1960), 39-40.

That many tragedies are concerned with these matters I take to be incontrovertible. Whether or not all tragedies are is a question which need not be opened here. What needs to be emphasized, however, is the intellectual and even didactic tone of such theories: tragedy no longer teaches us to avoid silly mistakes (like marrying Moors against our parents' better judgment), but it teaches us to know ourselves, our limitations and our strengths. And according to many theorists it reconciles us with what might at first seem a hostile and implacable fate.

In one sense eighteenth-century thought about tragedy is much shallower than this; it generally demands poetic justice, and if a "good" character suffers it either finds reasons why he ought to suffer or has the play rewritten to spare him. But in a different sense it is perhaps truer to the sense of tragedy that most people have in ordinary usage, something much more hopeless and irrevocable than the joyful enlightenment which we are sometimes instructed to perceive at the end of *King Lear*. In Geoffrey Brereton's useful statement of this common-sense view,

> A tragedy is a final and impressive disaster due to an unforeseen or unrealised failure involving people who command respect and sympathy. It often entails an ironical change of fortune and usually conveys a strong impression of waste. It is always accompanied by misery and emotional distress.[3]

Every word of this account, I think, would have been acceptable to Johnson and to most of his contemporaries, or if not they would at least have recognized it as familiar. And in its modesty it is closer to the kinds of tragic insight that Johnson does have than are more

[3] *Principles of Tragedy: A Rational Examination of the Tragic Concept in Life and Literature* (Coral Gables, 1968), p. 20.

elaborate theories, of which I have taken Heilman's definition as an example.

It is of course true that so modest and general a formulation tells us less about *Antigone* or *Othello* than a more complex one can; on the other hand, it tells us more than such a theory does about a tragic sense that we can imagine ourselves sharing with men of another age. And formal theories, useful as they are as critical instruments, suffer from a curious limitation if they are applied directly to the unorganized experience of actual life. As Richard B. Sewall remarks,

> Though the affirmation that suffering brings knowledge seems clearly one of the constants of tragedy, it is by no means true of life in general. All suffering does not lead to knowledge. Suffering leads often to a complete collapse of the personality; it can degrade and benumb.[4]

As has already been observed, tragedy gives shape to what in life is often frustratingly shapeless. But if we shift the focus from the tragic protagonist to the perceiving audience or reader, the apparent paradox here will diminish. The characters in *The Three Sisters*, if one had to define them, are doubtless pathetic rather than tragic. Yet their condition, as it is conveyed to *us* with all Chekhov's subtlety and skill, can be seen as deeply tragic, expressive of human waste and loss, goodness deadened, possibilities foreclosed—all the quiet despair which we believe millions of inarticulate and wholly unheroic people to feel. *The Three Sisters* is no tragedy in any traditional sense, and Chekhov himself denied that it was one; yet it may still say much, in this more generalized way, about tragic experience.

Something of this is apparent in Johnson's brooding about human suffering. Why does life destroy people

---

[4] *The Vision of Tragedy* (New Haven, 1962), p. 155.

like his humble amanuensis Peyton? Why are they ignorant of their destiny? The very fact that we do *not* learn
from suffering—from most suffering—is in itself tragic.

Again, one may suggest that in his impatience with
definitions of literary form Johnson was in a way anticipating an important tendency of later criticism. Aristotle said that poetry was more philosophical than history because it made sense of apparently chaotic experience. Modern criticism, despite its interest in
formal questions, tends to see art as complicating rather
than simplifying; in effect it transposes the Aristotelian
formula and sees poetry as more historical than philosophy. Instead of the Meaning we apprehend many
meanings, and perhaps even the impossibility of meaning. Thus Murray Krieger in his discussion of modern
tragedy praises Kafka for writing apparent allegories
which refuse to be worked out.

> If his terms do not translate into a single answer,
> it is not because he perversely and mockingly pre-
> fers to hide it but because he has not got it. As a
> poet who thinks in images, Kafka as fable maker
> sees the maddening nest of possible and yet incom-
> patible relations as somehow being out there in
> experience, embedded in it, but beyond rational
> extrapolation.[5]

Johnson is no Kafka, and certainly believes that life
makes sense, but he also believes that most literature
oversimplifies life. Shakespeare is specifically com-
mended for his fidelity to life's multiplicity, where
other playwrights impose narrow and systematic conventions (heroes in love, kings who must act like kings,
tragic scenes unmixed with comic ones).

Yet if Johnson's unconcern for tragedy as genre is
perhaps forgivable, one is left with the persistent sense

[5] *The Tragic Vision* (Chicago, 1966), p. 117.

that, despite all the ways in which he was open to tragic experience, his writings constantly strive to circumvent or go beyond it. More than most of his contemporaries he was aware of "an unknown fear" that haunts the imagination, but it was not a fear which he cared to dwell upon as much as one might expect. And at this point I should like to return briefly to the central problem of his criticism of tragedy, the failure to do justice to (or often even to notice) its metaphysical nature. The sort of thing I have in mind can be illustrated by a fine passage from Bradley:

> Everywhere, in this tragic world, man's thought, translated into act, is transformed into the opposite of itself. His act, the movement of a few ounces of matter in a moment of time, becomes a monstrous flood which spreads over a kingdom. And whatsoever he dreams of doing, he achieves that which he least dreamed of, his own destruction.[6]

Johnson might well have understood what Bradley means in relation to actual life, but it is impossible to imagine him writing like this about tragedy.

Each age values something different in those works which it describes as tragic, whether it reorganizes and reinterprets the dramatic form in some new way, or extends its meaning to embrace a generalized attitude toward existence, or laments that tragedy is dead. In any case, we do well to ask *why* men at various times have admired tragedy—to ask what they thought that tragedy could give. In the Middle Ages, for example, it was understood as showing that attachment to worldly objects must lead to a disastrous fall. Neoclassical theorists like Dennis conceived of tragedy as vindicating Providence by exhibiting the kind of ultimate justice that actual life so often fails to disclose. For Hegel,

[6] A. C. Bradley, *Shakespearean Tragedy* (London, 1905), ch. 1, p. 28.

tragedy showed that the defeat of apparent "right" was part of a larger historical process, very much as religious writers had traditionally explained suffering as part of God's mysterious plan.

All of these interpretations, different as they were, shared the assumption that the universe makes sense, and that tragedy could help to reconcile us to our fate by revealing that sense. Even Nietzsche, though he saw the universe as full of terrible and inexplicable cruelty, celebrated the unquenchable fecundity of which this was an aspect; in his view the Dionysian vision enables us to escape our individuality and, through "redeeming and healing" art, rejoice even in "the terror and absurdity of existence."[7] But recent writers have been more impressed with the existence of irrational evil than with the possibility that art can teach us to accept it. Admirers of tragedy are likely to reinterpret it in the light of modern experience, as in Jan Kott's chapter "King Lear or Endgame,"[8] or else to value it for showing a heroic dignity in the face of an implacable universe, which we find it hard to recapture today. "I am Duchess of Malfi still."

While much of Johnson's criticism seems totally innocent of this kind of thinking, there are moments, for instance his outrage at the death of Cordelia, that hint at a vivid awareness of the aspects of tragedy most emphasized today, even while denying the value of an art that could seriously entertain such possibilities. It goes without saying that he of all men was deeply aware of suffering and loss, but the question for him must be the end to which such experience is embodied in art. The modern critic may take Cordelia's death as an authentication of what many men have come to believe, that no amount of penance and redemption may

[7] *The Birth of Tragedy*, sec. 7, in *The Philosophy of Nietzsche*, trans. Clifton Fadiman (New York, 1954), pp. 985, 984.

[8] Jan Kott, *Shakespeare our Contemporary* (New York, 1966).

save us from an appalling fate, since "we inhabit an imbecile universe."[9] For Johnson her death is an inexplicable violation of the direction in which the play seemed to be moving, a gratuitous outrage far more horrible than "the extrusion of Gloucester's eyes," which at least had some semblance of deserved punishment:

> The Gods are just, and of our pleasant vices
> Make instruments to plague us;
> The dark and vicious place where thee he got
> Cost him his eyes.   (v.iii.170-73)

The eighteenth-century interest in catharsis is in part explained by the consciousness that tragedy presents a really frightening vision of the universe, one which most people were not willing to accept (just as today we may accept it uncritically, and Huxley has to remind us that tragedy is not the whole truth). If the real solution to the nature of catharsis is the idea of emotional equilibrium, then surely Schiller is right to argue that comedy is a higher form: "Its goal is the same as the highest aim of man's striving—to be free from passion, always to look with clear and tranquil eyes about and into oneself, to find everywhere more chance than destiny and to laugh at absurdity rather than get angry at malice or weep over it."[10] What looks like chance may turn out to be a manifestation of a resolutely benign destiny, like Fortune (which is really Providence) in *Tom Jones*, that central eighteenth-century work.

In the solemn generalizations of the *Rambler* and in the balanced harmonies of *Rasselas*, Johnson was able to treat these questions with detachment and perspective. In *Irene* only the guilty suffer, and nothing very

---

[9] J. Stampfer, "The Catharsis of King Lear," in *Shakespeare: Modern Essays in Criticism*, ed. Leonard Dean (Oxford, 1967), p. 375.
[10] Quoted by E. L. Stahl, *Friedrich Schiller's Drama: Theory and Practice* (Oxford, 1954), pp. 68-69.

251

terrible happens; an apostate who had every chance to save herself is destroyed by her own duplicity, and the government of the universe is systematically vindicated in the apportionment of rewards and punishments. There is little hint of the deeper fear which we know oppressed Johnson to the end of his life, that despite all a man can do he may be tried and found wanting: "Sent to Hell, Sir, and punished everlastingly" (*Life*, IV, 299). Fears like these are not to be exposed in art.

In a curious way, therefore, Johnson is receptive to the tragic but not to tragedy. While his emphasis on "truth to life" limits his understanding of tragedy as a distinct genre, his sense of the multiplicity of experience helps him to recognize the intolerable, inexplicable elements in it, rather than to impose artificial order upon those elements. He does not believe in the existence of a literary form that will justify the ways of God to men, as Milton thought that tragedy might do when he first conceived *Paradise Lost* as a tragic drama. Of course Johnson thought that God's ways could be justified, but *not by a literary form*. The point is important. The note of affirmation, of calm, or at least of resignation that is evident in many of the Greek tragedies is not, for Johnson, something that literature is capable of producing. Always he returns to religion, as at the end of his most tragic work, *The Vanity of Human Wishes*, as the only guarantor of meaning in an otherwise chaotic and often terrible universe.

In such a view some degree of optimism is necessarily present, and in Chapter 4 I have discussed the ways in which it militates against a tragic sense, but it is equally true that distinctions between kinds of optimism need to be made. That Johnson's religion was far from excluding tragic experience is particularly obvious if one compares it with Blake's apocalyptic Christianity. Denouncing the Lockean account of reality that Johnson accepted as a given fact, Blake believes that the unfallen world can be recovered by imaginative conquest: "Whenever any Individual Rejects Error & Embraces Truth, a Last Judgment passes upon that Individual."[11] Johnson believes that the world as we know it is irreducibly real, and that we can attain a better one only after arduous struggle and after surviving a Last Judgment that will be concerned with our moral actions rather than with our imaginative state. For him Blake's Beulah and Eden, if they exist at all, exist only in the future. Seeing man as irrevocably committed to the Newtonian world of time and space, he in effect regards Blake's world of Generation as the real one, and cultivates the faculty of abstract generalization which Blake consigns to icy Ulro. According to Blake the world in which we find ourselves represents a conspiracy to thwart our life-enhancing desires; for Johnson this world is an inescapable fact, not a swindle to be exposed, and human wishes can never be fulfilled in the present life. He sees the Bible as a collection of factual histories and moral precepts, not as an allegorical vision of Fall and Apocalypse, and it is not surprising that his solemn poem draws upon Ecclesiastes, which Blake must have regarded as one of the least imaginative books in the Bible. (Northrop Frye explicitly associates it with the chilling rationalism of Ulro.)[12]

If tragedy is not a single and isolable entity, neither is Christianity, and I have tried to show that no single formula can express the complicated relation between the two in Johnson. While he embraced the official dogmas that Blake derided, his religion was neither the sentimental benevolence of a Sterne nor the romantic religiosity of a Boswell. More generally, a mind as various as Johnson's, and as open as his to the contradictory nature of reality, cannot be reduced to a single attitude

[11] *Vision of the Last Judgment,* in *Complete Writings,* ed. Geoffrey Keynes (Oxford, 1966), p. 613.
[12] *Fearful Symmetry* (Boston, 1962), p. 317.

toward tragedy or anything else. In *The Vanity of Human Wishes* the conclusion is that since hope and fear can *never* find adequate objects in this life, they must be wholly redirected toward a future one. But in many of the periodical essays Johnson takes a secular line, and represents hope, even though illusory, as an essential element of life. "It is necessary to hope, tho' hope should always be deluded, for hope itself is happiness, and its frustrations, however frequent, are yet less dreadful than its extinction" (*Idler* 58).

That Johnson understood the *Oedipus Tyrannus* or *King Lear* so differently from modern critics is not, in the end, a function of his historical position. As I have tried to show in Part I, an intelligent though minor writer like Hughes on *Othello* could achieve a subtle awareness of how a great tragedy works. Johnson's deficiencies in this regard owe more to his assumptions about life and art than to any influence of "the age." To put it differently, when he came to write a tragedy he conceived of the genre in highly limiting neoclassical terms; when he criticized Shakespeare, on the other hand, he measured him not so much against neoclassical standards as against his own conception of the real state of sublunary nature. His gravest critical handicap was not the reduction of tragedy to narrow dogmatic terms, but his reluctance to reduce it at all. In his quest for a balanced perspective and comprehensive vision he chose to ignore the fact that art selects and intensifies certain aspects of experience at the expense of others. Joy and sorrow may be equally mingled in life as we know it, but by the very nature of the genre they cannot be mingled—or mingled in that way—in tragedy.

As has already been remarked, the literary form most deeply congenial to Johnson's assumptions was (whether he realized it or not) the emerging novel. Richard-

254

son's *Clarissa*, which Johnson admired,[13] offered nearly everything that he expected from tragedy: it is an affecting she-tragedy exhibiting deep understanding of the recesses of the human heart; it is sufficiently "domestic" to be apprehended by every reader; it is moral and indeed religious in its lesson; and, as a work of prose fiction, it is excused from the putative handicaps of elevated language. One may imagine further that the great achievements of the nineteenth-century novel would have been particularly attractive to Johnson. We have noticed an affinity between his notion of tragedy and George Eliot's in *Middlemarch*; a less obvious analogue but a suggestive one is Dickens' *Great Expectations*. In that work, knowledge and experience by their very nature imply an irrevocable loss of the Edenic world of Joe Gargery's forge (whereas in the comic *Tom Jones*, which Johnson detested on moral grounds, the fall from Paradise Hall is not permanent). Yet *Great Expectations* is no tragedy; it is full of real humor, and displays the chastened and balanced perspective of the sufferer looking back over his life in a later and quieter time. However deeply we are moved by Johnson's suffering and by his anguished expressions of it, some such breadth of vision as this must have been the ideal that he sought both in his writings and his life.

[13] Among various indications of Johnson's esteem for *Clarissa*, the reader may consult the following: *Life*, II, 49, and 174-75; *Miscellanies*, I, 282-83; *Life of Rowe*, II, 67. In the *Dictionary*, where living authors are seldom quoted, Johnson gives nearly a hundred illustrations taken from a compilation of moral sentences which had been selected from the novel: see W. R. Keast, "The Two *Clarissas* in Johnson's *Dictionary*," *Studies in Philology*, 54 (1957), 429-39.

APPENDIX

A Note on Sources

1. Periodicals

AMONG the various miscellaneous sources from which I draw evidence—biographies of actors, journals, letters, and so on—I have quoted a number of times from articles and reviews in magazines, notably the *Gentleman's Magazine*, the *Critical Review*, and the *Monthly Review*. For the *Monthly*, I have been able to supply the names of the writers, taken from Benjamin Nangle's valuable *Index*,[1] but otherwise they are inevitably anonymous. One must therefore be wary of evaluations of works as good or bad, since personal friendship or animus may dictate a reviewer's assessment. But if his opinions are quoted as evidence for a general view of tragedy, the problem is less important. When he wants to praise a work, he will praise whatever his system or tendency of criticism finds most valuable; when he wants to condemn, the way in which he does it will likewise be interesting; and in either case, his omissions—the things he never thinks to mention one way or the other—may for our purposes be most interesting of all.

Furthermore, the general public may be presumed to have read most of these reviews in good faith. Whatever private motives the reviewer may have had (and it certainly influences our opinion of a review relating to Johnson to know that Murphy or Burney wrote it), he is trying to recommend or disparage his subject in terms that he believes will carry weight with his read-

---

[1] *The Monthly Review, First Series: 1749-1789, Index of Contributors and Articles* (Oxford, 1934), and *Second Series, 1790-1815* (Oxford, 1955). Nangle has made positive identifications from a set of the *Monthly*, now in the Bodleian, which was annotated by the editor Ralph Griffiths.

ers; and since he seldom has space to expound any unusual theory of his own, we can assume that he thinks
he is treading on common ground.

Boswell complains that "instead of giving an accurate
account of what has been done by the authour whose
work they are reviewing, which is surely the proper
business of a literary journal, they produce some plausible and ingenious conceits of their own, upon the
topicks which have been discussed" (*Life*, IV, 215). This
practice was no doubt as maddening then as it is now,
but it is more useful to our kind of inquiry than a faithful summary would be. For this reason, incidentally,
the *Critical* is more helpful than the *Monthly*. Johnson
discriminated between them accurately in 1776 when
he told Boswell, "I think them very impartial," but went
on to say, "The Critical Reviewers, I believe, often review without reading the books through; but lay hold
of a topick, and write chiefly from their own minds.
The Monthly Reviewers are duller men, and glad to
read the books through" (*Life*, III, 32).

2. Johnsonian Sources

The canon of Johnson's writings is by no means settled, and I have sometimes had occasion to use material
that is not certainly his, though never without full indi-
cation of the fact, and never in such a way that my
argument depends on its being genuinely Johnson's. I
have also tried to be critical about some sources that
Johnsonian scholarship generally takes for granted. The
sermons, for example, are for the most part manifestly
by Johnson, but one of them and part of another have
been questioned, and in still others Johnson's friend
Taylor might conceivably have interpolated his own
thoughts (as he had every right to do) in sermons that
Johnson had written for his use.[2] But it is not likely that

[2] See J. H. Hagstrum, "The Sermons of Samuel Johnson,"
Modern Philology, 40 (1943), 255-66.

we can ever be sure in this matter, and the sermons as a whole are too valuable to dismiss. In any case I rest no argument upon them that is not corroborated by other evidence. I have also had to recognize, like other writers on Johnson, that the passages I quote were written in widely varying circumstances during a career of half a century. If some were the product of rigorous thought, others were the hasty efforts of "an attention dissipated, a memory embarrassed, an imagination overwhelmed, a mind distracted with anxieties, a body languishing with disease" (*Rambler* 208). I have therefore tried at all times to keep specific contexts in mind.

But the problem of sources only begins with Johnson's own works. The wealth of biographies, journals, and memoirs that record his conversation is astonishing, and obviously very uneven in reliability. Some recent writers seem to believe that the best solution is to exclude any evidence from Boswell or other reporters, but unfortunately this means excluding much that is very valuable indeed, and much that is already part of the mental world of anyone who studies Johnson. As for Boswell, his fidelity to the exact sense of what he heard, usually worked up from notes taken shortly afterwards, is so well established that undue suspicion is not called for. While one should be careful not to deduce too much from chance allusions in Boswell, the value of his record is too great to ignore, and indeed one may as easily misinterpret a passage in Johnson's acknowledged works as one in the *Life of Johnson*. For the other kinds of evidence the problem is much more acute. Strictly speaking it is impossible to defend a liberal use of the materials collected in G. B. Hill's *Johnsonian Miscellanies*, much of which Hill himself was not inclined to trust. However, Mrs. Piozzi—whom I refer to as Mrs. Thrale during the time of her friendship with Johnson—knew him in some very important respects better than anyone else, and has recorded anecdotes that are too excellent to ignore. Despite the habitual inaccuracy with which both Johnson and Boswell charged her, I have ventured, like many before me, to draw upon her testimony where it seemed appropriate. Of the other writers in the *Miscellanies* I have made very sparing use, and indeed they seldom offer much that is helpful for my study.

INDEX

Adams, Dr. William, 72
Addison, Joseph, 46; *Cato*, 20,
 21, 114, 118, 119, 137, 177,
 218n, 220n, 231-32, 241;
 Spectator, 16, 20, 35-36, 163,
 173n
Aeschylus, 184n, 245;
 Agamemnon, 34, 38, 40,
 183; *Persae*, 30; *Prometheus*,
 185, 193
Alembert, Jean d', 52
Alkon, Paul K., 157n
Alves, Robert, 59
Ariosto, Ludovico, 202
Aristotle, 5, 12, 13, 14, 36,
 164, 171, 173, 182, 191-92,
 196, 197, 204, 205n, 234,
 243, 248
Arrowsmith, William, 66
Auden, W. H., 98

Bacon, Sir Francis, 146
Banks, John, 119n
Barry, Mrs. (actress), 125
Barry, Spranger (actor), 26
Bate, W. J., 59, 60, 68n, 184n
Beaumont, Francis, 210n.
 See also Fletcher
Bentley, Richard, 35n, 41
Blair, Hugh (*The Grave*), 52
Blake, William, 252-53
Boethius, 157
Booth, Barton (actor), 177
Boothby, Miss Hill, 90n
Bossu, René Le, 12, 225
Boswell, James, 20, 53, 64-65,
 71, 89n, 93, 103, 107, 110,
 238n, 253; *Life of Johnson*,
 63-107 passim, 109, 110,
 133n, 147, 170-72, 173,
 175 ,176, 180, 183, 185,

185n, 191, 198, 199, 201,
 204, 209, 212, 228, 241, 252,
 255n, 257, 258
Bouhours, Dominique, 171
Bracegirdle, Mrs. (actress), 125
Bradley, A. C., 6, 7, 26, 95,
 221, 249
Brereton, Geoffrey, 246
Bronson, Bertrand, 64, 87-88n,
 111, 123, 128n, 130, 132n
Brooke, Henry, 119n
Brumoy, Pierre, 216
Buckingham, George Villiers,
 Duke of, 15
Burke, Edmund, 53-54, 163,
 170
Burnet, Bishop Gilbert, 140n
Burney, Charles, 4n, 195, 256
Butt, John, 225

Carlyle, Thomas, 61
Carroll, Lewis, 44
catharsis, 22-27, 171-74, 251
Chapin, Chester F., 76n, 90n,
 157n
Charles I, King, 13, 53
Charles XII of Sweden, 143-47
Chaucer, Geoffrey, 146
Chekhov, Anton, 97, 247
Cibber, Colley, 130n
Cohen, Ralph, 26n, 149
Coleridge, S. T., 7n, 178, 210
Colman, George, 222
Congreve, William, 18n, 122,
 125
Conklin, Paul S., 238n
Corneille, Pierre, 36, 116, 189
Cornford, F. M., 158-59
Cowper, William, 73
Cradock, Joseph, 186, 188
Critical Review, 16, 22-23, 33,

Critical Review (cont.)
46n, 82, 86n, 125, 177, 204-
205, 214n, 219n, 234, 237n,
256, 257
Cumberland, Richard, 14,
34-35, 41-42, 125, 184, 193

Dacier, André, 12, 172
Davies, Thomas, 16-17, 130n,
219n, 237n
Dennis, John, 12, 163, 203,
243; on tragedy, 10, 49, 232,
249; on *All for Love*, 17;
on poetic justice, 18-20; on
Antigone, 31; on *Oedipus*,
36-37, 187; on Shakespeare,
42-43; on Juvenal, 140n, 142
Dickens, Charles, 255
Dryden, John, 11, 80, 139, 163,
188, 202, 203, 243; on rules,
12; on drama, 13, 14, 21, 29,
31, 49, 165-66, 193-94,
225; on catharsis, 24-25; on
epic, 14, 25; on poetry,
209; on the passions, 44-45,
45n; on puns, 222; on
Shakespeare, 46; on Juvenal,
140n
    All for Love, 12, 17, 114,
120, 190, 191, 233, 241;
Aureng-Zebe, 113, 183n;
Conquest of Granada, 122,
189-91, 225n; *Conquest of
Mexico* (description of
night), 200; *Oedipus*, 35-38,
187; translation of Juvenal's
Tenth Satire, 140, 142, 144,
150, 153
Du Bos, Jean Baptiste, 171

Ecclesiastes, 78, 154, 155, 253
Eliot, George, 96-97, 255
Eliot, T. S., 145
Elton, Oliver, 3

epic, 14-15. *See also* Homer,
Virgil
Euripides, 31, 37, 118, 183,
183-84n, 185; *Alcestis*, 185;
Hippolytus, 29-30, 186;
Iphigenia in Tauris, 5; *Ion*,
28, 29; *Medea*, 184; *Orestes*,
19; *Phoenissiae*, 29, 184n

Fielding, Henry, 11, 28, 95,
251, 255
Fletcher, John, 42n, 189,
210n, 220
Franklyn, Thomas, 33-34
Frederick the Great, 52n
Frye, Northrop, 219, 253
Fussell, Paul, 53, 54n, 74-75n

Gardner, Helen, 134
Garrick, David, 25-26, 41, 42n,
51, 109, 115, 176, 212, 237n
Gay, John, 191
Gentleman's Magazine, 4n,
126, 132, 132n, 133, 134,
166, 179n, 195-98, 217, 218n,
227n, 256
Gibbon, Edward, 3, 41, 112,
116, 121, 129n
Gifford, Henry, 91n, 143n,
149n
Gildon, Charles, 11, 12
Glasse, G. H., 195
Goldsmith, Oliver, 104, 178-79
Goring, Charles, 132
Gray, Thomas, 66, 158, 197
Greek tragedy, 28-41. *See also*
Aeschylus, Euripides,
Sophocles
Green, Clarence C., 11n
Greene, Donald J., 61n, 166n,
179n, 195n
Griffiths, Ralph, 175n, 256n
Guthke, Karl S., 13n

Rothstein, Eric, 42n, 125
Rousseau, Jean-Jacques, 88
Rowe, Nicholas, 3, 31-32, 33, 50, 114, 122n, 170, 194, 218n, 220, 222n
Ruffhead, Owen, 34
Rymer, Thomas, 12, 18, 21, 24-25, 29-31, 41, 49, 50, 215

Sachs, Arieh, 60, 72n, 76n
Scaliger, J. C., 30
Schiller, J.C.F. von, 137, 251
Schoff, Francis G., 143n
Schopenhauer, Arthur, 26
Scott, Sir Walter, 142, 148
Sewall, Richard B., 247
Shaftesbury, Anthony Ashley Cooper, third Earl of, 209
Seneca, 29, 38-39
Shakespeare, William, 41-51, 94, 95, 114, 116, 119, 123-24, 142, 188, 189, 194, 248, 254
All's Well ("an unknown fear"), iv, 8, 249; *Antony and Cleopatra*, 42n, 114, 158, 208, 219; *Hamlet*, 27, 32, 39, 94, 126, 134, 135, 175, 176, 200, 208, 219, 220, 225-26, 227-28, 230, 238-40, 245; *Henry IV*, 128-29, 228; *Henry V*, 212; *Henry VIII*, 143, 220-21; *Julius Caesar*, 136-37; *King Lear*, 3, 18, 22, 26, 42n, 51, 62, 94, 183, 200, 206, 214, 218-20, 230-32, 235-37, 244, 245, 246, 250-51; *Macbeth*, 64, 134, 200, 213-14; *Measure for Measure*, 201, 226, 230; *Merchant of Venice*, 170; *Much Ado*, 213; *Othello*, 6, 18, 22, 37, 47-50, 177, 200, 202n, 214, 221, 222, 228, 247, 254; *Richard II*, 213, 228-30;

Richard III, 167, 234-35; *Romeo and Juliet*, 22, 212, 230; *Tempest*, 223; *Timon of Athens*, 218; *Twelfth Night*, 213, 217
Sherbo, Arthur, 166n, 195n, 217n, 220n
Sheridan, Thomas, 238n
Sidney, Sir Philip, 10
Smith, Edmund, 186
Solon, 5
Sophocles, 28, 31, 95, 184n; *Antigone*, 6, 29, 31, 247; *Electra*, 32, 33; *Oedipus Tyrannus*, 35, 38, 184n, 186-88, 193, 225n, 235, 245; *Oedipus at Colonus*, 37; *Philoctetes*, 193
Spectator, see Addison; by Steele, 217-18
Spenser, Edmund, 46
Spinoza, Benedict de, 5
Stampfer, J., 251-52
Steele, Sir Richard, 127, 217-18
Sterne, Laurence, 9, 253
Stone, George W., 42n
Sutherland, James, 96n
Swift, Jonathan, 3, 9, 45n, 95, 105-106, 141, 143-44

Tate, Nahum, 18, 51, 230-31, 237
Taylor, Dr. John, 257
Theobald, Lewis, 24, 37, 225
Thomson, James, 38-41, 136
Thrale, Mrs. Hester Lynch, 4n, 62n, 89, 91, 92, 100n, 118-19, 142n, 175, 183, 194, 209, 211, 258-59
Thucydides, 158-59
Tibullus, 90, 91n
Tickell, Thomas, 135
Tillotson, Geoffrey, 28-29n, 149